WILLIAM CARLOS WILLIAMS AND THE AMERICAN POEM

WILLIAM CARLOS WILLIAMS AND THE AMERICAN POEM

Charles Doyle

Professor of English
University of Victoria
British Columbia, Canada

First published 1982 by
THE MACMILLAN PRESS LTD
London and Basingstoke
Companies and representatives
throughout the world

ISBN 0 333 28484 4

Printed in Hong Kong

Contents

Acknowledgements

Acknowledgements and thanks are gratefully given to my late colleague, Professor J. C. Reid of Auckland University, to the late Professor Norman Holmes Pearson, and to Sister M. Bernetta Quinn. I should also like to thank the American Council of Learned Societies for a research fellowship, Auckland University, and the University of Victoria for leave and research grants, as well as Mr K. C. Gay, Curator of the Poetry Collection, SUNY Buffalo, and Mr Donald Gallup of the Beinecke Rare Book and Manuscript Library at Yale University.

Portions of this book have been published in somewhat different form in the following periodicals, to which acknowledgement is due: *Modern Poetry Studies, Perspective* and *West Coast Review.*

My thanks to Kathleen Cameron for typing the manuscript, and, once again, to my wife, for her patience and understanding as witness to the life of 'scribble, scribble, scribble'. Some fine work has been done in the past decade in the field of Williams studies, which illuminates even an introductory study such as the present one. The book's shortcomings are, of course, my own responsibility.

C.D.

List of Abbreviations

Names and titles frequently cited in the text are referred to by the abbreviations listed below. A bibliographical list of primary sources is omitted because full information is available up to 1968 in *A Bibliography of William Carlos Williams*, by Emily Mitchell Wallace (Middletown, Conn.: Wesleyan University Press, 1968). Since several extensive checklists of Williams criticism and commentary are also readily available, my bibliography of secondary sources is not intended to be exhaustive but to be relevant to the immediate concerns of my text.

AQQ   *Al Que Quiere!* (Boston, Mass.: The Four Seas Co., 1917).

Autob.   *The Autobiography of William Carlos Williams* (New York: Random House, 1951).

Buffalo   Poetry Collection (Williams items), Lockwood Memorial Library, State University of New York at Buffalo.

CEP   *The Collected Earlier Poems of William Carlos Williams* (Norfolk, Conn.: New Directions, 1951).

CLP   *The Collected Later Poems of William Carlos Williams* (Norfolk, Conn.: New Directions, 1950; rev. 1963).

CCP   *The Complete Collected Poems of William Carlos Williams 1906-1938* (Norfolk, Conn.: New Directions, 1938).

CP 21-31   *Collected Poems 1921-1931* (New York: The Objectivist Press, 1934).

GAN   *The Great American Novel*, in *Imaginations* (see below).

IAG   *In the American Grain* (New York: New Directions, 1956).

Imag.   *Imaginations*, ed. Webster Schott (New York: New Directions, 1971).

IWWP   *I Wanted to Write a Poem*, ed. Edith Heal (Boston, Mass.: Beacon Press, 1958).

KH   *Kora in Hell: Improvisations* (San Francisco: City Lights Books, 1957). (Also included in *Imaginations*.)

ND 16   'The Lost Poems of William Carlos Williams', ed. John C. Thirlwall, in *New Directions*, no. 16 (New York: New Directions, 1957).

ND 17   *New Directions*, no. 17 (New York: New Directions, 1961).

P   *Paterson I–V* (New York: New Directions, 1963).

PB   *Pictures from Brueghel and Other Poems* (New York: New Directions, 1962). Included in this volume are *The Desert Music and Other Poems* (1954) and *Journey to Love* (1955), both volumes originally published by Random House, New York. Referred to in conjunction with *PB*, these works are cited as *DM* and *JL*.

SA   *Spring and All* (Dijon: Contact Publishing Co., 1923). (Included in *Imaginations* — see above.)

SE   *Selected Essays* (New York: Random House, 1954).

SL   *The Selected Letters of William Carlos Williams*, ed. John C. Thirlwall (New York: McDowell, Obolensky, 1957).

VP   *A Voyage to Pagany* (New York: The Macaulay Co., 1928).

WM   *White Mule* (Norfolk, Conn.: New Directions, 1937).

Yale   Williams Collection in the American Literature Collection, Yale University Library.

1 The River

Among William Carlos Williams's unpublished papers at Yale are several typed and handwritten sheets which suggest that, at some late stage in his career, he intended to organize the whole corpus of his poems into a single, meaningful design. One sheet is headed THE COMPLETE COLLECTED EXERCISES TOWARD A POSSIBLE POEM (in 2 vols), another THE MODERN THEORY AND PRACTICE: FINAL COMPLETE COLLECTED POEMS OF W. C. W.

These titles declare the dominant preoccupation of Williams's life — poem as process, the making of the poem. Somewhat less obviously, the first title also suggests his view that to achieve a poem is to make a discovery. A global explorer like Columbus or a scientist such as Madame Curie, each in his or her own way, expands our view of the world and thereby renews it. Similarly the poet, through imagination, broadens and renews our consciousness of the world.

Williams's apparent intention in THE COMPLETE COLLECTED EXERCISES was to group his poems under six (or five) headings: (1) 'The River', (2) 'Kora in Hell: Improvisations', (3) 'Spring and All', (4) 'The Wedge', (5) 'The Poem as a Machine', and (6) 'A New Way of Measuring'. Each group was to be prefaced by a statement of his 'mode of attack' and his objective assessment of the degree of success achieved.[1]

Of the six headings, 'Kora in Hell' is either omitted or deleted from different typed versions of the scheme.[2] Williams himself had doubts about its status as a poem. Writing 'for relief, to keep myself from planning and thinking at all' (*Autob.*, 158), he later organized it by modelling it on a book Pound had left with him, Metastasio's *Varie Poesie*. Edith Heal records his describing *Kora in Hell* as a book of 'Prose Poems . . . I have always been puzzled by it. I realized it had poetic quality but without any form', but also his remark 'Perhaps this is the first thing to show me to be a prose writer' (*IWWP*, 31). As we shall see, however, *Kora in Hell* is a key work in the canon.

1

For a variety of reasons many of Williams's poems are impervious to critical explication by established methods. As the volume of critical response to his work increases, it becomes easier to define typical features of the poem, e.g. opacity, intensity, fluidity. It is much more difficult to determine which are the 'good' or successful poems and what attributes make those poems complete in a way in which others, just as typical, are not.

Part of the problem is that Williams made, or discovered, many different types of poem, from the improvisations of *Kora*, through the jaggedness of 'Perpetuum Mobile: the City' (*CEP*, 384), the deceptive simplicity of 'This is Just to Say' (*CEP*, 354), the range of approach in *Paterson*, and the easy discourse of the late work. All this is suggested by the headings for THE COMPLETE COLLECTED EXERCISES, which also group the work chronologically. Many linkages backward through the canon suggest that this chronology is not merely serial, but is cumulative. Regrettably, neither *Collected Earlier Poems* nor *Collected Later Poems* (either edition) appears to implement Williams's scheme. We have no way of knowing how the arrangement of these volumes (which is by no means strictly chronological) relates to the scheme. Nor have we the specific commentary, although a great deal of Williams's prose is relevant. Pragmatically, he may have felt that such an apparatus would give criticism and apologetics too prominent a place.

From early in his work a dichotomy suggests itself: the selective (although hidden) activity of the Imagist, and the passive immersion in the 'filthy Passaic' of local experience. Usually it is taken for granted that these, in Williams, complement each other. If so, the critical means needed to approach his poems may well be found by pondering how, and how well, the two parts are conjoined.

Two items are frequently quoted to establish a sense of Williams's attitudes to the world and to his craft: a letter to Marianne Moore responding to her sense of the 'inner security' manifest in his poems (*SL*, 147-8) and his early programme poem 'The Wanderer' (*CEP*, 3-12). Williams's 'anonymity', combined with his 'descent' into the Passaic River, are sometimes taken as showing that his 'resignation' was a surrender of the ego's assertiveness. J. Hillis Miller's fine study in *Poets of Reality*[3] rests on such an assumption and Miller's interpretation of 'The Wanderer' supports it. Yet Williams's development proves

X someone, A. Rich, suggested
this = a weak ego boundaries

ultimately to be not an abnegation but a re-ordering of the self. From one point of view, his 'sudden resignation to existence' resembles Keats's 'Negative Capability'. From another, since Williams himself saw it as 'a sort of nameless religious experience', it may be seen as a Zen-like acceptance of the here and now, a quality which accounts in part for recognition of Williams's greatness among many younger poets whose aim is the Zen *satori*.

Writing to Marianne Moore of 'a despair which made everything a unit and at the same time a part of myself', he suggests that he was 'about twenty' (1903) when for the first time he apprehended the universe and himself on equal terms. His first small volume, *Poems* (1909), nowhere evinces such 'despair'. Gauche as it is (amendments in the corrected issue, such as 'yclad' for 'y-clad', 'love-worn' for 'raptured', illustrate), *Poems* is permeated by Keatsian romanticism, and escapism, 'To worlds afar whose fruits all anguish mend'. Rod Townley, while tracing some complexity of organization through the book, perceives it as 'a collection of wish-fulfilments', though he adds that, paradoxically, the deepest wish the poet expresses 'is to be free of all his desires'.[4] A sense of 'resignation' is discernable only a few years later in some work included in *The Tempers* (1913). In retrospect at least, this inner state included a rejection of 'causes' (abstract) and a preference for work. 'The reason is that it seems so much more important to me that I am....As a reward for this anonymity I feel as much a part of things as trees and stones. Heaven seems frankly impossible' (*SL*, 147).

A notable feature of Williams's very early career is his imperviousness to Pound's influence. We have the well-known letters in which Pound reacts to Williams's tepid reception of *A Lume Spento*, where Pound provides early versions of some of his now famous instructions ('To paint the thing as I see it').[5] Seven months later, in response to *Poems*, Pound tells his friend what to read: 'I hope to God you have no feelings. If you have, burn this *before* reading. Dear Billy: Thanks for your Poems. ... As proof that W. C. W. has poetic instincts the book is valuable ...' etc. And the hortatory postscript 'And remember a man's real work is what *he is going to do*, not what is behind him. Avantie coraggio!'[6] Pound's words are cited here to evoke the link between the two poets early in their often difficult lifelong relationship. Each in his distinctive way was to manifest that *coraggio*.

Eventually, Williams became part of the second phase of the

Imagist movement, in the period after Hulme's dominance and before that of Amy Lowell, when Pound had established himself as the movement's spokesman (starting with H. D. and Richard Aldington in a Kensington 'bun shop'). When, in 1912, the *Poetry Review* (London) was the first periodical to publish Williams's poems, these were supported by Pound's 'Introductory Note', in substance a faint intimation of the famous 'A Few Don'ts for an Imagiste', to come a few months later. Pound had earlier been unimpressed by both his friend's 'studied Keatsian sonnets' and his 'quick spontaneous poems' (*IWWP*, 5).[7] Now, presumably in response to Williams's gradual peeling off of Keatsian pastiche, Pound felt himself able to say 'He apparently means what he says. He is not overcrowded with false ornament.' When Williams brought out his second book, *The Tempers*, it was Pound who found a publisher for it, Elkin Mathews of London.

A distinctly transitional book, in *Collected Earlier Poems* it is made to look stronger than it actually was (and is so treated by some commentators). The impressive portrait poems — 'Le Médécin Malgré Lui', 'To Mark Anthony in Heaven' and 'Portrait of a Lady' — were originally published much later (the last-named as late as 1920, when it appeared in the August issue of the *Dial*). Intermixed with pastiches of the English romantic lyric is evidence throughout *The Tempers* of a search for Poundian music, most typically in 'Homage' (*CEP*, 18), of which Pound said 'his verse is sound as a bell'.[8]

A certain technical eclecticism shows that Williams had learnt a great deal since publishing his first book in Rutherford. Yet this same quality reveals that he had far from found himself as a poet. Much is owing to Pound. Grammar, syntax, tone, use of archaisms and choice of titles (such as 'Mezzo Forte') are frequently Poundian. Besides imitating the Elizabethan lyric, Williams also employs free verse and the Browning dramatic monologue (in it, like Pound, usually being less interested in the 'character' than in what he himself has to say). Occasional lines even sound like Seamus O'Sullivan ('Over the five-barred gate, and will still be straying' — *CEP*, 25). Two distinct types of poem may be discerned throughout: one in a free verse line, tending towards colloquialism, and the other in a carefully wrought musical pattern.

The Tempers interests us chiefly for the latter. Pound presumably praises 'Homage' for its individual music, its fulfilment of his dictum that 'A man's rhythm must be interpretative, it will be, therefore, in the end, his own, uncounterfeiting, uncounterfeitable.'[9] Where Williams does not control his verse line with a sense of 'the musical phrase', it is dull. Yet some of the poems whose intent is obviously musical fail through their very obviousness. But, like later poets such as Louis Zukofsky, Robert Duncan, Cid Corman, Robert Creeley and Gary Snyder, Williams appears indebted to Pound for this particular sense of relationship between music and poetry. None the less, Williams was independent, as is shown by his early correspondence with Harriet Monroe, where some of his observations anticipate what was to become clear to him later, a need for 'brokenness' as one element in his own work: 'Now life is above all things else at any moment subversive of life as it was the moment before — always new, irregular. Verse to be alive must have infused into it something of the same order, some tincture of disestablishment. . . . I am speaking of modern verse' (*SL*, no. 13, pp. 23-4). In the same letter he shows himself to be virtually free of 'fixed iambic measure'.

Looking back, in 1958, he saw clearly that he was in 1913 'beginning to turn away from the romantic'. In December 1912 he married and settled at Ridge Road in Rutherford, New Jersey, where he spent the rest of his life. From the later vantage point in time, he speculated that the change of direction in his work was his great interest in the local, his experience of medicine and his 'intense Americanism'. Little of these actual qualities shows in *The Tempers*.

By the time he came to work on 'The Wanderer' (*CEP*, 3-12), Williams seems to have realized in full the disadvantages of free verse not controlled by an informing music. Much has been written already on this poem, first published in 1914,[10] which is the true beginning of Williams's career. Critics relate it to an earlier, lost[11] Keatsian poem based on a central figure (a Prince) who is out of tune with his environment and his fellows, i.e. with his *present situation*. 'The Wanderer', which has the sustained intensity of a mystical experience, is a rebuttal of these earlier attitudes, despite Williams's own later comment that 'It is actually a reconstruction from memory of my early Keatsian *Endymion* imitation' (*IWWP*, 25-6).

Immediately striking is Williams's command over line cadences. While it is perhaps an overstatement to speak of 'his wholehearted adoption of American vernacular speech' (as Guimond does),[12]

Williams certainly bases his line on conversational sentence structure, managing it with great ease. His 'story of growing up' is rendered in terms of ascent/descent, a sequence of movement which was to become centrally important to him. Urged to fly by his Muse (later recognized as his English grandmother) whom he encounters one day as he is crossing the Hudson River in a ferry, he follows her, accepting her, perceiving in her his destiny, she 'recreating the whole world':

> Saving alone that one sequence
> Which is the beauty of all the world . . . .
>
> (*CEP*, 4)

In flight, he follows as she leads towards the river. She strikes him and, he perceives below him, as if for the first time 'men as visions . . . Hasting-nowhere!' He realizes also the horrible power of the old woman, 'marvelous old queen'. At this point, the end of the poem's third section, there is a change of focus. Section four, 'The Strike', concerns the great Paterson strike which began in late January 1913, when 800 workers at the Doherty Steel Mills walked out in protest against the dismissal of some of their fellows who had attempted to pursue trade union activities.[13] Having 'hurried shivering/Out into the deserted streets of Paterson', the poet feels not sympathy but horror for what he observes, 'the low, sloping foreheads / The flat skulls with the unkempt black or blond hair, / The ugly legs of the young girls' (*CEP*, 7) all in contrast to 'the subtle' nature of the old woman. Thirty years later this horror will still be with him, and the roller mills will be his starting-point for *Paterson*. All his life the ugliness and 'filth' of the world around him presented Williams with a problem. Seeing that he must 'be a mirror to this modernity', how was he to do it? His Muse's Emersonian instructions, explicit in the poem's fourth section, 'Abroad', were that he was to draw people's attention to nature ('The tree in the wind', 'the myriad cinquefoil', 'the silent phoebe nest') and to life's simple realities which may also be beautiful ('the white house there, the sky!', 'boughs green / with ripening fruit within you!'). She warned him it would not be easy, but he had no alternative:

> For I knew the novitiate was ended
> The ecstasy was over, the life begun.
>
> (*CEP*, 10)

'St James' Grove', the closing section, is an initiation rite, a form of baptism, with the peculiarity that river and poet participate in it on equal terms. The old woman cries out:

> 'Enter, youth, into this bulk!
> Enter, river, into this young man!'
> (*CEP*, 11)

When the river enters his heart, the youth feels its rottenness and degradation:

> It tortured itself within me
> Until time had been washed finally under,
> And the river had found its level
> And its last motion had ceased
> And I knew all — it became me.
> (*CEP*, 11—12)

One final instruction issues from the old woman — 'Be mostly silent!', which prompts Hillis Miller's comment 'Here is attained that silence and anonymity which he describes in the letter to Marianne Moore. This silence is his marriage to all that is.'[14] The old woman speaks of her relationship to the river as one of 'marriage' and of the youth (poet) as product of that marriage. The poem is his baptism. His relationship to the river is one of 'interpenetration'. Not a loss of self is implied, but an extremely close identification of self and world, a detachment, a breaking down of the distinction between subject and object, not in the sense of assimilation of one into the other, but of acceptance. The opposite effect is achieved, to hedonism and self-alienation, by one who 'abides serenely in the here and now, and is above joy and grief, life and death'.[15]

To suggest, as Hillis Miller does, that Williams 'reaches at the age of twenty the place which Wallace Stevens attains only after decades of struggle to harmonize imagination and reality'[16] is to mistake a recognition for an accomplishment, although Miller's general thesis thereafter is profoundly right. Williams saw what his situation was, as a result of his 'despair' realizing for himself the vocation of discovering an order in human experience by means of the poem. In one essay after another, throughout most of his career, he explores the poet's role. Before turning to his next collection, *Al Que Quiere!*, let us look briefly at these explorations.

For Williams the poem is always related to people. 'I made up my mind', he wrote in the mid-thirties, 'that everything must come out of someone and relate to him, first and last. And it had to be for all, whether they liked it or not . . . . You build houses, for people. Poems are the same' (*SE*, 177–8). On the one hand he maintained a Keatsian sense of the unimportance of the poet's personal concerns, of his need 'to be nothing and unaffected by the results, to unlock and flow, uncolored, smooth, carelessly — not cling to the unsolvable lumps of personality . . . ' (*SE*, 72). On the other, he frequently asserted a Shelleyan view of the poet, as one

> dealing with actualities not with dreams. But do not be deceived, there is no intention to depict the artist, the poet, as a popular leader in the Rousseauian sense. Rather he builds a structure of government using for this the materials of his verse. His objective is an order. It is through this structure that the artist's permanence and effectiveness are proven. (*SE*, 213)

Many similar passages could be cited, claiming for the artist a socially useful, and therefore positively committed, role. Viewing the artist in relation to his material and his medium, Williams also finds there an active element. Primarily the task is an 'intense vision of the facts' and Williams often speaks as if all the artist need do is accurately record the 'vision'. Yet his sense of 'discovery' has as counterpart the concept of 'invention'. Though, in introducing Byron Vazakas's *Transfigured Night*, he suggests that a good poet 'doesn't *select* his material. What is there to select? It *is*',[17] yet Williams's whole view of the nature of form denies this. A passage in his essay on Charles Sheeler puts it succinctly enough:

> To be an artist, as to be a good artisan, a man must know his materials. But in addition he must possess that really glandular perception of their uniqueness which realizes in them an end in itself, each piece irreplaceable by a substitute, not to be broken down to other meaning. Not to pull out, transubstantiate, boil, unglue, hammer, melt, digest and psychoanalyze, not even to distill but to see and keep what the understanding touches — as grapes are round and come in bunches. To discover and separate these things from the amorphous, the conglomerate

normality with which they are surrounded and of which before the action of 'creation' each is a part, calls for an eye to draw out that detail which is in itself the thing, to clinch our insight, that is, our understanding, of it. (*SE*, 233)

Structural invention, therefore, entails separating the discovered material from 'conglomerate normality'. In this, too, the poet is an active participant rather than a passive recipient.

Williams's views of the poet as providing 'a rival government', as re-creating society (*SE*, 103), and his belief that one element of the poet's nature is to act as unquestioning receptacle, for the poem which alone 'focuses the world' (*SE*, 242), are matched by another romantic attitude, emphasis on an 'intense vision of the facts'. Pervasive especially in the earlier poems, it puts Williams squarely in the American tradition as a proponent of the sense of wonder.[18] He, like Emerson and Whitman before him, rejects analysis, backing the impulse instead. Not only with Emerson, but with Carlyle, Wordsworth, Blake and others, he shares the conviction that in the smallest object, intensely and truly perceived, the whole world may be discoverable. An essential part of the discovery is to attach to things their 'right names'. Hence it is that the artist 'must keep his eye without fault upon those things he values, to which officials constantly refuse to give the proper names' (*SE*, 231).

'Without today everything would be lost' (*SE*, 197), so Williams values present experience, joining Emerson in declaring for 'the everlasting NOW'. The two share also in realizing the importance of common speech in rendering that experience. 'Where else can what we are seeking arise from but speech? From speech, from American speech', says Williams (*SE*, 289), a point he makes many times in the course of his career. Instinctively he realized that one's language is intimately related to one's particular sense of reality. In this matter of language (although, it hardly needs saying, their styles are very different) he finds affinity with his contemporary, Wallace Stevens, and also with Whitman.

Williams's emphasis on the immediately present place and time ranges from subscribing to the Poundian Imagist dictum 'Direct treatment of the thing itself', to a whole host of attitudes shared with Emerson, Thoreau, Whitman and later writers such as Gertrude Stein. In the link with Stein we arrive at the paradox of shifting from the thing-in-itself to the ongoing process of things in being, of experience-in-itself. Stein's 'moment to moment emphasizing'[19] demonstrates the fluidity of experience, the breaking down of the object/noun and the point at which subjective and objective merge. Immersion in the process, however, does not mean subjugation by it, nor that a single reality has been achieved, merely that there is an oscillation between those moments when the 'thing' is singled out for intense scrutiny and those others when the scrutiny is so intense that the observer becomes caught up in the process he is observing. This phenomenon accounts for the bare clarity and hardness of some Williams poems in contrast with the fluidity of others.

An American, but only of the first generation, Williams was doubly cut off from the traditional past. Rejecting Europe, he could lay no easy claim to the American past towards which some of his contemporaries had begun to look for landmarks. He could not do that until he had established the viability of the *present* as a vital source of discovery for what goes into the making of America. Never a chauvinist or a regionalist, Williams's discoveries began from what was presented to his senses. His leading stratagem in *Al Que Quiere!* (1917) is to go directly and simply to the object of concern, but not passively. He partakes of it. Not anchored in mere logic or 'the finished product', he allowed scope to an element of incoherence which, when it served him well, invested his work with great vitality.

So much is made of Williams's 'objectivism' that his lifelong sense of the truth of subjective imagination is often passed over. Yet it is the central force of a poem such as 'Sub Terra' (*CEP*, 117), which opens *Al Que Quiere!* and concerns the search for the creative in the formless void. '— God, if I could fathom / The guts of shadows': the search is for nuances, a circumstance which gave rise to Stevens's gentle strictures upon the 'casual' and 'miscellaneous' character of *Al Que Quiere!* (*Imag.*, 15). Stevens sought a recognized order, but Williams was grappling with process, some elusive, indefinite and indefinable quality of life not to be discovered in the thing itself, but perhaps captured in the music of the poem. 'Danse Russe' (*CEP*, 148), energized in this way, is one of many self-abnegations. With approval, Kenneth Burke labels the poem 'crazy'. As elsewhere (e.g. 'Ballet', *CEP*, 169)[20] the poet is portrayed dancing, a joyous dance, in some degree narcissistic, celebrating artistic loneliness. In tension with his domestic setting, yet he can ask:

> Who shall say I am not
> the happy genius of my household?

Tapping the poet's 'store of madness' (in E. M. Cioran's phrase),
'Danse Russe' is kept under control with a touch of humour and
by musical pacing.

Sharing a humorous quality with 'Danse Russe', 'January
Morning' (*CEP*, 162) again depicts a solitary dance:

> The young doctor is dancing with happiness
> in the sparkling wind, alone . . .

The whole 'suite' is a dance of images, and also of all immediately
observable phenomena in the universe. Their discreteness is an
essential element in this dance. The young doctor, for the moment
at least, is their dancing-master, the intensity of his relationship
to them preventing a centrifugal tendency in the poem as a whole.
The dance becomes openly identified with the technique of exact
observation, the measuring, the imposition of order. Williams's
control is achieved largely through the same freedom of cadencing
as is observable in 'The Wanderer'. 'January Morning' closes with
the famous declaration to his Muse that this poem is intended as
something 'that you would understand'. Failing in that aim, any
poem is useless, even for the poet himself. 'But', he tells her, 'you
got to try hard.' American as it is, the idiom is employed to tell
how:

> the young girls run giggling
> on Park Avenue after dark
> when they ought to be home in bed

but also to evoke the natural scene and include the early exploration of America, and Shakespeare. To extend, not to
circumscribe, the sense of immediate reality — this is the necessity
of American speech in its own locale.

'Canthara' (*CEP*, 143) is a slyly humorous treatment of the
dance, the sexual dance of vigorous youth contrasted with the
dance of memory of the old man urinating, responding to the
'familiar music' with a wry music of his own. The deliberate
indelicacy of this scene sharply focuses one aspect of Williams's

sense of beauty, which he touches upon again in the fine opening lines of the otherwise sentimental 'Apology' (*CEP*, 131):

> The beauty of
> the terrible faces
> of our nonentities
> stirs me to it . . .

Taking his measure from the lives of everyday working people, combining it with his own 'nervous nature', Williams mastered the short line in *Al Que Quiere!*, basing it on speech rhythms.

Another feature of the book is a physical sense of colour. We may recall Williams's early desire to be a painter, his friendships with Demuth, Sheeler and others, his response to the 1913 Armory Show, recollected even long afterwards with excitement. All this is recognized in the closing pages of his *Autobiography* where he observes that 'It was the work of the painters following Cézanne and the Impressionists that, critically, opened up the age of Stein, Joyce and a good many others' (p. 380). Painterliness is observable in *Al Que Quiere!* in such well-known poems as 'Tract' and 'To a Solitary Disciple', which have a narrative or discursive sequence, but Dijkstra points to other poems — 'Dawn', 'Spring Strains', 'A Portrait in Greys' among them — 'in which the action occurs within the limits of a visual plane and within an instant of visual perception . . . consequently without a clearly defined narrative sequence'.[21]

A key poem, 'To a Solitary Disciple' (*CEP*, 167), is concerned with just the problem of distinguishing essential from secondary qualities. In part, it is an appeal to the disciple *to keep his eye on the object*, for the sheer practice of precise observation which he himself claimed for 'Gulls' (*CEP*, 126; also in *Al Que Quiere!*); but 'To a Solitary Disciple' goes far beyond that and beyond the Imagist doctrine which had been Williams's principal guide during the period when he was associated with Alfred Kreymborg and the *Others* group. A demonstration, it instructs the disciple to penetrate the surface image to essentials, to seek what Williams would later call 'the radiant gist'. Here he emphasizes not the accidental but the indispensable or universal qualities of the scene. Behind every injunction for us to *see* is Williams's realization that what 'is' differs from our experience of it; but true poems are made from the effort to bring these two facts of experience closer to each other. The cut back line, the 'short breath' measure, aids such a purpose.[22]

Curiously, in 'Gulls' (only part sheer observation) we find a fair example of the many impediments Williams was so soon to discard completely, like the conscious address to 'my townspeople', characteristic of a number of early poems, which is the poet too openly displaying one aspect of his sense of the artist — he the eagle, they the gulls. Addressing the people in a long, quite heavily punctuated line, he reports an event in his own life. Such a strategy, deliberately placing a barrier between poem and experience, would not satisfy Williams for long, as may be seen in many poems of that period, such as 'Dedication to a Plot of Ground' (*CEP*, 171).[23] Although by no means free of punctuation, it is organized, in line and syntax, in a dynamic thrust through to its rough, energetic, colloquial conclusion, which seems entirely fitting with all that has preceded it. Sometimes such a thrust is made almost without punctuation, as in 'Winter Sunset', 'Dawn' (*CEP*, 127, 138). This forward movement illustrates Williams's understanding of Aristotle, his insistence on the distinction between *copying* nature and *imitating* nature.[24] Art is a re-presentation, an 'enlargement of nature', a parallel action involving the imagination. The poem as an action re-presents nature as process — in 'Dawn', for example, as the verbal series 'pound', 'beating', 'rising', 'stirring', 'quickening', 'bursting', 'spreading', 'dividing', 'lumbering' — each in form and denotation conveying movement and energy.

Much of the strength of Williams's best work is drawn from his leaning to noun (thing) and verb (process). Deployment of the verb, to become one of his chief working methods, is related to what he later (in the Preface to *Paterson*) termed 'interpenetration'. Thus, in 'Winter Quiet' (*CEP*, 141), his own reactions to winter become part of the scene, of 'nature':

> Tense with suppressed excitement
> the fences watch where the ground
> has humped an aching shoulder for
> the ecstasy.

Technically, interpenetration is related to *juxtaposition*, a chief means of metamorphic poems. While not strictly a definition of interpenetration, a sentence from Hillis Miller's profound study of Williams may illuminate here: 'Sometimes the space of a poem is a multiplicity of things felt together and muscle against muscle.'[25] 'Drink' (*CEP*, 140) is an instance of juxtaposition being used to suggest an actual interpenetrative failure, while the sense of interpenetration is held in the poem's Whitmanesque closing lines:

> Where shall I have that solidity
> which trees find
> in the ground?
>
> My stuff
> is the feel of good legs
> and a broad pelvis
> under the gold hair ornaments
> of skyscrapers.
>
>   (*CEP*, 140)[26]

The poem's two elements, drink (instability) and rootedness (a prime virtue for Williams) are set over against each other, and that is the action/intensity achieved by deliberate association of unlike elements, in this instance dissolving into (and resolved by) free association. Yet even here the question, set in the middle of the poem, is a more direct approach than Williams would later prefer.

At this stage directness, combined with understatement, contributes considerably towards establishing Williams's world in the poem and his stance towards it, as two of the 'Pastoral' poems show (*CEP*, 121, 124). The first is an amplification of his sense of 'inner security':

> When I was younger
> it was plain to me
> I must make something of myself.
> Older now
> I walk back streets
> admiring the houses
> of the very poor:

Precisely cataloguing perceived objects, he concludes:

> No one
> will believe this
> of vast import to the nation.

Two overt contrasts are made in the second poem: between the
sparrows hopping on the pavement and the 'shut-in' lives of
humans, and between the movement of 'the old man who goes
about / gathering dog-lime' and that of the episcopal minister
(one of the more obviously sentimental comparisons of Williams's
earlier work). The poem concludes:

> These things
> astonish me beyond words.
> (*CEP*, 124)

In both poems Williams is actually offering us a self-portrait,
recording his own responses with a directness (i.e. a degree of
comment), which he would soon come to see as undesirable.
Unstated, but in the tone, is his view of the poem as a moral
commitment. This commitment is complex, involving the poet in
searching for the creative in formlessness ('Sub Terra', *CEP*, 117),
for harmony ('To a Solitary Disciple', *CEP*, 167), for the fugitive,
subtle quality of beauty which is to be discovered in the ordinary
as much as anywhere.

To pursue the search means often to reject the conventional
view, as in 'To a Solitary Disciple' and 'Tract' (*CEP*, 129), where
distinctions between essential and secondary are related to social
action. Separating conventional from essential at the funeral (in
'Tract') is to maintain contact with reality and thereby more
honour the dead. By analogy Williams is stating his practice as
poet.

A minor element of *Al Que Quiere!* is Williams's ambivalent
sense of 'dream'. In 'Libertad! Igualidad! Fraternidad!' (*CEP*,
134), a socio-political incident contains the activist 'It is dreams
that have destroyed us' and the fatalist 'dreams are not a bad
thing', which anticipates the observation in 'The Poem as a Field
of Action' that 'The poem is a dream, a daydream of wish fulfill-
ment ... the *subject-matter* of the poem is always phantasy —
what is wished for, realized in the "dream" of the poem ... ' (*SE*,
281). This conflict is handled with subtlety in the juxtapositions
of 'Good Night' (*CEP*, 145), where the objective reality of 'a glass

filled with parsley-crisped green' is set over against the romanticism of 'memory playing the clown', evoking pictures of 'three
vague, meaningless girls', their 'little slippers' and 'high-school
French'. Memory, the clown, has transformed them into
'phantasy', to which the glass of fresh parsley is said to be preferable. The poem is discovered in momentary circumstance but
'three girls in crimson satin' have dominated the poet's imagination. In some sense the object on the draining-board and the
subjective memory of the opera have equal value. They represent
an *inclusion* as well as a possible choice, the melding of objective-
subjective expressed in a key line of 'The Wanderer', 'I knew all
— it became me', to be repeated nearly half a century later in
Paterson V. From another point of view, this awareness of dream-
fantasy is a continuing sense of the 'subversive' in life. The chief
characteristic of *Al Que Quiere!*, however, is what Kenneth Burke
calls Williams's 'remarkable powers of definition, of lucidity'.[27]

2 Descent and Contact

What Williams regarded as, for him, a new kind of poem was the 'improvisation', examples of which he published in the *Little Review* in 1917 and 1918. For many years, at intervals he continued to employ the mode, but his most significant work in it was was formed into *Kora in Hell* (1920). He was influenced by Pound in using the Persephone (Kora)[1] myth, but it exactly complements another motif frequently repeated in his own work, the Venus.

'From "The Birth of Venus", Song' (*CEP*, 20) was first published in English in the *Poetry Review* (1912). The motif occurs again in *A Voyage to Pagany* (1928), and in *January: a Novelette and Other Prose* (1932) is 'The Venus', which Pound claims was 'written to occur somewhere' in *A Voyage to Pagany*.[2] Other allusions and references may be found in *Selected Essays* and *Paterson*. In *Collected Later Poems* we find 'Venus Over the Desert' and the long-lined 'The Birth of Venus'.

'Born again, Venus from the confused sea ... ',[3] Venus is the 'reduction to one'; ' ... she is one. Over and over again, she is one'. Venus is also 'beautiful thing', the 'radiant gist' of fully realized form, the 'fierce singleness' which is the opposite of 'divorce', separateness, the flux, multiplicity. Rising up through the waves in beauty, Venus is the classic wholeness, the 'direct object' which Williams valued so much in Marianne Moore's work, 'free from the smears of mystery, as pliant, as "natural" as Venus on the waves'.[4]

This acceptance of the *thing* unmodified, intrinsic in beauty, contrasts with the Kora motif, immersion in 'the filthy Passaic', descent to the 'formless ground'. Thus the 'improvisations' are complementary to Williams's short-lined, 'hard, dry' poems of 'accurate description'.[5] Together, the two motifs attest to Williams's intuition of the co-presence of ascent and descent, order and chaos, form and formlessness, that there can be no radium without 'pitchblende'.

17

Before City Lights reprinted *Kora in Hell* in 1957 an interesting exchange of letters (now in Yale) between Williams and Lawrence Ferlinghetti brought out certain things about the work. Ferlinghetti at first wished to select from the text to fit his series of small, 48-page saddle-back publications. Kenneth Rexroth, apparently offering his services as editor, suggested that the original prologue might be omitted as being too wordy. By then Ferlinghetti had come to think that the original document, as an entity, had historical validity, but Random House had included the Prologue in *Selected Essays* not very long before (1954). Finally Williams himself suggested printing without the Prologue and replaced it with another, much briefer.[6]

The original Prologue was written after the improvisations, differing greatly from them in character. A collage of anecdotes, letters received, fragments of poem, it is an important document and introduces the technique Williams was to establish as his *modus operandi* for a great part of his more extended work. Following up his well-known definition, 'seeing the thing itself without forethought or after-thought but with great intensity of perception' he attempts to ally his sense of the poem with the 'found objects' of Marcel Duchamp and Bob Brown's 'ready-mades'. What interests him is 'novelty' (both improvisations and prologue are under Pound's influence), so he rejects H. D.'s fervency: 'there is nothing sacred about literature . . . it'll be good if the authentic spirit of change is upon it' (*SE*, 10). (1M.13)

Seeing that 'change is mockery' to any sense of the poem as masterpiece or object of devotion, he says of the specific poem to which H.D. had plaintively objected: 'it filled a gap that I did not know how better to fill at the time'. Acutely conscious of the flux, Williams realized instinctively that his own work was part of it. He had to ensure two things: one, that 'what actually impinges on the senses must be rendered as it appears by use of which only, and under which, untouched, the significance has to be disclosed' (*SE*, 119); and two, that in the rendering, the thing itself remains part of the living flux, does not become an ossified museum-piece.   (1M.14)

Vaunting the 'thing itself', the true, against the 'associational or sentimental value . . . the false' (*SE*, 11), he saw lack of imagination as one source of sentimentality, another being the literary 'pastime' of creating similes. Both detract from the real object of the poet's search, undermining his crucial 'power which discovers in things those inimitable particles of dissimilarity to all other things which are the peculiar perfections of the thing in question' (*SE*, 16). Emphasizing, as he does here, his agreement with Pound's call for 'direct treatment of the thing itself', Williams appears to be repeatedly deflected, in the Prologue, from an accurate sense of what the improvisations meant for him. His thought oscillates between 'thing' and process. Appearing to accept (and misquote)[7] Pound's well-known response to the improvisation, 'The thing that saves your work is opacity', Williams knows that this quality comes to him from the nature of 'things' themselves, and that another aspect of opacity is escape from, rejection of, fixed or traditional forms in favour of 'broken' composition. Dependent in no way on a logical recounting of events, the poem does not even derive from *events* as such, 'but solely from that attenuated power which draws perhaps many broken things into a dance giving them thus a full being' (*SE*, 14). (IM. 17)

Both in his devotion to the object and in his pursuit of imaginative freedom in the improvisations, Williams, is, in a very real sense, anti-literary. When he suggests that 'The attention has been held too rigid on the one plane instead of following a more flexible, jagged resort. It is to loosen the attention, my attention since I occupy part of the field, that I write these improvisations' *Heisenberg* (*SE*, 11), he is anticipating McLuhan's criticism of the *lineal* M. 14 nature of modern American society (and, by extension, Western society as a whole). Some light is cast on Williams's work if we see him as intuitively in sympathy with what McLuhan was to call 'oral man', for whom 'all time is now', whose sense of the world is of 'simultaneity and inclusiveness'.[8]

Literariness is one outcome of literateness. Williams concludes a very early poem ('Immortal') with a pair of rhyming quatrains:

> And thou, beloved, art that godly thing!
> Marvelous and terrible; in glance
> And injured June roused against Heaven's King!
> And thy name, lovely One, is Ignorance.
> (*CEP*, 21)

In the *Kora* Prologue he speaks of 'The raw beauty of ignorance that lies like an opal mist over the west coast of the Atlantic, beginning at the Grand Banks and extending into the recesses of our brains' (*SE*, 16). As he makes clear, this is related to a passage

(IM.21)

in the main text. Both concern interpenetration, and explain his response to 'the terrible faces of our nonentities'. Ignorance, in his sense, is closely allied to innocence and that, in its turn, means an avoidance of being fundamentally intellectual. Favoured with such innocence man can more easily participate in 'the thing itself' and thus be more readily open to experience. Not riddled with half-truths, it is the 'ignorant' who are capable of that 'thousandth part of accurate understanding' and of discovering the music in things. 'Nothing is good save the new', a concept hinted at earlier in 'the new distance' of 'The Wanderer'.

Tension created by the opposition between 'thing itself' and 'the authentic spirit of change' is the central working principle of the improvisations, whose function is 'the shifting of categories . . . the disjointing process . . . '.[9] Williams recognizes that when a moment of balance does occur (which may be the poem), the poet retreats from it as from a doom, preferring the flux itself, which is life, 'the gross buffetings of good and evil fortune'. The furthest reach away from such a balance or stoppage is interpenetration. This is vital process, the dance of life:

> Ha, goodbye, I have a rendez vous in
> the tips of three birch sisters.
> *Encouragez vos musiciens!* Ask them to
> play faster. I will return — later.
> Ah you are kind. — and I? must dance
> with the wind, make my own snow flakes,
> whistle a contrapuntal melody to my
> own fuge [*sic*]! Huzza then, this is
> the dance of the blue moss bank!
> Huzza then, this is the mazurka of the
> hollow log! Huzza then, this is the
> dance of rain in the cold trees.
>
> (KH, 13)

In the imagination everything is held in another kind of balance or, rather, a dance, which the mind can order as it will, holding opposites to itself. Apart from its often-noticed relationship to Rimbaud's *Les Illuminations*,[10] this is akin to the first part of Bergson's aesthetic theory, summarized by Hulme as, 'the conception of reality as a flux of interpenetrated elements unseizable by the intellect . . . '.[11]

Williams has a good deal to say on the connection between imagination and reality. While, in art, imagination controls reality, it is also dependent on reality. Imagination is free of the time category, having *'neither beginning nor end'* so that *'it delights in its own seasons reversing the usual order at will. Of the air of the coldest room it will seem to build the hottest passions'* (*KH*, 15). The cold room, the dead young woman of intelligence and the murdered *'fellow of very gross behaviour'*, these are the 'array' of facts. Making no explicit moral distinctions, the poet sends them 'on their way side by side'. Imagination 'can instruct the mind' in the proper uses of emotions and experiences.

Imagination juxtaposes complementary oppositions, which may widen out into a total realization of the relativeness of all possibilities, hence perhaps the continuing fascination for Williams of his notion of Einstein. Was it Pope Clement who raped Persephone, or 'did the devil wear a mitre in that year?' (*KH*, 23). Such speculation is set off against the attempt to impose order through written 'history', 'an attempt to make the past seem stable and of course it's all a lie'. The relativeness of all facts is held in poise not by history but by art, which 'perfects' the facts it employs as substance: *'the perfections revealed by a Rembrandt are equal whether it be question of a laughing Saskia or an old woman cleaning her nails'* (*KH*, 24).

Repeated reference to hands (and fingernails) in *Kora in Hell* testifies to the importance of the sense of touch, which in turn is related to sexuality, the primary opposition. 'Your hands please. Ah, if I had your hands.' The hands are an offering of the self and (Williams universalizes the image through anthropology) are the instruments when 'the nights are long for lice combing or moon dodging — and the net comes in empty again' (*KH*, 36). Present touch, present sensation, NOW — these are the important things. Thus it is pointless to 'remember the weather two years back'.

Now, or two years back, at every stage the poet is Herculean, carrying the world upon his shoulders. In this way he transcends subjective and objective categories as 'the imagination transcends the thing itself'. Each imagination has its own 'weather' (as he will come to say that a community has a prevailing 'weather') (*SE*, 196ff.) in which *'The true seasons blossom or wilt not in fixed order but so that many of them may pass in a few weeks or hours whereas sometimes a whole life passes and the season remains of a piece from one end to the other'* (*KH*, 83).

Later, Williams himself saw the 'dislocation of sense' in the improvisations as a fault, but he realized that he had discovered methods and 'values' which could be extended. Karl Shapiro is, perhaps, going a little too far when he sees the method of *Kora in Hell* as 'identical' with that of *Paterson*,[12] but they have in common at least the juxtapositional technique. In fact, many foreshadowings of later work occur in *Kora in Hell*, and this interlinking was to become characteristic. There are notations for *In the American Grain*, a brief passage on the 'green-flowered asphodel', and, anticipating *Paterson*, drunkenness and Phyllis. Drafts of *Paterson* include material directly quoted from *Kora in Hell*. Most importantly, certain lifelong preoccupations are intimated or touched upon in *Kora in Hell*.

Freedom, instability, what he would later term 'carelessness', these characterize the poet's descent into 'Hell', which is himself. His aim is not self-exploration in the Romantic, egotist sense — but an attempt to cast aside the veil imposed on experience by ratiocination. No fixed line of reference is adhered to, even in terms of the conception of descent. Kora becomes Orpheus, but more often Hercules, whose burden is the world itself. Sometimes experience ('degradation'), sometimes age, is the descent — the depth as often as not proving to be a summit. Descent and ascent are one. They are aspects of the dance which holds all things in balance or relation. Williams had already used this image of the dance in early poems such as 'Ballet', 'Danse Russe' and 'January Morning', but in *Kora in Hell* it becomes crucial to the reordering of his perceptions and he makes it his central image for being fully alive. To be fully alive means to hold vitally balanced within oneself all possibilities. Williams also touches upon the importance of 'the language of the day' in the imagination's very texture (*KH*, 49), asserting that, otherwise, 'a poem can be made of anything', form created from formlessness. '*That which is known*' has form, but it has value '*only by virtue of the dark*' which is formlessness. The known is that which is totally assimilated into one's being, which '*passes out of the mind into the muscles*' (*KH*, 71).

Such a known thing is now related to the will in reacting to formlessness. Words, language are a chief agent of this reaction or 'vibration', but their value is not an absolute. A word, the 'one true phrase', is no more true than its opposite, every solid is an 'April zephyr', yet 'The particular thing . . . dwarfs the imagination, makes logic a butterfly, offers a finality that sends us spinning through space, a fixity the mind could climb forever, a revolving mountain, a complexity with a surface of glass: the gist of poetry' (*KH*, 82).

Kora in Hell is important not least for showing how Williams attempted to maintain concurrently a view of the primacy of the 'thing itself' and of the transcendent value of imagination, a view ramified in 'Notes from a Talk on Poetry': 'The world of the senses lies unintelligible on all sides. It only exists when its emotion is fastened to it. This is artistic creation.'[13] Here the 'fastening' of emotion to action is virtually identical with transforming it imaginatively, but there is another point of importance. Even a great scientific discovery (e.g. the Curies' isolating of radium) is 'stale, useless' once achieved. Only the very act of discovery engenders a live emotion. Adapting from Pound, Williams observes that 'a truth twenty years old is a lie because the emotion has gone out of it'. (Years later he will describe a corpse as 'a lie' for the same reason.) In contrast to this he introduces an idea which was to become central for the 'Objectivists': 'To each thing its special quality, its special value that will enable it to stand alone. When each Poem has achieved its particular form unlike any other, when it shall stand alone — then we have achieved our language.'

Achievement of a language, this is the poet's task. Experience becomes 'objective' only when it is made so for us by the discovery, invention, of the language proper to it. 'To discover and separate . . . things from the amorphous . . . calls for an eye to draw out that detail which is in itself the thing . . . ' (*SE*, 233). The poet is one with a talent for revealing the essential synecdoche, but elsewhere (in 'The Poem as a Field of Action') Williams points to language itself as the source, or origin, of discoveries: 'Where else can what we are seeking arise from but speech? From speech, from American speech . . . ' (*SE*, 289).

Words have the same integrity as other *things*, for they, too, are 'things'. Once more we encounter difficulty in Williams's thinking about the poem, and about experience. A dichotomy presents itself, again in terms of the distinction between *thing* and *process*, or object and energy. The poet's discovery of the form appropriate to his day is utterly dependent on what the common speech of his day happens to be. His role is to *recognize*.

Such recognition cannot occur without *contact*, as Williams and Robert McAlmon perceived when they started *Contact* in 1920. With Pound in mind, and presumably Dewey's essay on 'Americanism and Localism',[14] Williams produced a 'Sample Critical Statement' asserting that the artist's work must begin in 'the sensual accidents of his immediate contacts', in the achieving of a *locus*. Even great phases of other countries' art depend on their source localities. The locality is important because *contact* is important. This is the main emphasis of Williams's prose pieces for the magazine and is, in some sense, what the fictional character Evan Dionysius ('Dev') Evans stands for in the *Contact* story wherein he first appears, and also later in *A Voyage to Pagany*.

Contact of itself does not make art, but it is essential to art. No writing can be of value unless it derives from contact with experience, which means contact with other human beings. By definition, all experience must be local and will inevitably be affected by its location. To hold so is not parochial, and even memory and imagination depend intially on contact. 'What are its contacts?' is the most important, perhaps the only important, question to ask of any work. Despite the obvious fact that many American achievements — in building, machinery, manufacture, etc. — have been brought about by 'paying naked attention first to the thing itself', Williams observes that his fellows are timid in applying this principle to the arts. Even criticism, to be at its fullest value, must originate in the environment which has produced the work itself.

Williams described his next collection, *Sour Grapes*, as 'a mood book . . . poems of disappointment and sorrow' (*IWWP*, 33), but this can be misleading if it is applied to the focus of the poems rather than the impetus behind them. When the manuscript was under discussion with Edmund Brown of the Four Seas Publishing Company, it had the working title 'Picture Poems', which accurately attests to Williams's continuing imagism. 'I was lyrical', he said later, 'but I was determined to use the material I knew and much of it did not lend itself to lyricism' (*IWWP*, 35).

Placed as it is between *Kora in Hell* and *Spring and All*, both of which are landmarks in Williams's development, *Sour Grapes* seems something of a transitional work, with nothing especially to show in the way of new technical discoveries. Dominant is the poet's mood of dissatisfaction with the tenor of his everyday life. Poems focus on isolated figures, such as the doctor going about his medical duties in bad weather (in 'Complaint', for example), or baulked of human communication, as in 'Arrival':

> And yet one arrives somehow,
> finds himself loosening the hooks of
> her dress
> in a strange bedroom —
> feels the autumn
> dropping its silk and linen leaves
> about her ankles.
> The tawdry veined body emerges
> twisted upon itself
> like a winter wind . . . !
>
> (*CEP*, 215)

Subtle antithesis is made between such alienation and the artist's relatively 'happy' loneliness:

> When I am alone I am happy . . . .
> When I reach my doorstep
> I am greeted by
> the happy shrieks of my children
> and my heart sinks.
> I am crushed.
>
> (*CEP*, 213)

The long poem 'March' speaks of 'the happy loneliness of poetry',[15] and this mood also marks 'The Lonely Street'.

'Memory of April' (*CEP*, 207) represents another mood. In a letter to the mid-west poet, Alva Turner, in 1920, Williams wrote 'Disgust is my most moving emotion . . . . I am always, unhappily, knee deep in blue mud.'[16] Disgust permeates his sense of sexual experience in 'Arrival' and similar sexual disgust is an important element in 'To a Friend Concerning Several Ladies' (*CEP*, 216), another poem of the poet's desire to pursue his vocation while conscious of being impeded by the world. His passion for women and his feeling for the city are correlated. He is concerned to achieve a balance between these desires and to live a quiet writer's life, with 'a few chrysanthemums . . . a few people'. Too much 'city' leads to self-disgust, too much of writing to staleness, so that implicitly one is necessary to the other.

A good number of affirmative poems in *Sour Grapes* are

centred in flowers: 'Daisy', 'Primrose', 'Queen Anne's Lace', 'Great Mullen', 'The Tulip Bed', 'Blueflags'. 'Daisy' accumulates details of accurate observation concerning flower and scene (the daisy is 'the sun . . . upon a slender green stem') allowing these details to carry crucial hints of a larger world, the world of sexual love. 'Queen Anne's Lace' has the same larger theme. The woman's body is seen in terms of white flowers, but the poem is not so much metaphorical as analogical, its terms being kept separate. Woman and flowers share a quality of whiteness ('a clarity beyond the facts'), so that what is distinctive about them individually is a defining, unique radiance. Again, immediate attention has been paid to accurate observation.[17]

The same complex of sexual feeling expressed through minutely observed nature is characteristic of 'Great Mullen' (this group of poems is *CEP*, 208–11). More overtly an action, this poem is closely controlled in its punctuation and syntax. It jerks from one short, emphatic phrase to the next, in contrast with the declarative 'Blueflags' (*CEP*, 225), whose lines are organized in groups which Williams would many years later call 'the variable foot', thrust through from beginning of poem to end. Where in 'Great Mullen' the poet's consciousness is moving jerkily, disturbed (as befits the poem's sexual level), in 'Blueflags' the consciousness is serene, serial, causal, with the poem's interest held chiefly in the way line placement responds to causal pattern.

Yet another aspect of Williams's practice may be discerned in 'To Waken an Old Lady' (*CEP*, 200), whose opening anticipates that of *Paterson V*: 'Old age is / a flight of small / cheeping birds . . .'. Once on course this is a typical Williams Imagist poem, but the opening line endows it with somewhat different character. The phrase is similar in function to 'so much depends upon', which opens 'The Red Wheelbarrow', but in specifying 'old age' he has transformed the poem into a thought-out analogy (which one critic has even seen as an 'objective correlative').[18] This procedure is different from the customary Williams, not because his is an entirely 'unmediated vision'; he is not so totally free of metaphor as some critics (Karl Shapiro, for example) hold, but usually he presents his material 'objectively' before exploiting it metaphorically.

Before putting together *Sour Grapes*, Williams had offered criteria by which a reader might judge his poems: contact, the local, descent, the recognition of Venus, American speech. Yet the book itself offers difficulties. Contrary to often-expressed aims of tightness and accuracy, such poems as 'A Celebration', 'A Good Night', 'Overture to a Dance of Locomotives' and 'Portrait of the Author' (which McAlmon rescued from the wastepaper basket) are long-lined and diffuse. We cannot discover a single rationale or method for these pieces (two are grouped by Hillis Miller as poems of 'dissonance'),[19] and later Williams would avoid such syntactical and grammatical explicitness. On the other hand, his most baldly direct rendering of the object, 'The Great Figure' (*CEP*, 230) lacks the reverberation which so often makes his Imagist poems more than mere standard products of the kind. His next real advance towards the American poem is in the prose/poetry melding of *Spring and All*.

3 *Spring and All*

In method, *Spring and All*[1] is a step nearer to *Paterson*, its alternating prose and poetry combining techniques derived from the Cubist painters, especially Juan Gris. The prose sections, in particular, were also influenced by the Americans centred around the New York photographer Alfred Stieglitz.

Opening with a long prose section, *Spring and All* goes at once to the point, emphasizing *contact* and the rejection of past and future for *now* (this is following Stieglitz, along with Rosenfeld and Hartley[2]), the present moment. Then there is the puzzling assertion, reiterated at intervals throughout Williams's life, apparently inconsistent with his 'No ideas but in things', but working in quite a different direction:

> I love my fellow creature . . . but he doesn't
> exist! Neither does she. I do, in a
> bastardly sort of way.
>
> To whom then am I addressed? To
> the imagination.[3]

Here, and elsewhere, Williams is not suggesting that 'reality' exists only as a figment of his own imagination. For him the imagination intensifies a pre-existent reality. From this intensification comes the 'eternal moment' when we are truly alive. Thus it is, in effect, a Joycean epiphany. The season gives *Spring and All* its particular character, of a beginning, a birth, with cataclysmic power, expressed in a key image which was to become central: 'The rock has split, the egg has hatched' (*Imag.*, 97), here power, delicacy and beauty go together.

Part manifesto, part evocation, the prose opening focuses in the first poem, now usually titled 'Spring and All' (*Imag.*, 95–6). A poem of birth, it *embodies* process. As Dijkstra rightly says, its success is due to the careful selection of objective, natural detail

28

for 'a landscape, much like the brooding photographs in which Stieglitz presented elements of nature as equivalents to his innermost emotions',[4] yet the poem's force is carried in its form:

> By the road to the contagious hospital
> under the surge of the blue
> mottled clouds driven from the
> northeast — a cold wind.

Almost, but not quite, a metaphor, driven from the northeast over the patchy mud fields, this wind *is* the birth of spring. Objectively rendered, 'the stark dignity of / entrance' is the poem's core, for 'dignity' is the centrifugal point to which the emotion ultimately attaches, especially the dignity of the plants' 'entrance', as they, rooted, 'grip down and begin to awaken'. A process has been enacted (though perhaps in visual terms, as Dijkstra suggests, it is comparable with an Arthur Dove painting) and Williams also has described his own poetic method:

> One by one objects are defined —
> It quickens: clarity, outline of leaf.

The landscape is the same one Scott Fitzgerald had seen in terms of Eliot's *Waste Land* but Williams asserts it is a 'new world', the place or rootedness, wherein the poet, too, discovers his roots By paying naked attention to the details of landscape the poet has arrived, slowly and painfully, at definition — the discovery of words to 'quicken' the 'waste of broad, muddy fields' into true being.

Poem II (now called 'The Pot of Flowers' — *Imag.*, 96) is also of roots sources. Beginning with petals, going to the leaves and, finally, the 'dark' where the flowers are rooted, Williams is intent on conveying that this 'dark' is suffused upward through the plant, for even though the petals are 'radiant with transpiercing light', they are also of 'shaded flame' and 'darkened with mauve'. His sense of flowers as rooted in ground, but reaching out from it, is very strong and is sometimes used to give a special and peculiar sense of a human's place in nature, for example in 'Sympathetic Portrait of a Child' (*CEP*, 155), where the murderer's little daughter is described from the head downwards, with slanting, averted eyes, tendril-like arms, a flowered dress, thin twisting legs, her hair deflecting light and her hands holding out a straw hat.

'The Pot of Flowers' and the following poem, on 'the artist figure of / the farmer', are concerned with design. Rejecting tradition, the ensuing prose passage vaunts the new, particularly on the grounds that 'design is a function of the IMAGINATION' (*Imag.*, 98). The farmer's function (*Imag.*, 98–9) is analogous to the poet's, his sowing of the seed comparable with the poet's use of imagination. Ground and wind are the natural setting. The farmer imposes an order on the sowing, which might have come about naturally and haphazardly by means of the wind. His orderliness will make reaping easier for him. This orderliness is also a function of the imagination. Man's need for it is what makes nature, in a sense, his antagonist, for nature has its own order, which may not coincide with man's design. Sowing, then, is akin to the poet's action of discovery or recognition.

Regarded as a single work, *Spring and All* presents problems. Ostrom, for example, has argued that the poems are a unity (and in so doing has argued against explication, seeing Williams's typical poem as 'completely free from interpretation or comment — the images stand alone, the things in themselves, with only the method of their arrangement to give (implicitly) any understanding of their "meaning" (reality).'[5] He sees subsequent omission of the prose as a stripping down of the work to essentials, but in *Go Go* a *selection* of the poems was published as a booklet[6] and in *Collected Poems 1921–1931* the *Spring and All* poems are arranged in an order different from the original. The opposite view to Ostrom's is taken by Linda Wagner, for example, who claims that prose and poems are integral, but offers no compelling reasons.[7]

Williams himself, most ostensibly in his repeated rejections of 'subject matter', preferred that his poems be 'completely free from interpretation or comment'. His most useful of many statements of the position occurs in 'Notes in Diary Form', where he names the condition he is seeking, 'vividness':

poetry should strive for nothing else, this vividness alone, *per se*, for itself. The realization of this has its own internal fire that is 'like' nothing. Therefore the bastardy of the simile. That thing, the vividness of which is poetry by itself, makes the poem. There is no need to explain or compare. Make it and it

is a poem. This is modern, not the saga. There are no sagas —
only trees now, animals, engines: There's that.   (*SE*, 68)

This is the condition of his finest poems, but the very vividness
offers us something beyond itself. Yet *Spring and All* is organized
at least as a series. Even if such a poem as 'The Red Wheelbarrow'
can, as pure images, impinge on us by its 'vividness' alone,
Williams himself was conscious of something more being involved,
as his opening line to that small poem testifies. While the best
poems of *Spring and All* offer themselves 'free from interpretation', the work as a whole invites it.

   In the *Go Go* selection and *Collected Poems 1921-1931*, poem
IV, 'Flight to the City', is placed first. Its fragmentariness seems
to deny the meditative coherence of poems I-III, although it
shares elements eith 'The Pot of Flowers' (the light against a black
ground), and with 'The Farmer':

> > Nobody
> to say it —
> > Nobody to say: pinholes
> in the sky.
> > > > *(Imag.*, 99)

Reasons for the changed order are not readily apparent. Equating
the city with sexual love, 'Flight to the City' employs the same
variables as 'To a Friend Concerning Several Ladies' (*CEP*, 216).
The 'pinholes' are stars, but also where the seed is sown. Seen
against cityscape rather than 'blank fields', the poet's job is to:
'Burst it asunder / break through to the fifty words / necessary',
which appears also to be the lover's task in the city.

   Two things about the poem are worth noting: its brokenness of
line, apparently enacting the 'sundering', and its quasi-symbolical
use of the city. More than 'vividness' is involved in a perception of
'skyscrapers / filled with nut-chocolates'. Yet the prose passage
immediately following is an attack on symbolism (*Imag.*, 100-2).
In pursuit of 'the thing itself', Williams would continue to
condemn symbolism (for example, in his essay 'Against the
Weather', included in *Selected Essays* dated 1939) and yet make
use of symbols and quasi-symbolical motifs. A motif of *Spring
and All* is the wind, cold in the first three poems, 'dovetame' in
'Flight to the City'. The cold wind of 'Spring and All', herald of

birth, is also agent of destruction, explicitly so in poem V, 'The Black Winds' (*Imag.*, 102; titled 'The Immemorial Wind' later, in *An Early Martyr*). Here black/white is momentarily aligned with birth and death: 'Hate is of the night and the day / of flowers and rocks' but immediately Williams is aware of what is implied by writing in this way: 'Nothing / is gained by saying the night breeds / murder — It is the classical mistake', for 'There is nothing in the twist / of the wind but — dashes of cold rain'. Thus the poem is resolved into a comment on method, process, amplified in poem VI following, which states a central Cole-ridgean paradox in Williams:

> everything
> I have done
> is the same
>
> if to do
> is capable
> of an
> infinity of
> combinations

repeated in *Paterson* as the headnote, 'by multiplication a reduction to one'.

At this point refusal to systematize is, in fact, being used as organizational technique. What counts is energy and although 'energy *in vacuo* / has the power / of confusion', 'by the aid of the imagination' it may be combined so that the individual raises himself 'to some approximate co-extension with the universe' (*Imag.*, 105).

Carrying his sense of subject/object interplay into every ex-periential area, Williams perceives the artist as fixing 'the par-ticular with the universality of his own personality'. Form in art is imagination's response to the universe; naturally limited, 'the powers of man are so pitifully small, with the ocean to swallow', but imagination's fullness is nevertheless comparable with the ocean's plenitude. For maker and receiver, fruitful interaction with art shows the 'importance of personality'. When 'completed by the imagination', the individual's life has value even confronted by the immensity of the universe. Hence the futility of attempting to 'copy' nature rather than rendering it (Williams's usage of the Aristotelian theory).

Having just mentioned Juan Gris's attempt to separate paint from representation (imagination from a limited sense of 'reality'), prompted by Gris's Cubist painting 'Roses' (1914), Williams turns his attention to traditional symbolism in 'The rose' (poem VII, *Imag.*, 107-9), finding that, 'The rose is obsolete' (Marion Strobel, reviewing the volume in *Poetry*, finding it 'smart', 'tiresome', 'adolescent', notes, 'he even deprecates the rose'!).[8] Obsolete as a traditional symbol, the rose's 'each petal ends in / an edge'. (Gris's painting and the poem are both full of jagged edges.) Love, therefore, is to be discovered in an actuality which it shares with the petal's edge. As art, 'cold, precise, touching', the petal's edge is 'of steel / infinitely fine': 'The fragility of the flower / unbruised / penetrates space.'

Before passing on it is appropriate to emphasize the great admiration Williams had not only for Gris's painting, but for his thinking about it. Earlier this very year, for example, in 'Notes on my Painting', Gris declared: 'The world from which I draw the elements of reality is not visual but imaginative'.[9]

'At the Faucet of June' (poem VII, *Imag.*, 109-10) then presents the universe's potentialities as disparate elements, uncodified. Resemblances, leaps of the mind, are juxtaposed, exemplifying the immediate world, sun shining on a varnished floor surface, a song 'inflated to / fifty pounds pressure', J. P. Morgan as a satyr in Persephone's cow pasture. We may note in passing that this is a typical instance of Williams's use of the apparently irrelevant, or his sense that all things are relevant.[10] In the poem's conclusion (where the presence of the wind motif may suggest that its method, too, is acceptable relatively) the importance of *what happens* is stressed:

> . . . impossible
> to underestimate —
> wind, earthquakes in
>
> Manchuria, a
> partridge
> from dry leaves.

The co-presence of these details is a discovery of *order* among them, detached 'from ordinary experience to the imagination'. Direct realism in art is bewildering, the 'only realism in art is of the imagination'. These phrases occur in a long prose passage, which is largely a meditation on Gris's work. Today the serious artist must occupy himself in the 'invention of new forms to embody this reality of art' (*Imag.*, 111). This reality, the creative force of imagination, 'completes' science and enables the survival of intelligence. It is the vigour of a process, an accomplishment (suggesting identical means and end). In 'Young Love' (poem IX, *Imag.*, 113; titled 'Young Romance' when included in *An Early Martyr*) the process question, 'What about all this writing?' is answered with parallels — Kiki, the well-known Parisian 'model-songstress' of the twenties[11] and Miss Margaret Jarvis's 'backhandspring'. Against such clean, exact accomplishment is set fuzzy romantic possibility; evoking typical 'disgust': 'Pah! / It is unclean / which is not straight to the mark.' Dismissing such 'young love' (the incident occurs in the city and secretes that city/ artist opposition noted on several occasions) this links back to poem IV: 'Clean is he alone / after whom stream / the broken pieces of the city — / flying apart at his approaches.' Such is the artist, breaker and reintegrator, breaking the city apart, but by his very being drawing the pieces after him into new 'clean' unity. What applies to the artist applies, in some measure, to all men ('When we name it, life exists' — *Imag.*, 115).

Rejecting 'acquisitive understanding', Williams sees his own role as nominalist. As he looks back upon it here, his own intellectual limitations (inherent and circumstantial) caused a long repression relieved only by 'flashes of inspiration' and ultimately by the liberating process of the *Kora in Hell* improvisations, which led him to realize the work to be done in discovering 'new forms, new names for experience'. Simultaneously, it became clear to him that beauty depends on reality ('melon flowers that open / . . . about the edge of refuse'), universalized by imagination. 'The Right of Way' (poem XI, *Imag.*, 119) shows how universal and relative are one and the same, the theme of interrelation being carried through to the next poem, 'Composition'.

As if to prevent easy schematizing, test the tenuity of his view of order, Williams next offers the dissonances of 'The Agonized Spires' (*Imag.*, 124-6) but these tend to turn back on each other — sea / steel / coral / electricity / twilight / triphammers, etc. are interconnected, crucially:

The aggregate
is untamed
encapsulating
irritants
but
of agonized spires
knits
peace.

Imaginatively, death itself ('Death the Barber', *Imag.*, 126) is
included in the composition, leading to the Herclitean realiza-
tions of 'Light Becomes Darkness':

The decay of cathedrals
is efflorescent
through the phenomenal
growth of movie houses

But in our very beings we resist the process of mutability. This
desire to circumvent it is yet an aspect of it:

I can't die

— moaned the old
jaundiced woman
rolling her
saffron eyeballs

I can't die
I can't die
(*Imag.*, 129–30)

What Williams admires is the old woman's assertion of her own
individuality, so also in 'Shoot it Jimmy!' (*Imag.*, 130), the
jazzman's, 'Nobody else / but me — / They can't copy it'.
  Next, in the famous 'To Elsie' (poem XVIII, *Imag.*, 131–3,
'The pure products of America') Williams faces the peculiar
American problem: in what is the imagination to root itself, to
find nutriment? Manifesting in a high degree here his aim to
leave 'the thing itself' undistorted, the poem's core is a concern
for America's apparent lack of deep-rooted tradition. Fusion is

extraordinarily difficult,

> while the imagination strains
> after deer
> going by fields of goldenrod in
>
> the stifling heat of September.

The environment of 'chokecherry / or viburnum' is simply the location of some unspecified outrage, 'as if the earth under our feet / were / an excrement of some sky'. So that

> Somehow
> it seems to destroy us
>
> It is only in isolate flecks that
> something
> is given off

Here also are the 'Dirty satyrs' of 'Horned Purple' (*Imag.*, 136), but interpolated is the example of Pio Baroja, forsaking a limited, intellectual *milieu* to labour manually among 'the social class'. Workers are akin to the artist in possessing 'energy' (which is also 'force', 'rhythm'). Williams's concept of 'energy' is apparently connected with views attributed to Virgil Jordan, the New Jersey economist (husband of Williams's old friend, Viola Baxter) in a *Contact* piece entitled 'Patterns'[12]. Herein the individual is seen as a transformer of 'energy'. In a *creative* discharge of power, 're- sistance is overcome, form given to material, and the individual is in actual contact with the obstacle'. Creative discharge is the discovery of new patterns. In 'free' (truly creative) art 'patterns . . . are moulded to the material'. Artistic activity is the direct discharge of energy on material.

A 'Venus' poem at this point (poem XX) offers the woman's young body held aloft, afloat in clarity ('the sea that is cold') in contrast to 'Underneath the sea where it is dark / there is no edge / or two —' (*Imag.*, 136-7). Beyond the sea's edge (petal's edge) is multiplicity.

The brief poems XXI and XXII (*Imag.*, 137-8) modulate in stages to pure objectiveness. In 'Quietness' we have an objective image, which is disturbed by the single word 'lascivious' (a feeling also present through the hands in 'The Sea') serving to

this vividness alone per se

remind us of the Fall. This method, used in its immediate predecessor, deepens further our response to 'The Red Wheelbarrow', which is lifted above the status of a mere Imagist piece by
its suggestive opening phrase, 'so much depends upon' and, once
again, by the poem's organization on the page, everything physically depending from 'depends', with three nouns — barrow,
water, chickens — thrust at the reader in rapid succession, so that
in each case their 'vividness' carries the preceding 'description'
with it. Apart from its opening phrase, two other verbal elements
activate this poem. Its whole juxtapositional 'vividness' is concentrated into the single word 'beside'. Otherwise 'glazed' is an
energy source, given charge by the surrounding denotative
opacity. Visual colour is made tactile by the rain's glazzing
process. Thus the poem gives a startling clarity also to the prose
remark which follows it, that 'The same things exist, but in a
different condition when energized by the imagination' (*Imag.*,
138).

Vaunting imagination over reality, the poem over science,
poems XXIII and XXIV (*Imag.*, 141–3) enact the interaction of
nature / imagination, 'interpenetration, both ways' (XXIV ends
in recalling XI) reminding us of the remark to Marianne Moore:
'As a reward for this anonymity I feel as much a part of things as
trees and stones.'

While 'poetry feeds the imagination . . . prose feeds the
emotions', all writing 'deals with words and words only', an
assertion supported by 'Rapid Transit' (poem XXV), a series of
disjointed 'colloquial' fragments. Poem XXVI ('At the Ball
Game', *Imag.*, 147–9) reaffirms the necessary connection between beauty and reality, in this instance mixing good and bad
characteristics of the crowd in its 'spirit of uselessness'. Reality
'exists free from human action', but the imagination 'creates a
new object, a play, a dance which is not a mirror up to nature
but —'.

Several elements in 'The Wildflower' (XXVIII) occur throughout *Spring and All* (black/white, colour of flower like that of
bushes in opening poem, 'farmers who live poorly', 'The Pot of
Flowers') but it would be contrary to Williams's methods to end
with a summary. He simply stops, in keeping with his view of
process. Yet *Spring and All* holds an important place in his earlier
work because it brings a good deal of his method and thinking to
a coherency which has moments of true splendour.

4 Words and History

Setting out as if he were about to write a sequel to *Bleak House*, Williams achieved *The Great American Novel*[1] in about one-third of average novel length, including in the 'picaresque' adventures of his hero (a 'baby' Ford car) letters quoted from friends, anecdotes (but a minimum of story), aesthetic and theoretical discussion and an anticipation of much of the historical data of *In the American Grain*.

The early part of this work is concerned with *words* and the idea of 'progress'. Two decades later he would write of 'the concept of verbalism . . . the genius of a generation, the concept of words as things . . . '[2] and, for Williams, words were things. Sometimes, in fact, they were more than merely things. His sense of the power of words shares something with that of Mallarmé, and possibly it is Mallarmé's generation which had 'the concept of verbalism' as its 'genius'. The French orientation of much of Williams's work has been widely recognized — the influence of Rimbaud, for example, and (according to Rexroth[3]), of Max Jacob and Fargue. At the end of the twenties Williams would translate Soupault and, later still, Yvan Goll and Rene Char; but what Williams shares with Mallarmé is a sense of the word as magical. Early in *The Great American Novel*, he connects words with the Kora motif, but to this he adds the Heraclitean element, the sense of 'perpetual change' so centrally his: 'Words progress into the ground . . . . Now I am not what I was when the word was forming to say what I am' (*Imag.*, 158). Words *are* all the five senses, 'it is words you are made out of' (*Imag.*, 159). His method of proceeding is dialectical:

> Words are words. Fog of words. The car runs through it. The words take up the smell of the car. Petrol. Face powder, arm pits, food-grease in the hair, foul breath, clean musk. Words. Words cannot progress. Words are indivisible crystals. One cannot break them — Awu tsst grang splith gra pragh

38

og bm — Yes, one can break them. One can make words. Progress? If I make a word I shall make myself into a word. (*Imag.*, 159-60)

More of a pragmatist than a careful intellectual, Williams never felt the need to establish precise, fixed usages for his theoretical terms. It is simultaneously true that his concern is with 'what actually impinges on the senses' (*SE*, 119) and with his conviction that 'a poem is made up of words and punctuation, that is, words and the spaces between them'.[4] In a letter on the poem, to Kay Boyle in 1932, he declared: 'it deals with reality, the actuality of every day, by virtue of its use of language'.[5] While words 'have a contour and complexion imposed upon them by the weather, by the shapes of men's lives in places' (*SE*, 132) the value of a piece of writing does not therefore inhere in 'the sentiments, ideas, schemes portrayed' (*SE*, 109) but precisely in the 'vividness' with which the 'thing' is rendered. Making a poem is re-presenting one thing as another thing by bringing about an important structural or inventive change. 'Creation is speech. God spoke the world by uttering the Word. The poet, therefore, imitates the act of creation itself, in creating his poem, and what he creates is real: imagination is real.'[6]

The word must be free of past associations: 'Everything, no matter what it is must be re-valuated.' The novel itself is typically rejected as a 'fixed form', curiously perceived as 'pure English'. So, then, the important question is 'what should an American novel be?'. Revaluation, involving the dislocation characteristic of *Kora in Hell* is felt as living in hell, and is also a recognition that America can remain *Nuevo Mundo* only if it is not invaded by Europe, only if its newness is not tampered with. Rejecting progress, influence, the 'fad of evolution', the 'impertinence' of time, he extols 'the foamy crest of involution, like Venus on her wave' (*GAN*, 337), 'Nothing, save for the moment! In the moment exists all the past and the future!' (*GAN*, 337).

What Williams wants is for language to begin again, in American speech. This is the programme of *The Great American Novel*,[7] wide-ranging in its apparent aimlessness, a rejection of traditional fixities, patched together by Surrealism, naturalism, parody, irony. A rejection of Europe, it is a turning to some heroic moments in the American past only to arrive at a typical American success story of the poor immigrant who became rich, successful and famous and to cap this with an account of a typical shoddy product bred of such an individualist system. Williams will not have Europe, but neither will he allow any self-deception concerning America. Parodying himself and America, his beginnings do not become the great novel as advertised. En route to this non-achievement, sad realities are documented — foremost a negative version of 'contact', the plundering and spoliation of *Nuevo Mundo* by those without imagination except in greed.

Central to Williams's method in *The Great American Novel* is collage — a collage of facts, a distillation, a contrast of the aims of the American Union with its actual history, anecdotes, parodies — ultimately the method of juxtaposition first developed by Pound. Heavily allusive in Williams's hands, the method is employed in *The Great American Novel* for purposes of contrast — the aspirations of the American 'dawn' with present shoddinesses. Williams, it seems, had taken to heart Pound's observation that 'what saves your work is its opacity', for here he claims 'greater opacity, less erudition' (*Imag.,* 167), so his employment of allusion is for purposes of concrete objective comparison rather than erudite suggestiveness. Yet contrary to a common enough portrayal of Williams, his technique of allusive notation reveals considerable depth of reading, and an expectation of a similar depth in his own readers. The concerns of *The Great American Novel* and something of its documentary method recur immediately afterwards in *In the American Grain,* a crucial work in Williams's career and one now widely recognized as a grounding for the American sensibility.[8]

A major influence on *In the American Grain* was D. H. Lawrence's *Studies in Classic American Literature,* which preceded it by two years. Lawrence's sense of the blood-tie to a place or person fitted exactly Williams's need to find roots not only for himself but for America, in myths that would offer the feeling of a known place, which is why Donald Davie's label 'impressionistic history'[9] (and, more recently, Rod Townley's 'psychic prehistory') is less to the point than Dahlberg's characterization of the book as 'American canonical geography'.[10] By far the most penetrating immediate response to *In the American Grain* (the first edition of which was soon, sadly, remaindered) was Lawrence's substantial review in the *Nation* of 14 April 1926. Lawrence immediately perceived the importance of localism to Williams, and carefully distinguished it from both nationalism and parochialism. 'History in this book', says Lawrence, 'would be a sensuous record of the Americanization of the white man in America, as contrasted with ordinary history, which is a complacent record of the Europizing (if you can allow the word) of the American continent.'[11] From the beginning of his series of narratives Williams is sensible of a dichotomy, of two types of people. On the one hand were those, the Indians and some explorers, travellers and settlers, whose contact with the new continent was positive. On the other were those who voyaged to the new land to prey upon it and to return to the Old World with their plunder. Either that or, somewhat later, to settle on the land, as did the Puritans, and yet reject contact with it and inhibit the contact of others. Williams's belief in contact may well, in itself, owe something to Lawrence.

First conceived in the very early twenties, *In the American Grain* became Williams's attempt to discover 'what the land of my more or less accidental birth' might signify (*Autob.*, 178) by direct examination of the original records of American founders or 'heroes' (Williams uses the apostrophes). Before the second impression (virtually a new edition) was printed in 1939, with an introduction by Horace Gregory, Williams wrote a long letter to Gregory explaining 'how I came to write the book'. His main impetus was his mixed foreign ancestry and yet the feeling that he must possess 'the locality which by birthright had become my own'. He saw in the book 'as much a study of styles of writing as anything else' and attempted to compose each chapter 'in the style most germane to its sources', copying and using original materials, so that in some chapters 'no word is my own' (*SL*, 185-8).

Williams contends that history is as much a matter of language and imagination as of data. The past may be falsified by a misuse of language, failure to recognize its nuances, failure to perceive 'new contours' in 'old words'. In a headnote he informs the reader that he sought to draw from examined sources 'the strange phosphorus of life, nameless under an old misappellation'. His use of sources is somewhat of the same spirit as Pound's approach to translation. Williams is not afraid to compress, adapt or modify in order to express more strongly and succinctly the spirit of his subjects. Nor does he feel it necessary to provide scholarly footnotes explaining his method.

Implicitly rejecting the theory of American innocence, his two opening essays offer a polarization. Portraying Red Eric in strong verbal rhythms and concrete language, he indicates the contradictions built into America from the start, conveying in the undertow of his opening sentence the initial problem of the making of America, 'to take what is mine by single strength, theirs by the crookedness of their law' (*IAG*, 1), a sentiment which grew in the Revolutionary overthrow of Burgoyne and the British, the basis of American individualism.

Eric's departure from Norway was a rejection as well as a banishment. This dark opening sketch implies a contrast between Red Eric, around whom is an aura of displacement and discontent, and his son Leif Erickson, Leif the Lucky, a more successful adventurer. No proponent of the 'American Adam', Williams perceives evil as an inevitable part of the beginning, but he insists also on goodness and greatness, the two being compounded into one in the second essay 'The Discovery of the Indies'. The good, the vital, is expressed in a sexual image: 'It is as the achievement of a flower, pure, white, waxlike and fragrant, that Columbus' infatuated course must be depicted' (*IAG*, 7), yet the all-important first voyage results in discovery of 'a predestined and bitter fruit existing, perversely, before the white flower of its birth' (*IAG*, 7). Compressing and adapting from Columbus's Journals and letters,[12] Williams portrays a dedicated, purposeful man, pragmatic, single-minded, intent even in gravest peril on making his discoveries known and available, writing them on parchment, enclosing them in a cask, putting them in the sea to be found in case of shipwreck. To Williams it seems that Columbus was in the hands of a savage power, fate, destiny, process, 'A straw in the play of elemental giants' (*IAG*, 10), attempting to absorb into himself the immensity of the new world.

Somewhat over half the essay, the second part, is taken, with slight compressions and alterations, from the 'Journal of Columbus's First Voyage'. Thus Williams employs the 'borrowing' technique used by Pound and Eliot in poetry and here marshals it with great skill, placing the First Voyage last to make it his climax. More than half the remainder concerns the difficult fourth voyage, based on a letter to the King and Queen of Spain. Thus Columbus's later ill fortunes are told before the great discovery, lending poignancy to the account. This arrangement (noticed only by Waldo Frank — *IWWP*, 42) allows him to create a Columbus of depth, akin to the figure in Whitman's 'Passage to

India', in whom a growing despair is an inseparable part of his intense effort. Columbus continues as he does realizing that 'for a time it preserves us free from tedium' (*IAG*, 22), though the true 'end' of his life was the great moment at San Salvador, the discovery of the green land which was his 'beautiful thing' (*IAG*, 26). This moment will appear again for Williams in *Paterson* and provides a key motif for the poem.

Written 'in big square paragraphs like Inca masonry' (*IWWP*, 42), 'The Destruction of Tenochtitlan' and the following essay 'The Fountain of Eternal Youth' demonstrate the bloodlust, evil and despair attendant upon America's founding, Cortez's unfamiliarity and the coincidental timing of his arrival endowing him with godlike aura, his cold courage and implacability overriding Montezuma's tractable dignity. This, and Ponce de Leon's crass vanity: 'History begins for us with murder and enslavement, not with discovery' (*IAG*, 39).

Sexual imagery does not occur in the Columbus essay by chance. Williams saw the continent as a woman at once tender and cruel, and saw the positive response to the American land as a form of marriage (again thematically prefiguring *Paterson*). This is most overtly so in the De Soto material,[13] where 'She' opens the essay and is interpolated into the account of De Soto's adventures throughout, a presence not in the source material but quite possibly derived from it.[14] The Indians themselves have this feminine quality, but both they and 'She' exhibit a masculine defiance. At the very opining of the essay 'She' promises De Soto his acceptance, his 'immersion' into the American land (perhaps as intended, the figure recalls Williams's immersion in the Passaic) but only at death: 'you shall receive of me, nothing — save one long caress as of a great river passing forever upon your sweet corse' (*IAG*, 45). This finds a curious echo in *Paterson* itself:

> I wish to be with you abed, we two
> as if the bed were the bed of a stream.
>
> > (*P*, 35)

Writing about Raleigh, Williams finds something approaching an 'objective correlative' for England: 'his England had become a mouthful of smoke sucked from the embers of a burnt world' (*IAG*, 59), but he admires Raleigh, apart from his courage, for his pursuit of the beautiful thing: 'He conceived a voyage from perfection to find — an England new again; to found a colony; the outward thrust, to seek. But it turned out to be a voyage on the body of his Queen: England, Elizabeth — Virginia!' (*IAG*, 60). Writing in Raleigh's 'manner' (as he noted in a letter to Selden Rodman, who anthologized the piece as a poem[15]) Williams uses this trope, which reappears at intervals in his work, of perceiving the human body and the physical world in terms of one another.[16]

As he viewed it, the Puritans who ventured to America in the *Mayflower* belied their own ship's name. With an opportunity to flower, flourish in new soil, they did not do so, proving themselves capable of engendering only violence and despair, 'the secret inversion of loveliness'. Brought with them, their incapacity was something 'the wild continent' would not allow them to grow beyond. Williams laments the materialism of those dwelling in the 'stupefied jungles', always willing to trade for gain 'permanent values (the hope of an aristocracy)' (*IAG*, 68).

Based on another of the Original Narratives, 'The Voyages of Samuel de Champlain', the Champlain essay is somewhat perfunctory, using only a few pages of a long account. Williams appears to have attempted epitomizing Champlain as in an epiphany, his absorption in his task, his carrying the vision of France to the New World; but Champlain failed signally in the most important thing, to recognize the 'authenticity' of the new ground.

Two essays on the Puritans follow, 'The May-Pole of Merrymount' and 'Cotton Mather's Wonders of the Invisible World'. With minor textual differences (chiefly in spelling forms), the Mather material may be found in the Original Narratives. The other is a longish review of a reprint of Thomas Morton's *The New English Canaan*, prefaced by C. F. Adams Jr,[17] in which Adams's attitude to Morton is criticized on the ground that the minutiae of history may be even more important than 'to champion a winner'. Morton is in favourable contrast with the Puritans. Their loathing of Morton's womanizing is 'spiritless', while his stance is epitomized in the 'may-pole' itself. Morton accepted what was around him, while the Puritan strictures upon it led to madness and ultimately to the witchcraft persecutions recounted in Cotton Mather's *Wonders*.

It says much for Williams's writing tact that he can follow the piece from Mather with an account of 'Père Sebastian Rasles' which begins, breathlessly, as a résumé of a few weeks Williams spent in Paris,[18] and reports a conversation with the French critic Valéry Larbaud. Perhaps more even than Columbus, Rasles and Daniel Boone serve Williams's realization that greatness and loneliness go together. Vivid and moving, the account of Rasles is prepared for by a long exchange with Larbaud on American Puritanism. In many ways Rasles is the book's central portrait.

From admiring the Old World expedience of everyone's 'tearing his own meat', Williams is drawn by Larbaud to test his own view of the Puritans. Williams's response is concrete:

> Their sureness which you praise is of their tight tied littleness which, firm as it was, infuriates me today. It is their littleness that explains their admirable courage, close to the miraculous. It was good when through that first December they were going about in small boats in Cape Cod Bay, through rain and cold, under attack, when save for the finding of corn buried in the sand, they might not have had seed for the spring planting. (*IAG*, 110-11)

Larbaud sees the Puritan beginnings as magnificent, the protagonists as giants, 'cruel, but enormous, who eat flesh'; but Williams insists on their littleness. 'There was a maggot in them', he observes: 'It was their beliefs'. Because a Puritan preacher asked no material payment for promise of absolution, the Indians began to kiss his hand in gratitude, but he shook them off with distaste. Williams relates this trivial incident as the crux: ' . . . it is very ugly — and it is *that* which has persisted: afraid to touch!' (*IAG*, 119). Life-denying, this direct token of refusal of contact contrasts starkly with the young Puritan woman who, dressed in scarlet satin with a purple cloak, defiantly went to her wedding on a white horse. 'All that will be new in America will be anti-Puritan' (*IAG*, 120). Another sort of contrast, Rasles was a beautiful example of the goodness and effectiveness of tender, giving contact.

Rasles's selflessness allowed him to approach and accept the Indian in his reality, affording genuine contact and not the projection of the 'Noble Savage'. His descent contrasted with the Puritans' rapacity and cruelty. Rasles lived in personal physical suffering, totally absorbed in the Indian world, making no attempt to impose an ideology, but acting in deep accordance with his own Christian principles by *giving* himself to them. His was a life of devotion or, as Breslin so well expresses it, 'a combination of fierce independence and reverent self-effacement', typifying Williams's heroic indeal.

Williams's account of the 'Battle between the Bonne Homme Richard and the Serapis' affords a connection with Whitman, who dealt with the same battle in 'Song of Myself' (Chants 35-6). In transcribing John Paul Jones's report of the battle, Williams is not so much interested in the victory as in the ineptitude of its accomplishment. Victory was won despite some cowardice and lack of co-operation among the Americans, and the state of the shoddily outfitted vessel.

Writing about Aaron Burr in 'the Virtue of History' he makes an implied comparision with Washington, presenting Burr not as a danger to the state, but as one who attempted to prevent the narrowing down of freedoms. Williams's 'aristocratic' conception of democracy is nowhere more evident than here, where he observes approvingly of Burr, 'The common good he found common' (*IAG*, 203). Burr's relationships with women are seen as an aspect of his freedom. True, Burr was a failure, but he had style, and therein lay his value. So also did Jones have a certain style. Writing of Burr, Williams lacks the intensity of his approach to Red Eric, or Columbus, or Rasles, probably because in this instance he derived his material from secondary sources and, even so, seems not to have absorbed it slowly and deeply, as he had that for the most impressive parts of his book.[19]

'Whitman had to come from under. All have to come from under and through a dead layer' (*IAG*, 213), Williams declares in 'The Descent', a small but important piece on Sam Houston, who, in misfortune, begins to rehabilitate himself by taking 'the descent once more, to the ground', which is to say that he returned to the beginnings of things, in this instance to the Indians and Cherokees: 'He took an Indian woman for his wife' (*IAG*, 214). After many years he 're-ascended' for a second time, to become an American 'hero' at San Jacinto.

Using his occasion, Williams rails at the universities and the 'foreign congeries of literary claptrap'. His notion of 'descent', sometimes quasi-mystical, here becomes an appeal for rootedness in the American soil. 'It is imperative that we *sink*', for Americans there is no other choice but to begin at their own beginnings.

Since the publisher, Charles Boni, expressed doubts about a

book of American history without Lincoln in it, Williams provided his concluding page; but the real ending of *In the American Grain* is with Poe. The culmination of Williams's dig back through history to the real substance is to discover the making of the first true American poet. Shrugging off French aspirations for Poe, Williams claims him for America as 'a genius intimately shaped by his locality and time' (*IAG*, 216). Poe's distinguishing mark is his assertion of the *new locality*, his effort, in criticism and the poem, to clear the ground of all irrelevancies. Poe's provincialism compares strongly with J. R. Lowell's 'puerile sophistications'. Poe, in such pieces as 'The Philosophy of Composition' is discerned as a teacher somewhat in the Poundian fashion of three-quarters of a century later. Williams finds his own conception of the local in Poe: 'What he wanted was connected with no particular place; therefore it *must* be where he *was*' (*IAG*, 220). This is allied with Poe's lack of concern with poetry as a department of literature. Poe felt that poetry was, more importantly, related to 'the soul'. He wanted to 'tell his soul' and, forgoing 'the pleasing wraiths of former masteries' (a phrase for which Williams had a fondness, using it more than once), sought as a means of doing so 'to detach a "method" from the common usage'. Penetrating and refined at once, Poe's conception of the local was to advise against writing of the scene, trees, mountains, etc., 'to concentrate on the writing itself', thereby expressing the true local condition, that of the soul.

Williams concurs in Poe's assessment of Hawthorne as brilliant, but a localist in the wrong sense, doing for his own locality what many other artists of merit were doing for theirs, but copying others' methods to do it, originating nothing, inventing nothing. Against this, and against Hawthorne's notorious isolation, Poe's was a solitariness many shades deeper, awareness of himself in the very midst of chaos, battling against both formlessness and falsified form.

Because in some manner he reproduced in himself Poe's dilemma, Williams's comprehension of Poe's predicament is a moment of keen insight,[20] his Poe marooned in his own time, 'surrounded . . . by that world of unreality, a formless "population" — drifting and feeding' (*IAG*, 232), so that 'a huge terror possessed him', which manifested itself in his very technique: 'His passion for the refrain is like an echo from a hollow. It is his own voice returning' (*IAG*, 232). Ultimately, Poe's is a kind of individuality Williams can respect. For him it is a pervasiveness of woman which counts, but a 'fierce singleness' in men. Where we find our myths and rootedness in the past is in the lives and 'presences' of individual men, not in movements or traditions.

Reviewers of the time saw *A Voyage to Pagany*[21] as an extension from *In the American Grain*. 'In his new novel', wrote Morley Callaghan, 'he is still preoccupied with the word, still unsatisfied to offer merely the external fact and groping toward some kind of inner reality to explain the "fact" in a moment of blinding clarity.'[22] Callaghan perceives *A Voyage to Pagany* as Williams's version of the Jamesian expatriate's response to Europe, which he finds pallid and consequently longs for his own crass, chaotic society.

Callaghan finds the novel deficient in structure, and it is indeed episodic, with the episodes deriving from both changes of place and a sequence of encounters between the 'hero', Dev Evans, and a number of young women. Some reviewers of the time found difficulty in the fact that Dev's strongest emotional attachment is to his sister, Bess, who wishes him to stay in Europe (and who, surely, is his 'sister' in the sense of emblemizing that strong urge towards Europe). But Evans's European excursion serves to have him come to terms with his own soil, and the end of the novel is his true 'beginning' in that soil.

Several passages in *A Voyage to Pagany* concern Evans's consciousness of the Venus. Arriving in Rome, he is possessed almost to frenzy by the sense of Venus, momentarily identified with all he will reject but cannot forget: 'Rome starting alive from the rock. He felt it, he could touch the fragments. There IS the Venus. There, crouching at tht top of the stairs. But that is a stone. No, it is Venus! It is she. No it is a stone. It is she, I say. Venus! The presence is over the stone' (*VP*, 147). Equally here he is fascinated by a sense of process, discovery, invention. The *birth* of Venus, the Botticellian moment, holds him most of all. Thus, in the Rome chapter, when he sees the blonde, German girl again: 'it was *She* standing upon the shell; the hair, the eyes, the flesh that Botticelli had striven to imitate . . .' (*VP*, 148). Against this imagining of beauty's birth is set present reality, muddy Tiber; against oncoming spring, Rome felt as 'a motion of crumbling monuments'. Momentarily happy, Dev is conscious of his own resistance to being 'driven back', to 'the gilded Venus', a survival of the past invading his consciousness.

Rejecting history, as something which has ceased to proceed, Dev asserts that the 'thing that goes on and never stops' is beauty. He is disconcerted when his follow American, Grace Black, castigates their countrymen as lacking in depth, trying to palliate the fury around them with 'aeroplanes, radio and philosophies', living by a morality of amputation and prohibition (*VP*, 213-16). The whole novel offers, as part of its main concern, a glum view of America, which Dev, doctor-poet, attempts to offset by declaring: 'Art is a country by itself' (*VP*, 329). All his period in Europe is sea-conscious. Vouchsafed his vision of Venus, he is ready for his own emergence from the sea, close enough to shore to discern the Nantucket lightship: 'So this is the beginning' (*VP*, 338). He has discovered that his recognition of himself as American is at the beginning of all experience. Birth, and the struggle to be born, are of the first importance in Williams's work. So also is his view of woman as generative source, as is evident in both *In the American Grain* and *A Voyage to Pagany*.

5 Towards Objectivism

From *Spring and All* onwards Williams's writing became highly diversified. He continued to write poems and improvisations, essays, reviews and plays, and he added to these novels, short stories and an opera libretto. The early 1920s seem to have been for him a period of considerable literary energy, although Reed Whittemore sees them as only a relative rise in a twelve-year long depression which continued from 1917 to 1929.[1] A year of this, 1927/28, was a period of agreed separation from Flossie, Mrs Williams, and in the background of *A Voyage to Pagany* exists a dark, savage-minded journal titled 'Rome', which Williams kept on his 1924 six-month European sabbatical.

'The Descent of Winter', successor to *Spring and All*, occupied forty pages of Pound's *The Exile*, number four, in the autumn of 1928. A prose/poetry agglomeration, it was described by Vivienne Koch in 1950 as 'a temporarily barren stretch in Williams's development'.[2] Later, as he had done with *Spring and All*, Williams incorporated the poems from 'The Descent of Winter' into *Collected Earlier Poems*. The prose sections appear in *Selected Essays* as 'Notes in Diary Form'. Dating from the winter of 1927/28 'The Descent of Winter' anticipated by only a few months Williams's introduction, through Pound, to Louis Zukofsky. For a good many years after that meeting Williams directed his attention more to what he considered objective mimesis[3] and by 1932 he would go so far as to say: 'When we are forced by a fact . . . it can save us from inanity, even though we do no more than photograph it'.[4] Many of his poems of the late 1920s are no more than that: 'winter, winter / leather-green leaves / spear-shaped / in the falling snow' (*CEP*, 89).

The sparseness, even paucity, of that phase may be summed up by noting the contrast between the first chapter of *A Voyage to Pagany* and the same experience re-presented in the opening poem of 'The Descent of Winter' with its threadbare enumeration of numbers on a ship cabin's bulkhead.

Williams barely survives as a poet, in this group of poems, yet some sort of growth continues. His use of metropolitan, industrial and domestic 'landscape' widens and deepens. Many poems of the time have an undertow of anger and frustration, including much (though not all) of 'The Descent of Winter'. Most parts of this composite work are titled only with a cryptic date, month and day. The related prose, 'Notes in Diary Form', is similarly organized, but the most powerful effect of barrenness occurs in the first four sections of poem, pre-dating the 'Notes'. Unable to move beyond the baldest of observed factual data the writer, in a poem of unintegrated musings ('9/30'), is driven to consider his own work's lack of fusion, his doubts about it, 'waves like words, all broken'. Even some of the detailing lacks sharpness. The musing carries towards old age and death.

Counterpointed against these four poems by date proximity are three paragraphs of 'Notes' (10/23/27) beginning in a confident Steinian manner 'I will make a big, serious portrait of my time' (*SE*, 62) but faltering in tone, the statement modulating, expressing the writer's frustrated ambition.

To confirm the connection between poem and prose, a direct correspondence links the diary entry for 10/28 and the first of two small poems so dated. Manuscripts at Buffalo indicate that this diary entry is either excerpt or summary of an abortive novel titled 'Fairfield',[5] an uncompleted work which appears to be a specific forerunner of *Paterson*. Its immediate interest is in showing Williams as then bound down in a sleazy environment, his external surroundings concomitant to his interior life: 'The justice of poverty / its shame its dirt / are one with the meanness / of love' ('10/29'), *CEP*, 302).

With '11/2: a Morning Imagination of Russia', 'The Descent of Winter' reaches a more positive phase. At the corresponding point in the 'Notes' Williams breaks off into a consideration of Shakespeare ('about the best Shakespeare criticism there is' — Zukofsky[6]) including a statement Zukofsky afterwards turned to good Objectivist account: 'The only human value of anything, writing included, is an intense vision of the facts' (*SE*, 71), another iteration of Williams's concern for 'vividness'. Simultaneously, and for perhaps the only time in his career, he has considerable doubts about poetry, which all too often is 'a soft second light of dreaming' (*SE*, 67).

Grimness pervades Williams's poems of the middle and late

twenties, but they are shot through with affirmative flashes: 'Out of such drab trash as this / by a metamorphosis . . . .' 'Struggle of Wings', in which these lines occur, (*CEP*, 291-3, earlier version, *Dial*, July 1926) shows him casting about tentatively for shape. Its closing jingle, complete with rhyming couplets and archaisms, demonstrates uncertainty and strain. The *Dial* version particularly may serve to show some of the limitations of Williams's craft at a time when his work is below its best. His excellences at every period before *Paterson* are closely related to two characteristics: (1) control of the free-verse line, and (2) following Poe in concentrating upon a 'single effect'. 'Struggle of Wings' is not typical 'short-breathed' Williams. Its line is mostly long and slack. Tightening towards the close the poem falls into rhyming couplets, to maintain which Williams even employs an archaism to establish one rhyme ('bright / night', followed by 'alters / psalters').

A few months later 'Young Sycamore' (*CEP*, 332) also appeared in the *Dial* (March 1927, p. 210). Here is vigorous growth, to its 'hornlike' top — poem and tree involved in process, vaunting the new, quite alien to the rambling allusiveness of 'Struggle of Wings'. A majority of Williams's shorter poems, when successful, are *mimeses* of dynamic motion *now*, not reported or discussed.

Meeting Louis Zukofsky in 1928 re-focused Williams's work and his thinking about it. Imagist-oriented, he admired Zukofsky's early writing for being founded in words, language, rather than 'thoughts'. Williams may himself have invented the name of their group when he noted: 'Your early poems, even when the thought has enough force or freshness, have not been objectivized in new or fresh observations.'[7]

On the other hand, Zukofsky had discovered through the older poet the kind of poem he was looking for. Responding to *Spring and All* he said of Williams: 'his exclusions of sentimentalisms, extraneous comparisons, similes, overweening autobiographies of the heart, of all which permits factious "reflection about", of sequence, of all but the full sight of the immediate' (*The Symposium* essay, p. 81) manifest a "living aesthetic'. Yet the traffic was not all one way. Williams accepted helpful advice on his Stein essay and expressed admiration for Zukofsky's handling in the poem of 'abstract–philosophic–jargonist language'. Zukofsky anticipates, at one point, future ideas of Edward Dahlberg and

Charles Olson when he sums up the concept of Williams's 're-iterated improvisations': ' . . . it is a definite metaphysical concept: the thought is the thing which, in turn, produces the thought' (*The Symposium*, p. 69). Later, in his introductory material to *An 'Objectivists' Anthology* (1932),[8] Zukofsky included *Spring and All* on his list of essential reading, singling out poems in which 'objectification is to be found' (original numbering VIII, X, XVIII, XXVI), and including Williams's name with that of Pound, Stevens, Cummings, Eliot, Marianne Moore, Robert McAlmon and Charles Reznikoff.

Attempting a clear definition of 'objectivism', Zukofsky contrasts it with 'sincerity', a quality which relates to the personality of the poet, rather than to his poem, and which involves connotation and suggestiveness. In contrast, 'objectivism' affords a sense of 'rested totality' or 'objectification', which is 'the apprehension satisfied completely as to the appearance of the art form as an object'.[9] In Zukofsky's poem 'A6' an 'objective' is defined as 'rays of the object brought to a focus'.[10] This is allied to Poundian ideas of the connection between technique and sincerity. Both in his poem and his essay Zukofsky cites Pound's remark that 'a new cadence is a new idea', while in an undated note Williams asks Zukofsky for a phrase of George Oppen's 'about sincerity being not in the writer but in the writing'. These instances show the Objectivist spirit and its relation to the all but defunct Imagist movement.

An 'Objectivists' Anthology includes two groups of Williams's poems, some dating back more than a decade. Among them is a version of 'March' as rewritten by Zukofsky, placed in the anthology's closing section of poems by various people all 'revised' in some way by the editor! Zukofsky was not gathering the fully achieved products of a tendency, but was using the material in a Poundian, pedagogical way. Work selected is of various grades of accomplishment, having in common only manifestations of 'objectification'. Zukofsky's conception of an 'objective' was intellectual. A note (apparently from a later period) by Williams, at Yale, associates Objectivism to Imagism, but adds an important rider: 'The mind rather than the unsupported eye entered the picture.'[11] Paradoxically, Objectivism is subjective in its own way, as Zukofsky tacitly admits when he notes in the *Symposium* essay, 'Ultimately poetry is a question of natures, of constitutions, of mental colourings' (p. 71).

Williams's name was prominent among the Objectivists, but it would be foolish to attempt to see him as wholeheartedly (whole-headedly, perhaps?) in the movement, just as it is hazardous picking one's way among apparent inconsistencies in his thinking. Already in 'Paterson' (*CEP*, 233), which appeared in the *Dial* in February 1927, he had used his dictum 'No ideas but in things',[12] but he was never limited to the narrow objectivism castigated by Eugene Jolas, editor of *transition*: 'Pure objectivism fails because it is the antithesis of subjectivism. It follows the extreme swing of the pendulum towards a craze for actuality and factual experiences which can only end in artistic sterility and a return to the commonplace.'[13] With Jolas and his contributors Williams had in common a rejection of 'the King's English' and a Joycean approach to language experiment. Zukofsky, on the other hand, perhaps because he was more musically sophisticated than Williams, took from his language experiments the techniques of syllable and word count.

Williams had already reached, for himself, the Objectivist tenet of organic form. He shared the sense that only particulars could be communicated. Believing as he did in economy, process, he did not go as far as Zukofsky's injunction, 'Don't write, telegraph'.[14] An intellectual shade of difference marks the two men's views of the objectivity of writing; while Williams sees words *as* things, Zukofsky notes, 'tho it may not be harbored as solidity in the crook of an elbow, writing (audibility in two-dimensional print) . . . is an object or affects the mind as such'.[15] Zukofsky, and the Objectivist movement, had used as one point of departure Williams's Imagist poems. In turn Williams allowed himself to be influenced by Objectivism to the point where his presence is totally effaced from the poem. Thus 'The Red Wheel-barrow', an Imagist poem, includes his personal attitude in its opening statement, and may be contrasted with the equally well-known 'Poem' (first published in *Poetry* in 1930), a simple enactment of the movement which is its entire substance, a cat moving, paw by paw, carefully, over the top of a cupboard (*CEP*, 340).

Some of the poems in this manner record, baldly and without explicit or even implied comment, social and physical conditions of American life, thus prompting Stevens's remark that Williams's 'passion for the antipoetic is a blood passion'.[16] Williams had already deliberately rejected the attitude which this seems to imply. Towards the end of his essay on Marianne Moore, he declares that no 'special things and special places are reserved for art' (*SE*, 130), and therefore denies the possibility of a proletarian or aristocratic art. Stevens finds also in Williams's work 'a little sentiment, very little, together with acute reaction', and the presence of this quality in *some* of Williams's poems, in tension with their realism, may well make it seem that he is employing factual material as if it were anti-poetic, as in 'Brilliant Sad Sun' (*CEP*, 324) where, by Williams's own best practice at last the last three lines are redundant. He does seem to be effecting a deliberate contrast between the lunch counter and the rather 'grand' memory of an occasion of Adelina Patti's singing. Zukofsky might have regarded this as a poem which *includes* objectivity!

Many typical Williams poems are completely independent of paraphrase. Of these, perhaps best known is 'This is Just to Say' (*CEP*, 354). Much admired, this has also been used more than once to illustrate the basic triviality of both Williams's method and material. Yet such response is over-solemn. Here the immediate, small occasion is light-hearted, even comic, but the poem is much more than it seems: a celebration of the physical life, rendered with stringent economy but with a high degree of essential 'vividness'.

Williams's technique of *beginning* a poem with its 'conclusion' (as in 'To Waken an Old Lady', 'The Red Wheelbarrow') is a means of 'indirection' (roughly, presenting the object and letting it 'speak for itself') which also circumvents paraphrase. Just as in 'The Red Wheelbarrow' specific concrete details gain reverberation from the opening 'so much depends upon', so in 'The Bull' (*CEP*, 336), the whole poem's essential condition stems from the opening line's explanation: 'It is in captivity'. Otherwise the bull is the type of the physical life impeded, not (as in, say, Ted Hughes's 'Jaguar') the embodiment of frustrated rage, but of long term effects. That the bull is 'godlike' may convey awesomeness, but also divorce from physical reality; he is solitary, indecisive ('nozzles / the sweet grass gingerly'), time-killing, devitalized. 'Olympian commentary on / the bright passage of days' suggests both the bull's latent power and his remoteness from the 'bright passage'. Decorative: ' — The round sun / smooths his lacquer / through / the glossy pinetrees', he is, despite his 'ivory' hardness, a plaything for the wind. 'Milkless', he cannot reproduce his species nor have access to companions who can. Touching obliquely on 'divorce', this also concerns process and the necessity for wholeness, that the process may work properly.

Another poem on 'divorce' is the comic 'The Sea-Elephant' (*CEP*, 71), an animal also in captivity, separated from its just environment. Two refrains, the animal's 'Blouaugh!' and the human 'They / ought / to put it back where / it came from', are used to excellent effect, each successive usage changing in nuance. Towards the end of the poem the animal presence represents love, and rejection of the sea-elephant is fear of love, fear of involvement, a prime cause and circumstance of 'divorce'. The sea-elephant is in fact a comic Venus, love — but also art. Though it may seem so, the concluding, 'and Spring / they say / Spring is icummen in' is neither slight nor wilful. Included in the 'Primavera' section of *Collected Poems 1921-1931*. 'the Sea-Elephant' ends by affirming the beginning, which is love, the vital principle. Counterpoised against it is 'Death' (*CEP*, 78), in which, devoid of life, divorced from it, the man has become no more than 'a godforsaken curio' incapable of contact because 'love cannot touch' him any more:

> he's dead
> the old bastard —
> He's a bastard because
>
> there's nothing
> legitimate in him any
> more
>   he's dead
>   . . .
> He's nothing at all . . .

Legitimacy, 'vividness', being alive, this is important. Asked, in a questionnaire, 'Why do you go on living?', Williams answered, 'Because I have an enjoyable body for my pleasure.'[17] He felt, as Stevens did with him and for him, that in the flux of time, 'we have only our own intelligence on which to rely'.

Another work of Williams's from this period is *The Embodiment of Knowledge*. Begun after completion of 'The Descent of Winter' in 1928 and worked on sporadically until early 1930, it remained unpublished until 1974, when New Directions issued it

with an introduction by the poet Ron Loewinsohn.[18] Responses to
this work have so far been few, but varied, and it is not likely that
it will radically affect either the critical approaches to Williams's
work or its general estimation. Joseph N. Riddel (possibly
following Zukofsky) declares that 'it contains some of Williams'
most fundamental thoughts on education, literature (especially
Shakespeare), and history',[19] but makes virtually no use of the
book himself. Rod Townley, in contrast, finds it 'at once
fascinating and extremely boring' and perceives Williams as
wreaking 'compulsive sabotage' on his own reflections, in a work
which 'can only help prolong the current fashion to deride
Williams' critical writings'.[20]

The Embodiment of Knowledge is juxtapositional and anti-
systematic in method, an anticipation of the injunction in
Paterson to 'write carelessly, so that nothing that is not green will
survive'. Its aesthetic is one of ongoing process, immediacy,
potential flashes of illumination. Its concerns may be said to anticipate, in a random and personal way, those of Ivan Illich, John
Holt and others, in that it attacks the gap between real
knowledge of a subject and the formal learning of that same
subject in a school context (Williams was irate because his son
fared badly in French at Rutherford High School even though he
had spent a year in Europe speaking French).

Williams's Shakespeare, the 'hero' of the work, was 'obscure',
'unevangelical', and unscholarly, unlike Bacon (Williams chipped
in on the Shakespeare–Bacon controversy), but presumably like
the way Williams saw himself. This version of Shakespeare
attends upon the pages of *The Embodiment of Knowledge*, now
and then emerging into the forefront.

Apart from this pervasive figure, the 'focus' (an odd word,
perhaps, in the circumstances) of Williams's interest is modernism. The book includes a customary attack on Eliot, and musings
on many of the figures who appear also in *Selected Essays* and
Imaginations, such as Joyce, Gertrude Stein, Pound, John Dewey.
Behind the text, as Paul Mariani points out, are readings of
Whitehead's *Science in the Modern World* and, to a lesser extent,
of *The Education of Henry Adams*.[21] Shot through the whole
work is, in fact, a sense of poetry at once humanistic and quasi-
vatic:

Science is a sham to him who sees his city destroyed by

gunfire. Philosophy is a cheat to him who has lost that which he loves and knows no better than to weep. Poetry at such moments is terrible, an overwhelming summation of life and the world — never perhaps to be set down, the type of a peculiarly humane knowledge. (*EK*, 39)

Ron Loewinsohn sees poetry for Williams as an act of self-definition, self-assertion, a struggle therefore against convention and tradition. In contrast, science and philosophy are pointed towards some hypothesized (and dehumanized) future. Poetry is, pre-eminently, the act of dwelling acceptingly in the present (and Loewinsohn draws the parallel with Williams's 'first master', Keats, and negative capability). True knowledge is *embodied* in the sense Williams had already suggested in *Kora in Hell* when he said 'A thing known passes out of the mind into the muscles' (*Imag.*, 74). Yeats once pondered 'Man may embody truth, but he cannot know it.' To this Williams might well have replied that the only 'truth' is whatever is embodied by man in the process of his life. Yet as far as *The Embodiment of Knowledge* is concerned, a problem remains for the reader, that despite its incidental insights concerning art, literature and education, the probing of Williams's 'precarious convictions' is more or less random, and ultimately inchoate. Not that the details are in themselves unclear, but they are nowhere marshalled into the larger, cogent whole which would justify their presentation as a book. Yet this difficulty, as for the whole canvas of Williams's work, turns back upon itself. Here as elsewhere, even in an instance where Williams himself did not prepare the final manuscript for publication, the *ad hoc* nature of the venture attests to its 'wholeness'. We are once again implicitly invited to re-examine our notions about the 'wholeness' of an artist's work, in the total context of human knowledge, not as one of its finished products, but as part of its continuing process.

6 Into the Thirties

Although its reception was mixed, *Collected Poems 1921-1931* shows in range and depth, perhaps for the first time, what Williams could do as a poet. During the 1930s he also produced, in *The Knife of the Times* and *Life Along the Passaic River*, two fine collections of short stories. Besides these, and related to them in its objective naturalism, is his 1937 novel *White Mule*, first of the Stecher trilogy. For Williams the period immediately before the Second World War was a complex including his link with the newly formed publisher, New Directions, and his libretto for a proposed opera by George Antheil. These were the years, when correspondents sometimes addressed him as 'Comrade Williams', of his associations with the *New Masses*, *New Republic* and, latterly, *Partisan Review*. He contributed rather earnest assessments of slim volumes by the proletarian Sol Funaroff and the 'Missouri dirt farmer' H. H. Lewis to *New Masses* and, in answer to yet another of the ubiquitous questionnaires, supplied the ironic two-liner:

> What's wrong with American literature?
> You ask me? How much do I get?

When the 'Stalinist' *New Masses* squabbled with the 'Trotskyist' *Partisan Review* Williams became directly involved, but was apparently rehabilitated when he answered yet another questionnaire for *Partisan Review* in 1939. To the *New Republic* he contributed both poems and reviews, including 'The Yachts' and a piece on Walker Evans's *American Photographs* where he reiterates the importance of individual place, which should be regarded as 'everywhere'.

When we come back to the question of Objectivist aesthetics which were central to Williams at this time, we may observe, first, that they were much akin to the ideas Fernand Léger expressed in the *Little Review* in the mid-1920s. Léger clearly perceived the distinction between 'plastic' beauty and 'sentimental, descriptive or initiative values', held that every object has its own independent value, but also that the creative act is a mysterious struggle between objective and subjective. The artist's task is to attempt to see objects '*in isolation* — their value enhanced by every known means', thus enabling them to take on a degree of personality never before realized.[1]

Williams must have known these essays. His mid-1940s definition of poem-as-a-machine[2] resembles Léger's thinking and also derives from Objectivist theory. A decade before *The Wedge*, reviewing George Oppen's *Discrete Series*, he wrote:

> It is the acceptable fact of a poem as a mechanism that is the proof of its meaning and this is a technical matter as in the case of any other machine. Without the poem being a workable mechanism in its own right . . . it will remain ineffective.[3]

Despite some contact and concern with social propaganda, Williams continued to accept the exigencies of the poem as preeminent, so (following his penetrating essay on *A Draft of XXX Cantos* — see *SE*, 105ff.) he introduces his assessment of 'Pound's Eleven New "Cantos"' by defining poetry as 'a construction which embodies among its concepts, its words and the form of their composition, the deep and serious aspirations of man' (*SE*, 167), an attitude close to that stated in *The Embodiment of Knowledge*.

Although it retains its basic character, established through the 1920s, much of Williams's 1930s poetry lacks buoyancy. Both his Alcestis Press publications, *An Early Martyr* (1935) and *Adam and Eve and the City* (1936), are mélanges of poems whose dates of initial composition range over a fifteen-year period. Many were subsequently placed near the beginning of *Collected Earlier Poems*, though a considerable number are scattered throughout that volume. One found its way into *Collected Later Poems*, while two — one a strangely personal piece called 'Genesis' — remain uncollected. *An Early Martyr* cannot be judged solely by Objectivist criteria. Williams's qualified acceptance of work by such people as Funaroff and Lewis should warn us not to look for propagandist poems, yet some of his more successful pieces here have a socio-political relevance, including the title-poem (which, however, dates from the early twenties).[4]

Approximately one-third of *An Early Martyr* — mostly poems published in periodicals in the mid-thirties, and including 'To a Poor Old Woman', 'Proletarian Portrait' and 'The Raper from Passenack' — is socially preoccupied. (Marxist critics of the period included 'The Yachts' in this group. A proportion of the remaining poems had been printed earlier in *Spring and All* or 'The Descent of Winter'.)

Many of these poems lack the energy of line so important and vitalizing in earlier work. They sound flat and are sometimes over-explicit. Probably it is true, as Linda Wagner and others suggest,[5] that Williams was disillusioned with humanity at this time, but as early as *Sour Grapes*, he had written of bare and broken trees, etc. (a melancholy counterpart to his sense of blossoming flowers). To say that for him then 'even nature became cold and lifeless' is to overlook chronology. Winter trees appear to have been, for Williams, almost an 'objective correlative' for consciousness of mutability, so a poem like 'Tree and Sky' is not characteristic of this period only.

Yet, in poems such as 'Invocation and Conclusion' and 'Late for Summer Weather' his attitude, combining sympathy and objectivity, contrasts with the then common romanticizing of the proletariat. 'To a Poor Old Woman' (*CEP*, 99), similarly based, may suggest the pitfalls of 'interpreting' Williams (as Parker Tyler, for example, interprets 'The Red Wheelbarrow' in *Briarcliff Quarterly*[6]). A kinetic poem, the 'action' is recreated almost solely by line disposition:

> They taste good to her
> They taste good
> to her. They taste
> good to her . . .
>
> . . .
>
> a solace of ripe plums
> seeming to fill the air
> They taste good to her.

A chief Williams method of making a poem fluent while maintaining rapidity and lightness was drastic reduction of conventional punctuation. (This discarding of punctuation has become a post-Williams convention.) Early in his career he had jettisoned as unnecessary the practice of line capitalization. This, too, helped with the flow, but the verse in some instances, shaped more through his ear than anything on the page, became an apparently endless flux. Next he began to experiment, restoring capitals but not full stops, breaking poems up into visual units (thereby imposing a 'punctuation' on the *reader*). In this practical way he arrives, on many occasions, at instances of two-line or three-line units. His most common punctuation device at this period was the dash — though, somewhat surprisingly, he did not employ it to indicate breath groupings. He adopted a method of capitalizing to mark out image-units or thought-units, a practice which seems arbitrary in 'An Early Martyr', but successful in other poems, such as 'A Portrait of the Times' or 'To a Poor Old Woman'. Varying the practice on occasion, he resorted to the time-honoured custom of capitalizing a key word.

In 'The Raper from Passenack', 'Invocation and Conclusion' and 'A Portrait of the Times' is discernible a co-extension of social depression with 'the immemorial tragedy / of lack-love'. More penetrating than the others, 'The Raper from Passenack' (*CEP*, 103) concerns alienation, 'divorce'. An objective account of 'facts', it is also something deeper. Ostensibly the raper is a criminal, the girl his victim. For both life lacks 'vividness' and, in some sense, each is most fully alive during the rape and its immediate aftermath. The rape is touch, is their *contact*, the rapist more whole than his victim. Partially at least, he recognizes this when he says 'I took care of you' (an idiomatic phrase facing both ways, towards life and towards death). His act has endowed him with self-assurance, a measure of fulfilment, affirmation of his own existence, which the girl has neither before nor after the violation. The sexual act is here a gross token for love. Only through pursuing a 'lower' kind of contact, substitute for love, does the man achieve some kind of self-realization. The girl cannot do even this. To her the act has nothing to do with love. Contact, in her case, brings fear of disease.

Williams is not here yielding to a male sentimentality. He uses the irony of the situation most effectively: 'I suppose it's my mind — the fear of / infection. I'd rather a million times / have been got pregnant.' The girl's existence is lived too much in her 'mind'. She has some vague intimation that pregnancy would be a better outcome than the disease she fears so much, but this is not because it could be the fruit of true love, the means of over-coming alienation. For this girl, in her very being, sexual congress is a main focus of fear. Her attitude to it is a precise index of her alienation. Williams will later use this sense of sexual contact as 'dirty' many times as a figure of 'divorce . . . in our time'.

Several poems from *An Early Martyr* had been printed together (*Poetry*, October 1933) as an ineffectual sequence, 'In the American Style'. Williams broke the grouping down, presumably recognizing that even the '4th of July' section (*CEP*, 194) was not 'in the American style' in any fully effective sense. Further, he rewrote one section, 'The Locust Tree in Flower' (*CEP*, 93, 94), cutting back already very short lines, reducing a 'thin' poem to half its original length. Together, the two versions are ample demonstration of his concern for form. For all its terseness the first version (*CEP*, 94) fails, in being too explicit without making its explicitness 'do' anything except state itself. *Not enough is omitted* to involve the reader actively in the poem, thus circumventing one of Williams's own primary requirements. Resonance and response are forfeited through over-specification.

In the shorter version the implications of a technique are developed to their logical end. Single word lines, here, are not the product of Williams's 'short breath', but a rigorous stripping of verbal redundancies. The result is an example of his instinct for process. Its force is a force of *words*, words as things, and clearly so. 'Among', the opening gambit so to speak, is not an incom-pleteness or an abstraction, but an *action* or part of an action. It suggests discreteness, disposition of separate elements, just as 'of' suggests partaking. As is intended, the first two lines read antithetically, excluding each other. The poem is set up as a polarization, offering choices, but in the action the choices disappear as the brief poem runs its course. This is intentional, since the white flowering of May cannot 'choose' to bloom (as is suggested in the resolution 'Again'), but what is enacted therefore is a hesitancy, on the very threshold of budding. The poem's very shape is that of a branch still bare. May, as it comes, will be multiplicity, as the only verb in the poem suggests. The process of spring blossoming is at once single and multiple, a matter of old and new, broken and green, side by side. As the poem's implications arrive for him, the reader works out this action graph for himself.

Published in May 1935, in the *New Republic* (a possible

reason for the number of Marxist interpretations it has had), 'The Yachts' (*CEP*, 106) is, technically and otherwise, a far remove from 'The Locust Tree in Flower'. Of this much anthologized piece Williams wrote to a correspondent in 1961:

> This is the one consciously imitative poem I ever wrote. . . . I felt ashamed to have forgotten the American idiom so completely. As yet I was not sufficiently grounded in the variable foot, though I was consciously enough grounded to make me feel that something had gone amiss. I was unhappy at the result. I felt ashamed of myself. I have never forgotten it.[7]

The American idiom apart, 'The Yachts' succeeds as movement, the run of the verse being as the deployment of yachts in heavy seas. First apprehended visually, next in the line itself as motion, 'The Yachts' is interpenetrative, the water's swell felt in terms of human movement. This movement derives naturally from the contemporary ambience, coloured by the time's social afflictions, human efforts to 'keep afloat' or 'get aboard', but the poem's ultimate force is more than social. The 'ungoverned ocean' is the flux, chance, in which all humanity lives out its life. 'Mothlike in mists, scintillant in the minute / brilliance of cloudless days', the yachts of human life, beautiful though they may be (and this is part of the yacht symbol), burn quickly away. Placed as it is, the word 'minute' carries visually connotations both of extreme smallness and of a brief unit of time. By mid-poem the yachts symbolize products of the human, built to race (the poem uses connotations of 'race' also), but ultimately getting beyond the control of their makers. The sea which 'the skillful yachts pass over' is a Dantesque 'sea of faces'. Seeking criteria by which to judge Williams's poems in general, the reader is not helped by an untypical poem like 'The Yachts', which contains verbal redundancies and yet succeeds as a rhythmical effect. Williams establishes and maintains a powerful pattern of rhythm, backing it up (in the first and third stanzas, for example) with suggestions of rhyme. These effects are gained at the expense of going against his customary position, that a genuinely American poem may be discovered only in and through the American idiom. Similarly, his quasi-symbolic consciousness of the yachts endows the poem with a quality at once discursive and non-objective. Overanthologized as it is, 'The Yachts' has a certain compelling quality which may be because it 'was written right off',[8] dredged up from the 'unconscious self', discovered therein, so to speak, and written down without a word being changed. This is again, the obverse of Williams as Imagist–Objectivist. All the same, it is an essential aspect of his identity as poet, the writer of *Kora in Hell: Improvisations*, but at a later stage.

Two poems in *An Early Martyr* offer quite distinct accounts of the poet's role, 'Hymn to Love Ended' (*CEP*, 108) and 'A Poem for Norman MacLeod' (*CEP*, 114). The first, an 'imaginary translation from the Spanish', discusses the traditional isolated bard ('Villon beaten and cast off'), but one related to 'the streams released to flow'. The second expresses his 'pose', his ultimate position: 'The revolution / is accomplished / noble has been / changed to no bull' and its conclusion is close to Stevens's 'I am what is around me'. 'You can do lots / if you know / what's around you', says Williams. Through his insight Stevens controlled his *mundo*. Williams here expresses only one pole of his poems' strong internal tension, his awareness of the 'objective'. At the other pole, even his own improvisations, written 'carelessly', partook of such objectiveness simply because they had come into existence and, as themselves, could not be different from what they actually were.

Allusive, and again untypical, 'An Elegy for D. H. Lawrence' (*CEP*, 361)[9] owes a little to a reading of Lawrence's 'The Snake'. It touches Lawrence at a point central to both writers, the need for human love. Through

> The serpent in the grotto
> water dripping from the stone
> into a pool.
> Mediterranean evenings. Ashes
> of Cretan fires. And to the north
> forsythia hung with
> yellow bells in the cold

Williams gives us

> Poor Lawrence
> worn with a fury of sad labor
> to create summer from
> spring's decay.

But Lawrence himself, finally, must be numbered among the 'Men driven not to love / but to the ends of the earth'. An artist unloved in his own country, he failed, in Williams's conception, to bring about the 'summer' he envisioned, so that the serpent of vitality gives way to the cricket:

> Greep, greep, greep the cricket
> chants where the snake
> with agate eyes leaned to the water.
> Sorrow to the young
> that Lawrence has passed
> unwanted from England.
> And in the gardens forsythia
> and in the woods
> now the crinkled spice-bush
> in flower.

Throughout the poem Williams has maintained and reinforced the elegiac mood by means of skilful juxtapositions. Just as the shorter version of 'The Locust Tree in Flower' works on purely verbal juxtaposition, the present poem puts together allusions, responses, articulating them into a coherence centred on, and indeed dependent on, Lawrence himself.

In 'How to Write',[10] a key essay of the period, Williams appeals to the source of art, of writing, as 'the night of our unconscious past', instructing that the writer 'must thoroughly abandon himself to the writing'. Though followed by a phase of 'ratiocination', this 'anarchical phase' is the most important in writing. Such thinking is not diametrically opposed to Williams's 'objectivism', although it may seem so. It does, however, differ from it, allowing purely subjective, even surreal, images such as the closing lines of 'Flowers by the Sea' (*CEP*, 87):

> the sea is circled and sways
> peacefully upon its plantlike stem

— much more effective than the earlier version printed in *Pagany* (Fall 1930, p. 5):

> the thought of the sea is circled and
> sways peacefully upon its plantlike stem.

One of Williams's most beautifully realized lesser-known poems, 'Flowers by the Sea' goes beyond both Imagism and the American idiom, and is a subjective projection (with the images of sea and pasture inverted, as it were) in a recognizably international idiom.

As his Imagism (which Thirlwall says persisted until Glenn Hughes's *Imagist Anthology*, 1930[11]) modulated into Objectivism, so simultaneously Williams maintained his interest in Surrealism and quasi-Surrealism. While Zukofsky's expatiations, finally, offer no single clear definition of 'Objectivism' it is certainly not intended as a diametric opposite to something labelled 'Subjectivism'. The interest centres on 'object' (including poem as object) and 'objective', but Zukofsky more than once refers to participation of the poet's senses and intelligence. Yet Williams's improvisatory side may at times seem to run counter to *the facts* in which he professes such interest. His critical prose is not notably consistent and, besides, varies in sharpness; but his instinct to 'write carelessly' actually complements his drive to render precisely 'bricks and coloured threads'. The carelessness is to circumvent *thought about* the object or action of the poem, which dims its 'vividness'.

Adam and Eve and the City is a more cohesive book than *An Early Martyr*, with a ground theme — the futility of desire. Of fifteen poems (a group of five Spanish 'versions' counting as one), 'Adam' and 'Eve' are placed centrally and 'The City' last. Portrayals of his mother and father constructed along a narrative line, both 'Adam' and 'Eve' are unsatisfactorily prosy, lacking tension as poems. 'The City' (later titled 'Perpetuum Mobile: the City', *CEP*, 384) combines narrative with metamorphic technique in a poem of contact. The 'two' of the poem, man and woman, go together to the city, object of their 'fused' dream ('a little false'), but which disappears by day when they arrive. Again the city has a symbolical function, as desire for love. Yet this 'love' is perhaps limited to sexual desire and is expressed through a kaleidoscope of violence, city sewage, gross human appetites. Contrasted with it is a stunted but immediate nature: 'Over the swamps / a wild / magnolia bud — / greenish / white', a sketch of New Jersey landscape, foreground to distant Manhattan highrises and skyscrapers. Man and woman finally leave the city again, and by indirection we have learned that the city's 'stars / of matchless / splendor' too easily, even on a summer's day, dwindle 'in a wall of / rain'.

Several shorter poems in the volume are more fully realized than these longer pieces, and perhaps most of all 'To a Wood Thrush' (*CEP*, 367). Brief as it is, the poem is in three parts: a particular moment described in five lines, followed by a five-line comment, thus putting Williams's values in due precedence — that the *fact* of the thrush's singing is 'more / than my own thoughts'. There is a third shift, which dismisses his opening description as poeticizing the occasion. The incident's true point is elicited, its presentness, making the observer subject to the moment ('What can I say?'), focusing his emotions: 'Vistas / of delight waking suddenly / before a cheated world.' The poem's whole validity is merely in pointing.

Its only value-judgment offered in the title, 'Fine Work with Pitch and Copper' (*CEP*, 368) exhibits the same verbal structure of present action. A sense of the artist's pride in his work is conveyed through the closing triad. Still lunching, a workman: 'picks up a copper strip / and runs his eye along it'. Later, Williams himself suggested that this poem is 'about' his struggles with technique, search for a regular stanza pattern (*IWWP*, 57). The quest for that particular kind of order is here reflected in capitalization, used still for punctuation, breaking the poem into three sections, a mathematical diminuendo (9, 6, 3 lines), each fresh sentence beginning with the line.

Philip Horton, in a review attacking *Complete Collected Poems of William Carlos Williams 1906–1938*,[12] turned Stevens's 'anti-poetic' and 'sentimental' against Williams. Horton saw Williams's 'Objectivism' as a 'deliberate stylization of the anti-poetic state of mind', but claimed that, while 'overtly' objective, Williams was really sentimental, attempting to solve his own inner conflict by substituting the impersonal for the personal. While such a procedure may be 'spiritual hygiene' it is not poetry, which is produced not when conflict is eliminated but when it is sustained in equilibrium, 'made to function as a physical law of the poet's universe'.

Stevens's subtle, well-intentioned, well-mannered insights of 1934 had become a stumbling-block in the appreciation of Williams's poems. Horton apparently missed the point of Williams's stripped form.

Irritating as Williams found it, Horton's was not the only significant review. Among others were reviews by Horace Gregory, Paul Rosenfeld, Yvor Winters, R. P. Blackmur, and an overview in *Poetry* by Ruth Lechlitner. Gregory, for example, noted that Williams's work was remarkable for its combining American images and the American idiom. Taking a different line Winters saw Williams as a romantic and forecast that he would be regarded (with Stevens) as 'one of the two best poets of his generation'.[13]

Usually any sentimental element in the poems (an identification with the 'subject') is slight, turned to good purpose, held in austere tension against the poem's form. In 'Young Woman at a Window' (*CEP*, 369), for example, the verb tense of present action is strongly reinforced by line structure, the poem reading in a single continuous movement of eye and mind. The two-figure group is perceived in an instant of time, the woman crying, the boy, 'his nose / pressed / to the glass', giving a strong sense impression of grief caused by longing, deprivation, the pair shut off by the glass from the outside world. Clarity of presentation offsets any sentimentality, while linear tension lifts the poem above the merely Imagist.

Moving from 'warmth, variability' to: 'the gold hawk's-eye speaks once / coldly its perfection', 'The Rose' (*CEP*, 369) is a representative, if not highly successful, poem of process, as also is the long, more fully realized 'The Crimson Cyclamen' (*CEP*, 397), dedicated to Charles Demuth. Such a poem serves to show that Williams was involved in process, as Pound was, in the sense suggested by A. N. Whitehead: 'We should start from the notion of actuality as in essence a process.'[14] It can never be overlooked that while one side of Williams's interest in actuality was the object, the other side was more complex: flux, perpetual change, spontaneity, disorder, the evanescence of vitality. Out of this process, life:

> out of the sea —
> the Venusremembering wavelets
> rippling with laughter —
> freedom
> for the daffodils!
>   (*CEP*, 379)[15]

Similarly, the opening of his novel, *White Mule*,[16] introducing the child, the central figure, a flower:

>   She entered, as Venus from the sea, dripping. The air
> enclosed her, she felt it all over her, touching, waking her. If
> Venus did not cry aloud after release from the pressure of that
> sea-womb, feeling the new and lighter flood springing in her
> chest, flinging out her arms — this one did.   (*WM*, 1)

As he continued to develop as a poet, Williams was also writing
his short stories, novels and plays. Of *White Mule* he observed
that he had 'started without too much forethought, the way I
always do' (*IWWP*, 60), but what distinguishes his prose fiction is
its directness. He is specific, always. The Stecher trilogy embodies
his dictum: 'No ideas but in things' and is part of the same effort
as *In the American Grain* to capture an unfalsified sense of
America. His finest single collection of short stories, *Life Along
the Passaic River*,[17] concentrates more direct social concern than
any of his poetry. Complementing his Objectivist approach to the
poem, his fiction is behaviourist and environmentalist. Circumstance plays a key part in activating many of the stories, while
some are constructed by a juxtapositional method comparable
with that employed in the poems.

Where his fiction shows Williams's preoccupation with the
quality of American life, his dramatic work is chiefly interesting
for its concern with form. Each play is experimental and one in
particular, *Many Loves* (originally *Trial Horse, No. 1*),[18]
manifests his interest in process, the flux, multiplicity, the shift of
focus upon the theme, and kinds, of love being in itself
metamorphic. Besides exploiting the juxtapositional techniques
later employed in *Paterson*, both of Williams's major plays, *Many
Loves* and *A Dream of Love*, are, thematically, a foreground to
his last and greatest period as a poet, with human love as the
central value.

With occasional exceptions, such as 'Elegy for D. H. Lawrence',
Williams's poetry in the 1930s continued to avoid discursiveness
and to keep the poet's personal attitudes well in the background.
Largely, it was still concrete and imagistic, but (perhaps through
social, as well as personal, circumstances) it became less vital and
much grimmer in its tone and concerns. Temporarily at least, the
joy in 'vividness' seems to have disappeared. 'It grew more serious,
austere, and obscure', as James Guimond suggests.[19] A sort of
bouncy, lighthearted satire typical of the earlier work had, for
the moment, dissipated. At times during the 1930s Williams must

have come as close as he ever came to extinction as a poet, but he survived into the decade when he was to begin serious work on the 'epic' *Paterson*. Seen in the long perspective of his whole career perhaps the respectful critical reception then was a turning-point, even though it immediately preceded the hiatus brought about by the onset of the Second World War.

7 Poem as Machine

Much has been written in recent years, by James Breslin, Robert Coles, Linda Wagner and others,[1] about Williams's development as a prose writer. With *Life Along the Passaic River*, the first two novels of the Stecher trilogy, *White Mule* (1937) and *In the Money* (1940), would seem to show that his development at this time was as a fiction writer, particularly if *Complete Collected Poems, 1906–1938* is regarded as a watershed rather than a further move forward. If, however, our concern is 'the American poem', the fiction of the 1930s and 1940s is not pertinent in the way that *In the American Grain, The Great American Novel* and even *A Voyage to Pagany* certainly are.

In the best of Williams's fiction — the two volumes of short stories published in the 1930s and the first book of the Stecher trilogy, *White Mule* — the strength lies in its realism, accuracy of observation in the accounts of the day-to-day strains of a general practitioner's life, or of the pressures in the lives of immigrants making their way. In some important respects, Williams's sense of the nature of poetry may be discerned as complementary to all this, at a different level of engagement. In essays of the time, he pointed more and more to the importance of art in life, the focal essay being 'Against the Weather',[2] in which art is claimed as the only unchangeable, while the 'only world that exists is the world of the senses, the world of the artist' (*SE*, 196). Civilization's most important product, art, also creates and shapes civilization, containing 'new conceptions of government'. The artist, besides being 'objective' must also be 'sensual'. He needs the latter quality to 'produce' vital experience and the former to prevent ego or thought from predetermining its structure. Both qualities are dependent on *where* he is, simply because he happens to be there, and on his local idiom, whatever it happens to be — in Williams's case, the American idiom.

As a natural outcome of his interest in process, his interest in the thing became involvement in the thing in action. Movement and structure of many poems in *The Wedge* (1944)[3] are testimony of this. One typescript of the book, at Buffalo, has as alternative titles, *The Language* and *The (Lang) WEDGE*. Zukofsky pointed out that these were over explicit, and also advised against inclusion of a number of prose passages, suggesting they be omitted or remade into poems. The advice was good as the passages in question deal in somewhat stale Joycean language effects, which could only dilute a book the central concern of which is the word.

In the Introduction Williams declares that man is *used by* language and not the reverse: the poem has a more objective quality and presence than man himself. The Freudian theory of poem-making as self-therapy (which he elsewhere subscribes to) is here rejected, a metamorphic view of man offered ('Hamlet today, Caesar tomorrow', *SE*, 256). The nature of the poem, however, is fixed, as 'a small (or large) machine made of words'. Again Williams is rejecting Stevens's imputation of sentimentality, and in 'sentimental' he includes, by implication, 'rhetorical'. The poet's building of his machine is anti-rhetorical. He makes it from 'words as he finds them interrelated about him' (*SE*, 257) and it is in the resulting composition, 'the intimate form', that 'the exact meaning' of any work of art is to be discerned.

'A Sort of a Song' (*CLP*, 7)[4] states the point about language by, perhaps unexpectedly, using two seemingly unrelated metaphors. Like a waiting snake, words are 'slow and quick, sharp / to strike, quiet to wait, / sleepless'. Presumably the idea offered in this figure is that words exist actively. Seemingly, but only seemingly, at a tangent, the poem concludes: 'Saxifrage is my flower that splits / the rocks.' Another metaphor for words, the language, the poem, this is the wedge, more delicate, beautiful, than gross actuality (the rock), driving into the rock, smashing it, beginning its crumbling to fruitful soil. The flower, in Williams, commonly suggests woman, so here is a reversal, or rather a *completeness* of role, whereby the flower, beauty, drives in, planting seed, enriching soil. These are metaphors. The poet aims ' — through metaphor to reconcile / the people and the stones'. This seems to contravene his often-stated tenet rejecting 'the bastardy of the simile', 'the word as symbol', etc. Clearly evident as it is that he sought first 'vividness', nominalistic or cubistic clarity, not 'the word as symbol' but 'the word as reality'

(*SE*, 107), yet he used metaphor in a variety of ways. Things having 'one-thousandth part of a quality in common' (*SE*, 11) may be apprehensible in themselves by 'great intensity of perception', but they may also invite metaphor, since metaphor is an 'idea' discovered in a relation of 'things'. Williams's various fulminations against such devices have behind them a distrust of literariness, the literary kind of metaphor which does not result in the common illumination of two objects but merely in verbal staleness. Metaphor, for him, is not an exercise of the intellect but a special way of comprehending, or responding to, reality. Reviewing Rexroth's versions of *One Hundred Poems from the Chinese*,[5] he uses the phrase 'total metaphor', observing 'These men . . . were looking at direct objects when they were writing, the transition from their pens or brushes is direct to the page.' His own sense of the world, and of metaphor, is akin to this. The impulse of Williams, Marianne Moore and some of their contemporaries to omit connectives is, of course, directly related to Fenollosa's observation that 'All nations have written their strongest and most vivid literature before they invented a grammar.' Fenollosa also points out that metaphor does not depend upon causality, abstraction, logic, but upon perception or recognition.[6]

For Williams the insistence on analogy, in its various forms, is a falsification of experience. 'No symbolism can be permitted to obscure the real purpose, to lift the world of the senses to the level of imagination and so give it new currency' (*SE*, 213). But otherwise in *The Wedge* he makes another shift in his deployment of the line. Often his poems present themselves more didactically or polemically than hitherto, his line, varying to accommodate the change of tack, is more obviously (in Cid Corman's phrase) 'along a prose arc'. 'Prose can be a laboratory for metrics', Williams had told Kay Boyle in 1932 (*SL*, 130). For a long time, he had resorted to prose-writing as a loosener, and appears to have turned instinctively to it whenever he lost creative intensity.

Any tracing of his career as a poet will show that his high periods came fitfully, bursting through at intervals. Naturally enough for a pediatrician, a recurring theme or motif in his work is that of birth, and this is the focus of several poems of the period, including 'Catastrophic Birth' (*CLP*, 8). Presumably the parallel between the human life-cycle and the cycle of creativity must at some time have occurred to him. 'Catastrophic Birth' is a poem of process, which repeats the image of the rock splitting. There are three 'births': (a) the child-bearing of an Italian woman of gross proportions, (b) the action of a volcano, (c) the activity in a chemistry laboratory. Each of these brings about change. So? 'The change reveals — change.' This is a way of saying that the flux of being exists in its own right and for its own sake. Yet the products of process (in this instance, violent) must be complete, whole, in themselves: 'Unless each remain inflexible / there can be no new. The new opens / new ways beyond all known ways.' Each change, therefore, is a metamorphosis. Through the 'she-Wop' we learn that change 'cleans you up / makes you feel good inside'.

The volcano's metamorphosis brings a complete change to its world, fallen 'into a heap of ashes'. The 'revelation' spoken of is also a revolution, in which 'Only he who had been confined / in disgrace underground is rescued alive'. This, too, is a birth. All the births attest to the fact of change and an attendant violence, and the 'catastrophic' of the title is ironic, for change, although it is inevitable and is no more than change, is also welcome. In an adjacent programme poem, 'Paterson: the Falls' (*CLP*, 10), rock is again the substance undergoing change, with water the transmogrifying agent.

These poems of process and metamorphosis are followed by 'The Dance' (*CLP*, 11), a poem of movement, which yet suggests unity, stability, measure, comprehended in the work of art. The peasants' movement is circular and continuous, and this is emphasized in the physical shapes of people and objects evoked. The poem's single full stop, followed by 'kicking' conveys a change of movement rather than a halt. The brief whole is framed by a static line repeated at opening and close. Its verbal subtleties include the participial series, the motion carried in the reiterated 'l' and 'r' sounds ('rolling'), the bluntness of the repeated 'k' and 'b'. This sense of the dance (going back as far as *Kora in Hell*, foreshadows 'The Desert Music' (*PB*, 109):[7]

> Only the counted poem, to an exact measure:
> to imitate, not to copy nature, not
> to copy nature
>
> NOT, prostrate, to copy nature
>   but a dance! . . .

and will be the culmination of *Paterson.*

A new discursiveness is most plainly evident in 'Writer's Prologue to a Play in Verse' (*CLP*, 12). Williams's interest in the drama was at its strongest at this period and there is evidence of a general change of involvement towards, broadly, interaction of people, forces, elements, world and mind. This poem explores the changes, suggesting the human importance of imagination, which can provide all the settings and actions to accompany them. In one Buffalo draft the opening line has 'can', 'In your minds you can jump from doors', and its omission in the final version indicates Williams's intention to show the power, spontaneity and immediacy of imagination. He insists on the existence of concrete details alongside the mind (and noticeably at this period 'the mind' was a crucial object of Williams's contemplations):

> You see it
> in your minds and the mind at once
> jostles it, turns it about, examines
> and arranges it to suit its fancy.
> or rather changes it after a pattern
> which is the mind itself . . .
> (*CLP*, 12)

The poem (in the general sense, Williams usually preferred this terminology to 'poetry') is the mind's peculiar speech, ultimate manifestation of the individual person: 'Would it disturb you if I said / you have no other speech than poetry?'

Paragraph two is the writer's imaginings (as *dramatis personae*) advising the reader to seek the poems in himself, some coherent sense of his being beyond the merely hedonistic. For such a discovered truth, the ultimate sense of oneself, the first shock provides no language, but when the language comes it is poetry.

'Burning the Christmas Greens' (*CLP*, 16) combines Williams's characteristic mode of observed actuality with this newer sense of people acting in concert, in this case almost ritualistically. The mind is a means of facing outwards towards the world, as well as in. An insistent greenness in this poem offers both solid actuality and peace. Source of reassurance, it is where 'small birds hide and dodge / and lift their plaintive / rallying cries . . . '. Yet this green must be matched, balanced by red, this peace by violence, this actuality by imagination. As in 'Catastrophic Birth', violence brings the new. In the flames' roar the used-up actuality of the Christmas greens bursts to a new, brief, vivid life. Green is transformed:

> to red, instant and alive. Green!
> those sure abutments . . . Gone!
> lost to mind
>
> and quick in the contracting
> tunnel of the grate
> appeared a world! Black
> mountains, black and red — as
>
> yet uncolored — and ash white,
> an infant landscape of shimmering
> ash and flame and we in
> that instant, lost,
>
> breathless to be witnesses,
> as if we stood
> ourselves refreshed among
> the shining fauna of that fire.
>
> (*CLP*, 18)

This vivid act of imagination anticipates and has affinities with the *Paterson* sequence of the bottle in the fire. Their shared theme is that out of destruction (by fire) comes new life, created by imagination.

Greater emphasis than before is given to process rather than object in *The Wedge*. Much now is seen to depend on the cyclical nature of experience, birth–death–rebirth, and this experience is frequently violent. Clearly, however, as in the plays 'love / will rise out of its ashes if / we water it . . .' (*CLP*, 19). Both violence and gentleness are stressed in 'The Monstrous Marriage' (*CLP*, 53, Williams's odd 'Leda and the Swan'). With obviously gentle intent the woman in the poem reaches to rescue a wounded pigeon, but her touch goads it to fury. Attempting to win it over to gentleness 'she stilled it for the moment / and wrapped it in her thought's / clean white handkerchief', but the outcome is to say the least ambiguous, 'she adopted a hawk's life as her own', while from his side the pigeon-turned-hawk tries to learn from her love. He appears to be desolated by his transformation, but she protects him, adapting her love to his new, violent life. This is a strange fable of unresolved metamorphosis.

Little critical notice was given to *The Wedge* at the time and general assessments of Williams's poetry tend to leap from *Collected Poems 1921–1931* over to *Paterson*. If we are thinking of 'the American poem', it is easy to see why this is so even though, reviewing *The Wedge* in *Partisan Review* in 1945, Randall Jarrell declared of Williams, 'He is the America of Poets', and felt that his poems epitomize 'one of the great mythological attitudes of our country: Brooklyn, the truck-driver looking shyly at the flower'.[8] Clearly, this is not the poet of such poems as 'The Monstrous Marriage'. That is a poem of fancy, deriving from long primitive and mythological traditions of marriage between human and animal, or bird. When, a few years later, Williams's *Collected Later Poems* (which includes much of the work from *The Wedge*) was reviewed in England, there was respect and a recognition of difference, but no especially helpful exploration of that difference. *The Times Literary Supplement* reviewer, for example, locates the American manner in terseness, and says 'Dr Williams is never diffuse';[9] but in fact much of Williams's poetry of the 1940s is both more discursive and more fanciful than earlier work. In a nice image, the reviewer sees Williams's poems as resembling 'the unpromising figures of pruned rose trees', adding, 'He does not use the ordinary combinations of sounds such as we are accustomed to in English poetry.' But what does he do? Well, many of the poems of this period approach nearer to an iambic matrix than Williams's poems of the 1920s, but they elude it. The rhythms do indeed move 'along a prose arc', reinforcing the detachment the reviewer also notes (which is, in fact, no more than Pound's 'opacity'). 'It would be hard to say exactly what his style is' and yet the emphasis is on form, but a fluid and highly adaptable form.

Writing in the *Yale Review*, David Daiches located the projectivist nature of Williams's approach to poetry, as 'an intensely individual structuring of language to correspond to a perception or state of mind of the author. It is not the expression of a state of mind so much as the construction of a pattern of words which at the same time resolves it and bears witness to it; and the emphasis is always on the integrity and the uniqueness of the finished poem.'[10]

Indicative of contemporary responses outside the immediate American context, these comments are useful, and Daiches's remark is especially penetrating as an attempt to establish that the poems may be attempts at enactment (projection) and objectification.

To return, then, to the poems. Discursive, non-imagistic (and, I believe, adequate to illustrate my remark above about the 'iambic matrix'), 'To All Gentleness' (*CLP*, 24) considers polarization: violence, gentleness, poetic, anti-poetic. The oppositions are put expressionistically:

> Secure in the enclosing rain,
> a column of tears borne up by the heavy
> flowers: the new and the unlikely, bound
> indissolubly together in one mastery.

Both 'the new and the unlikely' may be the so-called anti-poetic, to ignore which is to lose contact with half the world. Williams's method here is juxtapositional, pointedly placing together the poles of his discourse. The gentleness of

> to buy, shall we say, the
> grass, or a small cloud perhaps (in
> whose shadow a lifting wind whirls) or
> if Queen Blanche, a pond
> of waterlilies or the rain itself

is set against the violent beauty of human birth, the mother being 'forewoman to gang at the ship foundry':

> Never had a backache.

> Not the girth of thigh, but
> that gentleness that harbors all violence,
> the valid juxtaposition, one
> by the other, alternates, the cosine, the
> cylinder and the rose.
>
> > (*CLP*, 29)

He is saying that, in the fullest experiences, the human body 'knows' the external world inwardly or, put another way, 'enters into' the external world. 'A thing known passes out of the mind into the muscles.'

Such poems are none the less a considerable distance from Williams's earlier mode, which Gorham Munson had summed up as 'an arbitrary composition characterized by *independence*. He is attempting to leap straight from contact (sharp perceptions) to the imagination (order in the highest sense) . . . .'[11] The staple poems of *The Wedge* are unlike this. Some sense of the difference may be gained by comparing 'The Right of Way' from *Spring and All* (*CLP*, 258) with 'The Forgotten City' (*CLP*, 49). Each poem concerns a drive by car, but the earlier is all observed detail, while 'The Forgotten City' describes the driver's sense of strangeness and isolation as he drives through an unfamiliar area in the aftermath of a storm, so the latter is nearer to involvement in a process, which may account for one commentator's remark that Williams drew few clear pictures.

This poem figures the *persona* Dr Patterson, as does 'Eternity' (*CLP*, 36), where an assignation results in his feeling isolated and alienated: 'Night, greater than / the cataract / surged in the cisterns of Noah's / chest.' Darkness becomes so tangible he has a sense of swimming in it. The outer world (and his inner world) become unreal. Night externalizes an inner solipsism. He is moved from one encapsulation of light to another. Since he finally halts 'under a / street lamp to make / some notes' the assignation apparently resolves itself into the poem, to the woman's (Olympia's) relief. They return to the world of 'Break-fast / at seven'.

At this quite late stage Williams had not fully related his poems to speech, as is evident from the Buffalo drafts of 'Raleigh Was Right', e.g.

> What can the small violets
> tell us that grow on furry stems
> in the long grass among
> lance shaped leaves?
>
> . . .
>
> Empty pockets
> make empty heads. Cure it

> if you can but do not believe
> that we can live today
> in the country . . .

Zukofsky advised him to 'realign' the poem for 'spoken cadence' (the result being the lineation in *Collected Later Poems*).[12] Thus Williams's central criterion was not always, as he suggests, idiom. 'Perfection' (CLP, 40),[13] for example, appears to be organized by letter count, a technique Zukofsky had attributed to Williams in the *Symposium* essay a decade earlier, nearer to musical notation than spoken idiom.

Objectors to Williams's treatment of the line commonly point to his line culminations in words such as 'and', 'a', 'the', 'so', etc. Use of such endings is deliberate, and is part of his effort to revitalize the poem. As a poem is a 'thing in itself', so also is each word. From that point of view all words possess equal reality. Claiming that the full reality of a word is established in its *relation* to other words, he nevertheless felt that each word exists in its own right, part of the poet's task being to use it so (*SE*, 128, 129). Speech cadences apart, Williams often employed syntax to display the autonomy, the 'thingness' of individual words. This procedure, of itself, thrusts energy back and forward through the line, the syntactical/ lineal arrangement often being reinforced by a deliberateness of rhythm to the same end:

> No one
> has moved you
> since I placed you on the porch
> rail a month ago
> to ripen.
>
> (*CLP*, 40)

This technique denies conventional interdependence of rhythm and grammar. Where it is customary for each of these elements to confirm the other's *rightness*, Williams typically sets them in tension. Besides asserting the active presence of specific words, the resulting dissonances have the more subtle effect of refusing, rather than satisfying, the ear's expectations (see, for example, *CLP*, 56, 'Silence'). An obvious case here is the break at 'and' in line 3. Prepared by the opening words, we might have received a more portentous, or dramatic, statement, but the 'yellow leaves' attach us firmly to objective reality while establishing the poem's immediate scope. Following this, 'disturbs' opens out to further possibilities, denied after the line break, while 'the green leaves' could be as much as a forest. A small instance, but word and line placement have been used here to excellent effect. A poem of a year or two after *The Wedge*, 'When Structure Fails Rhyme Attempts to Come to the Rescue' (*CLP*, 79), both sums up and exemplifies Williams's viewpoint:

> The old horse dies slow.
> By gradual degrees
> the fervor of his veins
> matches the leaves'
>
> stretch, day by day. But
> the pace that his
> mind keeps is the pace
> of his dreams.

His technical sophistication is clearly evident in the two versions of 'Sparrows Among Dry Leaves' (*CEP*, 458 and *CLP*, 55) where he sacrifices some degree of sharply-defined individual detail for the sake of rapidity and an effect of unity of action.

Overshadowed as it is by *Paterson* and the fine late poems in 'the variable foot', there is much value in Williams's shorter poetry of the late 1940s. His mastery of the imagistic poem continued, as in 'The Manoeuvre' (*CLP*, 88)[14], 'The Motor-Barge' (*CLP*, 92); but in practice he did not always scorn the simile, as in 'The Horse' (*CLP*, 89) or 'The Flower' (*CLP*, 104). In some instances intensity of human involvement renders his poem an epiphany, for example 'The Act' (*CLP*, 96). Two published versions of such an epiphanic poem are an illuminating comparison. These are of 'The Girl' (*CLP*, 123) and an earlier version:

> THE GIRL
> with big breasts
> in a blue sweater
>
> was crossing the
> street bareheaded

reading a paper
held up close

but stopped, turned
and looked down

as though
she had seen a coin

lying
on the pavement.[15]

Though verbally more explicit, this earlier version is less precise
and immediate, in fact descriptive rather than epiphanic. In this
type of poem, objective rendering which reverberates emotion-
ally, Williams's most sustained success of the time was 'The
Semblables' (*CLP*, 244).

Ranging far beyond Imagism and his terse, tight, short line, he
composed freely discursive poems such as 'Russia' (*CLP*, 93-6),
his ability for objective recording helping him to keep his musings
in focus. Sometimes he moves discursively even in space of a short
poem such as 'Raindrops on a Briar' (*CLP*, 99) and again, taking
a hint from Surrealists such as Hans Arp, he can mock such
discourse, as in 'For a Low Voice' (*CLP*, 105). But his new
flexibility of approach was not uniformly beneficial. Two poems
dealing with related material, the city, are a revealing contrast.
'Approach to the City' (*CLP*, 177), is in a mode typical from *Al
Que Quiere!* onwards, 'naked attention to the thing itself', an
affectionate rendering with the observation 'I never tire of these
sights'. On the other hand, 'A Place (Any Place) to Transcend all
Places' (*CLP*, 113) ponders the evil, artificial city, compared with
the good, solid rootedness of the country. The approach is that of
the metamorphic 'Perpetuum Mobile: the City', but here the
conception fails through being nakedly abstract. Williams's
remark of this time, 'I was in my stride now. I thought I had
found my form' (*IWWP*, 74), is true enough but his early work in
the new form had its failures.

Contemplativeness accompanied a deepened awareness of the
value and necessity of love, and a new sense of the mind, the
imagination, the work of art, as shown by many of the poems,
such as 'Labrador' (*CLP*, 68, originally 'The Bath'). Williams

rejects explicitly such mental abstractions as 'heaven', 'the ideal state', preferring as always the near at hand, observed 'cat / threading a hedge' (*CLP*, 80); but the mind's products can lift us above material limitations, handicaps: 'the music leads them . . . cleansing from each / his awkwardness for him to blossom' (*CLP*, 83). Unless it can be transformed in 'voyages' of the imagination, the physical world is pointless, yet for other levels of experience, in the face of love's desire, for example, the mind is 'a trivial / and momentary clatter' (*CLP*, 87), at once the breadth of personality (*CLP*, 72) and rigid boundary of existence. 'The Mind's Games' (*CLP*, 109) fundamentally affect, even control, our responses, as they are focus of our extension into the world. Similarly (*CLP*, 124, 'The Clouds') our mind is our extension into, and possession of, the past. Here, evoked by the visual image of racing clouds, comes thought of immortality, rejection of the specious ideas of it held by conventional religionists. True immortality is discovered in the continuing relevance of work done by past men of imaginative genius, 'fresh in our thoughts, their / relics, ourselves' (*CLP*, 126).

Para-symbolically, 'The Mind Hesitant' (*CLP*, 118) shows how an experience may be simultaneously held in the mind and be part of the objective world, the two in balance. The mind in adequate relation to the external world, a form of that world may then assume autonomous existence in the mind itself. In this sense mind includes the world, love, the image of Venus (as suggested in the opening lines of 'A Crystal Maze' — *CLP*, 167). In the mind 'Anger can be transformed / to a kitten — as love / may become a mountain' (*CLP*, 169).

> The mind's a queer sponge
>   squeeze it and out come bird songs
> small leaves highly enameled
>   and moments of good reading
> (rapidly) Tuck, tuck, tuck, tuck, tuck!
>   (*CLP*, 195)

'Choral: the Pink Church' (*CLP*, 159-62) gave its original title to a separate collection of Williams's poems.[16] Earlier (Yale) drafts of 'The Pink Church' show that it was discursively conceived, but as we have it in *Collected Later Poems* its great virtue is in its singing, its 'choral' quality. Williams himself suggested the 'the pink church' was, wrongly, interpreted as a symbol for Communism (*IWWP*. 76). Rather it is an affirmation of living in the present, a denial of Original Sin, a hymn to those who 'take no thought for the morrow', a contrasting of the end-products of the Philosophy Departments with sexual man, 'bringer / of pure delights'. Above even the teaching of thinkers Williams himself respected (Dewey, Whitehead, William James) stand the pragmatic facts of the Pink Church, a double symbol: of humanity itself, and of the beauty, which men:

> Sing!
> transparent to the light
>   through which the light
> shines, through the stone,
>   until
> the stone-light glows,
>   pink jade
> — that is the light and is
>   a stone
> and is a church . . . .
>   (*CLP*, 159-60)

Despising both Calvinistic torturers and the false plumage of the 'liveried', the poet celebrates, even in man's suffering, 'Joy! Joy! / — out of Elysium!' The 'joy' now seems more in Williams's head than it had twenty years earlier, but its affirmation remained a true possibility. The complexity of the continuing struggle towards it is the matter of *Paterson*.

8 *Paterson*: the First Stages

Any account of William Carlos Williams's quest for the American poem must culminate in *Paterson*, which is widely, though not universally, held to be his major work, the quintessential product of his Americanism. As early as February 1927 his 'Paterson' (*CEP*, 223-5) appeared in the pages of the *Dial*.[1] Fourteen lines of this poem survived into *Paterson I*, and these contain several important items: the figure of Mr (Dr) Paterson, the dictum 'No ideas but in things', and the macrocosm/microcosm ('Inside the bus one sees / his thoughts sitting and standing', *P*, 18).[2] As further evidence of long, if sporadic, germination, a poem of the 1930s, 'Paterson: Episode 17' (*CEP*, 438-42),[3] in modified form became the 'Beautiful Thing' motif of *Paterson III* as also a number of 'details' intended for that poem appear in *An Early Martyr*, *Complete Collected Poems 1906-1938* and *The Broken Span*. To Pound in 1936 Williams spoke of 'that magnum opus I've always wanted to do: the poem PATERSON' (*SL*, 163). Nearly a decade earlier, in 'The Simplicity of Disorder' (*SE*, 94) he implied the planning of a long poem.

The genesis of *Paterson* may begin very early in Williams's career as a poet, as Stuart Peterfreund had interestingly argued in 'Keats's Influence on William Carlos Williams'.[4] Williams's development is commonly seen as a prolonged psychomachia between the Keats and Whitman influences in him, which took its final positive direction when Whitman prevailed. Some critics, however, such as Rod Townley and Peterfreund, see the influence of Keats continuing much later into Williams's career, and Peterfreund draws interesting parallels in theme and structure between *Paterson* and *Endymion*.

Two notes in the Buffalo Collection suggest that Williams's final successful drive to realize *Paterson* was connected with his interest in drama, which developed strongly in the 1940s.[5] That apart, he resorted to his now well-tried melding of prose and poem, noting an explicit distinction between two kinds of

86

material:

> There are to be completely worked up parts in *each* section —
> as completely formal as possible: in each part well displayed.
> BUT — juxtaposed to them are unfinished pieces — put in
> without fuss — for their very immediacy of expression — as
> they have been written under stress, under LACK of a sat-
> isfactory form — or for their need to be just there, the
> information.   (*Yale*)

His sense of the poem had been much the same long before when
he wrote in 1913 to Harriet Monroe that 'life is above all things
else at any moment subversive of life as it was the moment
before'.[6] His supreme effort at synthesis, *Paterson* none the less
includes the Bergsonian sense that disorder is simply an
unfamiliar order. 'Words form a new city', Zukofsky had written
in 1930.[7] As Doctor Paterson and the city of Paterson are one, so
the creating of the word-city is the poet's 'primary effort' to
make himself. A headnote for *Paterson I*[8] (virtually paragraph 1
of the 'Author's Note' to the complete edition)[9] outlines the whole
project, in which 'Part One introduces the elemental character of
the place'.

By now, there is a substantial number of *Paterson* explications
and commentaries, but it seems fitting to sum up the poem's
methodology from Randall Jarrell's extraordinary 1946 review.
Jarrell saw *Paterson I* as 'the best thing Williams has ever
written . . . the organization of *Paterson* is musical to an almost
unprecedented degree: Mr Williams introduces a theme that
stands for an idea, repeats it over and over in varied forms,
develops it side by side with two or three more themes that are
being developed, recurs to it time and time again throughout the
poem, and echoes it for ironic or grotesque effects in thoroughly
incongruous contexts'.[10]

Book I itself is presented with an important, oracular headnote
(applicable to the whole poem — *P*, 10) and a Preface, opening
with the declaration that 'Rigor of beauty is the quest', and the
aim formulated elsewhere through Williams's response to Dewey
and Whitehead:[11]

> To make a start
> out of particulars

and make them general . . . .
(*P*, 11)

The whole poem is a conflict between Williams and his own experience of chaotic, pluralist America, resulting in a number of polarizations: marriage/divorce, man and woman, convention and instinct, ideas and things, art and nature. In every instance he seeks a fusion, or a resolution based on the dominance of the preferable alternative.

His means are complex, as progression through the text will show:

> Sniffing the trees,
> just another dog
> among a lot of dogs. What
> else is there? And to do?
> The rest have run out —
> After the rabbits.
> (*P*, 11)

Paterson is not a narrative but 'a dispersal and a metamorphosis' (*P*, 10), its coherence carried in themes and motifs. One such is the 'dog motif', the dog having a quasi-symbolic function as the thoughts (or as a metamorphosis), of the doctor–poet Paterson/Williams. The lines quoted are a covert reference to the Pound–Eliot quest in Europe, and Williams's own refusal to follow them. For him, 'the lame', the preferable alternative is 'a reply to Greek and Latin with the bare hands' (*P*, 10 headnote). Refusing to chase the typical American success, he endorses his own championing, in *In the American Grain*, of the man who refuses such 'success' in favour of loving the American land and living fully in it *now*. Features of this are his rejection of Old World tradition and (a refrain in *Paterson*) of the kind of 'knowledge' purveyed in the university, inimical as it is to touch, contact.

Determinedly local, Williams chose to base his poem on Alexander Hamilton's 'Paterson, the federal city', his own city of Rutherford lacking the same degree of historical interest. In her excellent pioneering study of the poem,[12] Sister M. Bernetta Quinn has shown how much of Williams's intention is present in the very name, 'Paterson' suggesting as it does father and son, generator/generated. Homonyms 'son'/'son' suggest self-generation, and also Williams's microcosm/macrocosm conception: 'man is both subject and object in the design of reality, since through perception, according to Williams, he creates what lies about him'.[13] Paterson is also the 'father of sound'.[14]

Williams's key statement of method in his headnotes is 'a dispersal and a metamorphosis'. His poem's focus, the giant man-city Paterson, undergoes many radical transformations and yet in some sense remains the same for, seen from one point of view, he is the Joycean 'inclusive consciousness' whose thoughts and experiences change rapidly and repeatedly, although it remains the same consciousness throughout.[15]

A Preface parenthesis immediately offers a sexual connotation for 'dispersal':

> (The multiple seed,
> packed tight with detail, soured,
> is lost in the flux and the mind,
> distracted, floats off in the same
> scum)   (*P*, 12)

but in 1919 Williams had spoken of the 'dispersive quality' of modern poetry, its going 'into all corners, into every emotion, down as well as up',[16] thus participating in the 'perpetual change', metamorphosis. Such a perception is of a piece with his Passaic immersion, elimination of subjective/objective categories, the 'interpenetration' of man and environment.

In the metamorphic cycle:

> — today is tomorrow is yesterday
> is time reversed, circuitous
> (*Yale*, 186/3)

the movement of *Paterson* is from the 'nine months' wonder' to 'the final somersault / the end' (after which comes Book V and the sketch of VI!). Cyclical pattern was originally more overt in emphasis, through correspondence between the four books and the seasons. Man and environment are interpenetrative, thus the simultaneous presentation of Paterson as man-city; but the whole of reality is metamorphic in this way — qualities manifested in their opposites — in a way reminiscent of T. E. Hulme's summary of Bergson's philosophy in the first of its two parts: 'the conception of reality as a flux of interpenetrated elements unseizable by the intellect ...'.[17]

Drafts show that 'rolling' (besides relating to cycle) is connected with manufacture, rolling mills, intended to exemplify a 'horrid' means employed to further a wrong (material) conception of beauty. The quotation opening the published Preface is completed in draft: 'Rigor of beauty is the quest. But how will you find beauty when it is locked in the mind past all remonstrance? It is not in the things nearest us unless transposed there by our employment. Make it free, then, by the art you have, to enter these starved and broken pieces' (*Yale*, 186/2).

Two lines follow:

> My beautiful shirt is worn out? Where shall I get another?
> The mills, the mills, the horrid mills, rolling . . .[18]

Conscious of the dangers of over-explicitness, Williams may have realized that such lines could raise anew the whole irritating question of the 'anti-poetic'.

By structuring the 'starved and broken pieces' by such 'addition and subtraction' the poet 'renews himself'. Discovering and accepting the design, he avoids his craft's being 'subverted by thought'. Throughout his work Williams repeatedly takes this stand against analogical poetry, a position beautifully summed up by his follower Denise Levertov at the close of her 'Letter to William Kinter of Muhlenberg':

> I saw
> without words within me, saw
>
> as if my eyes
> had grown bigger and knew
>
> how to look without
> being told what it was they saw.[19]

The Preface is pervaded by mathematical terms culminating in the phrase 'from mathematics to particulars' (*P*, 13), in a context of repeated references to Einstein and relativity. Mathematics was a subject of discourse for David Lyle and Williams, so that we find Lyle citing Korzybsky's supposed correlating of mathematical symbols and the central nervous system and Lippmann's view of the Good Society, 'as awaiting the issuance of a new language from somewhere out beyond the more recondite Math . . .'.[20]

Lyle also quotes Havelock Ellis's 'thinking is counting'. Once again we cannot tidily summarize Williams's attitude to mathematics nor even find a consistent view. Obviously it was important to him in several ways. In 'The Poem as a Field of Action' he asks 'And what is reality? How do we know reality? The only reality that we can know is MEASURE' (*SE,* 283). The relativity of all histories and cultures is discoverable in measure, which is in itself relative. Each 'world' or era calls for a different measure: ... 'our prosodic values should rightly be seen as only relatively true. Einstein had the speed of light as a constant — his only constant — What have we? Perhaps our concept of musical time ... ' (*SE,* 286).[21] In America itself this concept of musical time in poetry relates back to Poe, but certainly owes something to Pound and to Williams's long-standing friendship with Zukofsky, who correlated music and the poem throughout his career and latterly influenced such poets as Robert Duncan and Robert Creeley in this direction. The phrase 'from mathematics to particulars' suggests that, for Williams, *measure* has the place which light-speed has for Einstein, establishing the relations between objects being a means of establishing the objects themselves. This is one sense of the headnote 'by multiplication a reduction to one' (*P,* 10), which is close to Coleridge's 'rendering multiplicity into unity of effect'. (Poe's criterion for the true poem is the establishing of a single poetic effect.)

The same headnote phrase relates to Dewey's dictum that 'the local is the only universal', while the 'one' is also 'Beautiful Thing', or Venus who 'is one. Over and over again, she is one' (*A Novelette,* 31). Oneness, in the sense of a single ongoing process, is also characteristic of Williams's work ('All I have ever done has been one' — *A Novelette,* 25): work from the abortive novel 'Fairfield', in the 1920s, found its way into essays, into *White Mule* and *A Dream of Love* and *Paterson.* Laughlin suggested *Life Along the Passaic River* as a source for *Paterson,*[22] while *In the American Grain* is quoted in the text and *Kora in Hell* and *White Mule* figure in drafts of the major poem.

Opposite the giant, the man–city Paterson, are 'innumerable women, each like a flower' (*P,* 15). Drafts include a specific 'bouquet' and a suggestion of colour symbolism little of which remains. Garrett Mountain, the rock, is a woman. The Passaic, life-principle, River of Life, is also woman, prefigured in

'Fairfield' as Dolores Maria Pischak, counterpart of Anna Livia Plurabelle.[23] The 'innumerable women' include the poetess whose letters are quoted through the first two books of *Paterson*, helping to define the difficulty of conjoining poem and 'reality'. This use of prose material (there are over one hundred prose items) has been widely misunderstood, prompting suggestions of the poem's inability to cope with the range of contemporary experience, including the breakdown of language itself. Rather, the opposite is the case, for the prose is an important structural element. Williams's whole career demonstrates that for him the dividing line between prose and poem is an artificial one. His own best critical defence occurs in a remarkable essay on Pound's *A Draft of XXX Cantos*:

> His excellence is that of the maker, not the measurer — I say he *is* a poet. This is in effect to have stepped beyond measure.
>
> It is that the material is so molded that it is changed in *kind* from other statement. It is a *sort* beyond measure.
>
> The measure is an inevitability, an unavoidable accessory after the fact. If one move, if one run, if one seize up a material — it cannot avoid having a measure, it cannot avoid a movement which clings to it. . . .
>
> That is the way Pound's verse impresses me and why he can include pieces of prose and have them still part of a *poem*. It is incorporated in a movement of the intelligence which is special, beyond usual thought and action . . . .
>
> It is that which is the evidence of invention. Pound's line is the movement of his thought, his concept of the whole. (*SE*, 108)

Williams uses prose of all kinds as an importation of 'reality' directly into the poem, instances of the 'thing in itself'. A weapon against literariness, it affords repeated opportunities for direct transcription of the language. He found his early model for alternating verse and prose in 1909 when he and H. D. read *Aucassin and Nicolette* together (*Autob.*, 52).

A brief passage from *Kora in Hell*, 'Of Ymir's flesh / the earth was made and of his thoughts / were all the gloomy clouds created' (*KH*, 44), occurs in verse form in some Yale drafts of this early part of *Paterson*. The early placing of this passage, which gives clarity to some otherwise obscure points (e.g. *P*, 193, 'This dress is sweaty'[24]) offers the possibility that, besides creating his own myth, Williams intended to make (perhaps even a systematic) use of classical mythology. Some passages of mythological significance remain, but they are made purely incidental.

As we move into the poem proper (I, i), Paterson's thoughts are equated with the river's movement and the fall of water. The river is at once the stream of (human) consciousness and a certain faculty of intuition above and beyond it. This opening passage is interrupted first by an excerpt from the poetess, raising the issue of life versus art, and later interrupted again by the prose account of David Hower's discovery of pearls in Notch Brook (*P*, 17). In 'the low mountain' may be discovered 'Coloured crystals the secret of those rocks' (*P*, 17). *She*, low mountain with Park as head, lies sleeping:

> Pearls at her ankles, her monstrous hair
> spangled with apple-blossoms.

The central tenet, 'No ideas but in things' is contrasted with sophistries:

> Twice a month Paterson receives
> communications from the Pope and Jacques Barzun
> (Isocrates).
>
> (*P*, 17-18)

Falls and river, source of thoughts, are also therefore source of speech, language, self-naming ('PISS-AGH! the giant lets fly!'). An obscure reference to '*Muncie*' in this passage may offer yet another dimension of Williams's approach, a rather striking kinship with R. S. Lynd's sociological studies of 'Middletown' carried out in the 1920s and 1930s. Lyle wrote to Williams about *Middletown in Transition*,[25] a study based, at least partially, on the small mid-west town of Muncie, Indiana.

The cryptic reference in *Paterson* may offer more than it seems to. In *Middletown*, for example, Lynd notes that:

> an outstanding characteristic of the ways of living of any people at any given time is that they are in process of change, the rate and direction of change depending upon strong centers of cultural diffusion, the appearance of new inventions, migration and other factors which alter the process. (p. 5)

As *Paterson* focuses on a city created by United States industrial expansion, populated partly by migrants and an example of typically American socio-cultural development, there is an obvious parallel. Referring to his use of documents, Lynd explains that one of his techniques is 'using as a groundwork for the observed behavior of today the reconstructed and in so far as possible equally objectively observed behavior of 1890' (p. 5). This is equally true of *Paterson*.

Looking for a city as locus, Williams rejected Manhattan as too complex, Rutherford as lacking in historical and social depth. In a comparable search, though with different central aims, Lynd's two main objectives were remarkably similar to Williams's:

(1) that the city be as representative as possible of contemporary American life, and
(2) that it be at the same time compact and homogeneous enough to be manageable in such a total-situation study. (*Middletown*, 7)

Williams's use of population statistics etc. can be matched in Lynd and is typical of such sociological studies. Lynd's pointing out of the quality of nineteenth-century life, the belief in traditional remedies etc. is in the same spirit as passages of Williams on the 'wonders' (e.g. *P*, 19). Middletown's gas boom of the 1880s had effects similar to those of the Society for Useful Manufactures in Paterson. Lynd gradually realized the primacy of money and the economic conditioning of all aspects of life in the society, 'the tendency of this sensitive institution of credit to serve as a repressive agent' (*Middletown*, 47). To this correspond Williams's Poundian economics of the later books of *Paterson*.

One of Williams's major themes, 'Divorce is / the sign of knowledge in our time' (*P*, 28), is prefigured in a passage in *Middletown*:

. . . a value divorced from current, tangible existence in the world all about men and largely without commerce with these concrete existential realities has become an ideal to which independent existence is attributed. Hence the anomaly of Middletown's regard for the symbol of education and its disregard for the concrete procedure of the schoolroom.   (p. 221)

Lynd also writes of the 'divorce' brought about by mass-production employments and the need to travel to work. He stresses the importance of talk, discussion, sermons, oratory, and of libraries and reading, all of which anticipates *Paterson*, while his note on the decline of religious observance and of attention to preachers is matched in the public reception of Klaus Ehrens in *Paterson II*.

These correspondences suggest that Williams was familiar with *Middletown*. It would be gratifying to discover in Lynd's book a source for *Paterson*, and one might begin from the walking motif of *Paterson II* (and Lynd's observation of walking as a common Middletown pastime) or by comparing the 'weather report' in *Paterson II* (104), with one of Lynd's cited typical diary entries of late nineteenth-century Middletowners. The important point, rather, is that Williams wanted to give *Paterson* a sociological 'presence' and, as we have seen, from the depression onward part of his concern in writing was social. His whole view of its value was one of social usefulness.

Turning again to the *Paterson* text, three passages from New Jersey history follow (*P*, 18-20), the first describing a monstrous-headed dwarf who, later in the poem, is metamorphosed into a figure of the poet. Between this and a report of the catching of a large fish (headlined in the *Paterson Advertiser*, 'The Monster Taken') is the brief account of the growth of a polyglot 'heterogeneous population' — thousands originating in the ten house hamlet Alexander Hamilton had seen by the Falls. Presumably this, too, is a monstrous growth.

Now in a brief, fused poem several 'themes' are made explicit: 'They begin!' (*P*, 20). Human relationships — sexual, marital, social, psychological — are figured in a traditional flower-bee metaphor, deriving from 'each like a flower'. The bee fails, the flowers 'sink back into the loam / crying out'. 'Marriage' has 'come to have a shuddering / implication', while what is lacking is a sufficient means of communication:

> The language is missing them
> they die also
> incommunicado.

> The language, the language
> fails them
> They do not know the words
> or have not

The courage to use them
(*P*, 20)

— the language
is divorced from their minds . . . .
(*P*, 21)

A prose passage (*P*, 21-2, on the Ramapos) next contrasts 'the setting's natural beauty with the clamour and violence of the people: Indians, British army deserters, negro slaves, Irish women — all contributing to the polyglot babble. While indicating the pluralism of American society, Williams also possibly suggests the vitalizing effects of marriage, backing this up by an account of a picture of the wives of an African chief found in an early *National Geographic*.[26] In contrast, marriage and death are combined in the passage in Mrs Sarah Cumming's disappearance over the falls (*P*, 23-4). The unctuous tone of the account of the lady's death embodies 'a false language' (a falls language). Repeated from the opening passage, where it is Paterson's, the 'stone ear' (since she is a rock) is also the woman's. Mrs Cumming died because she found no 'redeeming language', only 'the voice of distress'. This is the fate of all men not redeemed by the Word.

Some *Paterson* drafts contain more overt religious reference. Thus, for the compound Sam Patch / Noah Faitoute Paterson, Williams (while working on Book I) apparently read Noah Davis's *The Narrative of a Coloured Man* (1859),[27] for his notes include a five-page summary of 'Chapter III — Religious Experience — Conviction — Conversion', an account not unlike parts of William James's *The Varieties of Religious Experience*. Patch, who occurs at this point in the text as another Paterson metamorphosis, was an actual person. Born in Rhode Island in 1807 he was a cotton spinner in the Hamilton mills at Paterson who became famous for daredevil diving feats from cliffs and other similar heights. Thus Noah is the flood survivor, Faitoute is based on one of Patch's two frequent saws: 'Some things can be done as well as others.' 'P for short' (*P*, 25) is a partially disguised verbal pun, the initial of Paterson, but also a reference to the Passaic ('PISS-AGH!'). Similarly, 'Crane, who had charge of the bridge' (*P*, 26) may be Williams's humour.[28] Like Mrs Cumming, Patch climbs 'the hundred steps'. His final jump, not into the Passaic but the Genesee,[29] is preceded by an inadequate speech. In this failure of speech he *is* America: 'A great silence followed as the crowd stood spellbound' (*P*, 27).

Carrying over directly to I, ii, this is the reiteration of 'I / cannot say. I cannot say . . . ' (*P*, 28), the divorce of language and reality, and an echo device — how (howl), disposal (proposal), our ears (arrears), which simultaneously suggests a partial apprehension of language and yet enriches the text. Particularizing the language/reality divorce, 'the sign of knowledge in our time', interwoven into the text at this point are suggestions of 'stone ears', 'deaf ears', the deafening tumble of the river (life and language) 'inducing sleep and silence'.

Exemplifying the 'innumerable women', the two 'halfgrown girls' (*P*, 29) are also the 'beautiful' and the language, the falls. Standing for the femaleness of the poet's opposition, his lyrical evoking of them as individuals is broken by the banal 'Ain't they beautiful!'. Randall Jarrell noticed the mythological aspect of this passage:

Girls walk by the river at Easter and one, bearing a willow twig in her hand as Artemis bore the moon's crescent bow,

> *holds it, the gathered spray,*
> *upright in the air, the pouring air,*
> *stroking the soft fur —*
> *Ain't they beautiful!*

(How could words show better than these last three the touching half-success, half-failure of their language?)[30]

In the face of this half-language, the next passage, on the 'robin' and Erasmus, is a rejection of the culture of the European past and of an English name for an American bird, token of a 'subtle transformation' of his ground. Now the 'giant' Paterson is metamorphosed into Paterson/Williams, the doctor–poet, dismissing the validity in the poem of his own personal life, recognizing that his 'theme' must find fit language (with a hint forward — *P*, 30 — that this *may* be discovered among the common people in the park in *Paterson II*). One headnote is repeated, localized, the task ' . . . a mass of detail / to interrelate on a new ground, difficultly' (*P*,30) which is, in some sense, a summary of method.

River and bush are then correlated, followed by emphasis on the colour white (suggesting the passage's epiphanic intensity), which here could be a vestige of a system of colour symbolism. Paterson cannot be fully convinced of beauty's existence merely by thinking of it. Echoing the 'death' he has contemplated, the language available to him is 'stale as a whale's breath'. Pondering the 'silent, uncommunicative' fates of Mrs Cumming and Sam Patch, Paterson feels he has at last begun to,

> know clearly (as through clear ice) whence
> I draw my breath or how to employ it
> clearly
>
> (*P*, 31)

Repetition, here and later, of 'clearly' carries the burden of the whole poem, the quest for a clear, unfalsifying, unequivocal language.

Now Paterson is momentarily metamorphosed into a tree, first a gale-swept juniper and then (interpenetrantly) a sycamore. The tree's branches are the 'innumerable women' (*P*, 30, 31). One 'mottled branch' exhibits the same 'giraffish awkwardness' as the 'first wife' of the African chief (*P*, 31–2, but also *ante P*, 22) suggesting that the wives on the log are 'branches' of a tree, an image of the form of society. At both points (*P*, 23, 32) the women survive among 'thick lightnings', which could strike a tree down. A pun at this point (on 'sum', S. U. M., Society for Useful Manufactures), repeated from the Preface, may be read as opposing the natural force of women to the effect of industrial forces: 'in sum, a sleep, a source, a scourge'.

His thought moves to the university, 'a green bud', potential source of true growth, but in practice a prime example of the divorce of knowledge (language) from reality ('Now come the Universities, the conformists of all colours . . . ', *IAG*, 124)[31], then back to the two women, sisters, the cry for divorce, reality in 'the indifferent gale'. The 'first wife' becomes a flower, 'a flower within a flower'[32] (a possible momentary identification of Muse and Venus), but the flower's 'history' 'laughs at the names / by which they think to trap it' (*P*, 33). Defiant of the 'rifle-shot of learning', 'history' becomes a fanged monster, living in its own odours and language. Following this is the image of 'the snow falling into the water', the white clarity of (realized) form being lost in the flow of language. Some, however, falls upon rocks and dry weeds. At this point (*P*, 34) the natural scene is evoked in imagistic detail:

> The vague accuracies of events dancing two
> and two with language which they forever
> surpass . . . .

A sexual 'replica' follows, given an air of *carpe diem*:

> we sit and talk
> I wish to be with you abed, we two
> as if the bed were the bed of a stream
> (*P*, 35)

This image echoes the opening of the De Soto essay in *In the American Grain*, 'Earth' speaking: 'And in the end you shall receive of me, nothing — save one long caress as of a great river passing forever upon your sweet corse' (*IAG*, 45). As the lovers sit and talk, in contrast the 'silence speaks of the giants / who have died in the past' (*P*, 36): but another element, air (wind) has suggested throughout this section an intransigence man encounters, bringing him both 'rumours' and experiences of 'separate worlds', embodied in several examples of alienated human beings, one in a letter from T., showing through paucity of language the crude limits of his contact with life. This letter introduces the fire element.

Following the specificities of a grocery list, the final verse passage of I, ii (*P*, 39) contains a number of Eliot echoes, an approach to Eliot's less concrete procedure, in a 'delirium of solutions', or a flurry of objective concretives! So the final cut-off of the passage, 'No ideas but / in the facts . . . ', not only repeats (in slightly different, more circumscribed form) a central dictum, but is a check by Williams on his own method.

An excerpt from an Edward Dahlberg letter closes I, ii.[33] Lining up with the poetess 'C' ('Cressida'), Dahlberg accuses Paterson/Williams of turning away 'the few waifs and Ishmaels of the spirit in this country', of being merely irritated by men's suffering, and of literariness. As the aim of *Paterson* is marriage of language with reality, to quote this passage is partially a confession of failure; but it has a charge of irony, since the passage itself illustrates that, in his own fashion, Dahlberg is at least as 'literary' and self-involved as his correspondent.

Possibly echoing the opening of Joyce's *A Portrait of the Artist as a Young Man*, I, iii sets up an opposition between red rose (imagination) and green rose (the facts). The 'idiot' reminds himself that 'The rose is green and will bloom / overtopping you' (*P*, 41). He concludes:

> My whole life
> has hung too long upon a partial victory.
>
> But, creature of the weather, I
> don't want to go any faster than
> I have to go to win.

The 'weather', from the mere fact that it sets conditions, is usually a curtailment of freedom. To complete his victory necessitates his lifting his effort from the merely aesthetic to the moral realm (the making of *Paterson* being such a lifting).

Now he is metamorphosed again into a tree (*P*, 42–4 top: one draft of this passage is titled 'The Sycamore'). His thoughts are raindrops pouring from the leaves. This is his version of 'the child is father to the man', a notion he both accepts and rejects. His sense of 'everybody has roots' raises again the question of living's purpose, a dismissal of the university and its upstart 'clerks':

> spitted on fixed concepts like
> roasting hogs, sputtering, their drip sizzling
> in the fire
>
> (*P*, 44)

Their conceptions resemble reality, which, however, is 'something else the same'.[34]

Documenting the knowledge/reality divorce, the next passage is a vignette of a doctor displaying the wrong kind of detachment, followed by the small, desperate voice of the coloured woman asking 'Will you give me a baby?'. These alienations are shown to be at the very *root* of our way of life.

Statistical facts are used to evoke material preoccupations and wealth, epitomized in 'A special French maid / her sole duty to groom / the pet Pomeranians' (*P*, 45). The ensuing prose passage appraises the 'goods and chattels' of one Cornelius Doremus (whose name is possibly a concealed irony), exemplar of the materially provident. Contrasted is the spoliation of the lake (*P*, 46–7), first drained of water, then emptied of fish and eels, an action produced through men's ignorance, the restriction of knowledge, and willingness to exploit nature for material gain.

The verse following thematically echoes the Preface's 'lame dog' passage (*P*, 11):

> Moveless
> he envies the man that ran
> and could run off
> toward the peripheries —
> to other centers . . .
>
> a sort of springtime
> toward which their minds aspired
> (P, 48)

while his own condition resembles that of Sam Patch's body frozen in the ice, waiting for the spring thaw. Another brief prose account of a falls death follows and, after it, an evocation of the river's industrial pollution, 'the gravel of the ravished park', screaming children, the determinacy of 'the convolutions of the sexual orchid / hedged by fern and honey smells . . . ' (*P*, 49), and the 'pathetic souvenirs' of unhappy marriage. All are:

> A chemistry, corollary
> to academic misuse, which the theorem
> with accuracy, accurately misses . . .
> (P, 49)

An exchange between P. and I. (confusingly, P. here is Pound)[35] asserts Paterson/Williams's interest in process rather than end-product. Then Paterson, 'among the rest', drives out to the convent of the Little Sisters of St Ann,[36] his musing about its pretended 'mystery' shifting from irritation, through horror to a sense of tranquillity, a statement of his apprehension of beauty in the grossest quotidian.

We move next ('He shifts his change') to a very brief prose account of an eighteenth-century earthquake, the rock-splitting which is primary metamorphosis (*P*, 51), then the closing poetry of *Paterson I*. Thought (but not speech) clambers 'upon the wet rock'. This and the final excerpt from Symonds's *Studies of the Greek Poets* (*P*, 53) both concern speech: one, describing how the 'pouring torrent' shrouds in its din 'Earth, the chatterer, father of all / speech . . . ' (*P*, 52).

Repeating the figure of the poet as 'dwarf or cripple', the Symonds passage points to the 'harmony which subsists between crabbed verses and the distorted subjects with which they dealt' (*P*, 53). At first reading a defence, this reiterates rejection of the idea of 'anti-poetic'.[37] Yet the poet is not fully at grips with his reality, his poem, reconciling 'the green and / dovegray countries of / the mind' (*P*, 43), himself, with the roots. All is, at this point, 'a flickering green / inspiring terror' (*P*, 52).

9 *Paterson II*

Despite receiving the Loines Award of the National Institute of Arts and Letters for Book One, Williams had difficulty in moving to *Paterson II*,[1] apparently at one time stopping work on it for many months. He then planned to use as an 'interlude' between the two 'books' the poetess's letter which now closes II. He considered centring it on the Paterson strike, while in another draft it is subheaded 'summer' — with a parenthesis: '(Pleasure. Happy, happy, happy!)'. In the same set of drafts (*Yale*, 185) he insists in one place that 'The Whole Poem is / *ONE* / . . .', describing it in another as a somewhat long episodic poem'. Episodic it is, as he himself came to recognize, but paradoxically *this* is its 'single effect', the rendering of flux.

II, i, in the event, is an articulation from the ending of Book I, beginning with musings in the 'moist chamber' of Paterson's mind, but asserting the external objectivity of the world, moving out to it:

> concretely —
> The scene's the Park
> upon the rock,
> female to the city
> (*P*, 57)

Paterson is there with his dog ('the dog of his thoughts'). Young men and women in the park are characterized by lines from the strike passage in 'The Wanderer':

> . . the ugly legs of the young girls, pistons
> Too powerful for delicacy!
> the men's arms, red, used to heat and cold,
> to toss quartered beeves and

Thus begins presentation of the 'modern replicas', and next is

103

introduced the 'Walking' motif (*P*, 59), its basic source a medical or quasi-medical textbook. A clipping with the Buffalo drafts opens: 'Walking is one of the simplest and most fundamental actions and may serve as an example of dynamic posture.' The last two words have been underlined, and the last four verse lines on *P*, 59 are a quotation from the cutting. Later, Paterson is identified with Audubon walking, and in *Paterson V* occurs the injunction:

> WALK in the world
>   (you can't see anything
> from a car window, still less
> from a plane, or from the moon!?
>   (*P*, 249)

Behind this connection between walking and seeing is that whole special attitude to experience, which prizes the immediate response of the senses as opposed to mere classification by the intelligence. Thoreau expressed it when he mused: 'I must walk more with free senses. It is as bad to *study* stars and clouds as flowers and stones. I must let my senses wander as my thoughts, my eyes see without looking.'[2] Tony Tanner perceives this sense of experience in a succession of American writers, from Emerson and Whitman, through Thoreau and Twain, to Hemingway and Williams, as a prime characteristic of the American literary tradition.

Williams's introduction of the walking motif is interrupted by an excerpt from one of the poetess's letters, which undercuts Paterson's 'I'm still the positive', making his 'dynamic posture' an irony. Paterson's relationship with the poetess has ended in 'divorce', yet she now realizes she cannot create without man. An exchange of questions follows, appearing to suggest that Americans are more interested in function than in the individual,[3] but Paterson refuses the point, answering the American form of the question (the unassigned pronouns allow him to participate in both sides of the exchange):'*What do I do? I listen, to the water falling. (No sound of it here but the wind!)*' His reception of language is impeded by the wind's insistence on a different language (from elsewhere, foreign).[4] Interpolated into the ensuing prose passage of local history is Alexander Hamilton's scornful phrase for the people, 'a great beast'.[5] (This sense of them is matched in the verse following, a crow under attack from a swarm of small birds.) The Demos of Williams's *The First President* is the same beast. Here and in several other passages on the crowd, or mob, Williams is asserting the rights of the individual and, by implication, especially the artist.

Still walking, Paterson crosses the disused pastureland, now stubble, the labour put into it 'a flame, / spent':

> When! from before his feet half tripping,
> picking a way, there starts
>   a flight of empurpled wings!
>   (*P*, 62)

suggesting a flight of true imagination ('from the dust kindled / to sudden ardor!'). Imagination is then metamorphosed into a 'grasshopper of red basalt'. Led forward, by the 'announcing wings' (which do not need to 'unfold for flight') Paterson is stopped by an interpolated protest, again one of the poetess's letters (the prose working actively to impede the sense of flight); but this flight is not to be stopped, continuing in an identification of love and art:

> Love that is a stone endlessly in flight,
> so long as stone shall last bearing
> the chisel's stroke
>   (*P*, 63)

Through imagination Paterson participates in stone (rock), the necessary passive principle, recalling the remark in the *Kora* Prologue that 'The world of action is a world of stones' (*SE*, 14) [and see forward: '(Thus the mind grows, up flinty pinnacles)' *P*, 68]. This verse passage (*P*, 63-4, which may be related to poems from *The Wedge*, such as 'A Sort of a Song' and 'Catastrophic Birth'), is to the effect that art outlives the flesh, but that love also combats death. Placed as it is, the prose account of the mink 'chase' has an 'objective correlative' effect, as a figuring of the elusiveness of imagination.

A 'high' passage of verse, 'Without invention nothing is well spaced' (*P*, 65), follows. Perhaps inspired by Pound's 'usura' Canto, it is Williams's amplest statement of his concept of invention.[6] Most often elsewhere he relates the concept to structure, but on occasion he goes beyond this, as in 'Against the Weather', where he says, 'After a while they will run out of bombs. Then they will need something to fall back on: today. Only the artist can invent it' (*SE*, 197). Today is, and must be, one's immediate environment. Each day the positions, and the relative positions, of the stars change and need to be 'new measured' — the measure and the imagination are in some sense interdependent ('unless there is / a new mind there cannot be a new / line'. *P*, 65). Williams is taking his customary position of affirming the present, or the possibilities of the present.

Specifically, the imagination's calling forth of the witch-hazel bush becomes a 'present' scene, Paterson observing two lovers, 'modern replicas' of the delineated giants, feels their 'frank vulgarity. / Minds beaten thin / by waste . . . ' (*P*, 66) and that 'SOME sort / of breakdown / has occurred'. As 'their pitiful thoughts do meet / in the flesh', so they are his 'pitiful thoughts' and, as such, not 'undignified' (nor anti-poetic). True, 'they sleep', but equally they are 'surrounded / by churring loves. Gay wings . . . ', and can be transformed by the imagination.

Continuing his walk, Paterson meets the collie and her master, a 'clean-dog', as distinct from Musty (echoing the 'musty bone' of the Preface). Figures of the flux, the variety of fate, the all-encompassing nature of thought, imagination, these are like the picnickers' voices in the Park, 'multiple and inarticulate', the 'great beast' come to sun himself' (*P*, 70), gaily, since 'it is all for pleasure'. The gaiety is endowed upon the scene by Paterson himself, for otherwise the picnickers are 'aloof' or indifferent to their surroundings and to each other. Perhaps to suggest this misrelation of Paterson's expectations and the other participants in the scene, Williams introduces a 'lift' into the vocabulary, using language which remains highly concrete, but which is uncharacteristic of the environment ('escarpment', 'abutting', 'stanchions', 'rampart' — details in the scene, but untypical of the ethos). Obliquely, these details and the trumpet sound are put in perspective parenthetically:

> Stand at the rampart (use a metronome
> if your ear is deficient, one made in Hungary
> if you prefer)
>
> (*P*, 71)

At 'the core of gaiety' a young man plays a guitar while Mary, the old Italian woman, dances (*P*, 73) matching 'the sun in frank vulgarity' (*P*, 66 *ante*), chiding the other people for lacking her own vitality. Her dance has a Bacchanalian quality, affirmative, gay, fertile, carrying forward to IV, i and the closing note of V (see below). It contrasts with, and complements, the goatish wooing of a couple surrounded by indifferent children playing. The pervasive dismayed hedonism is juxtaposed to recollection of Russian peasants:

> the peon in the lost
> Eisenstein film drinking
>
> from a wine-skin with the abandon
> of a horse drinking
>
> so that it slopped down his chin?
> down his neck, dribbling
>
> over his shirt-front and down
> onto his pants — laughing, toothless?
>
> > Heavenly man!
> > (*P*, 74)

Human use of the natural setting is also contrasted with an earlier purity:

> oaks, choke-cherry,
> dogwoods, white and green, iron-wood:
>
> humped roots matted into the shallow soil
> — mostly gone
> > (*P*, 77)

The section ends on a contrast in which the poem's method is pointed to as 'an elucidation by multiplicity', whereas the crowd is marshalled by traffic police. Benjamin Sankey[7] interprets the sign 'NO DOGS ALLOWED AT LARGE IN THIS PARK' (*P*, 77) as representing both social order and the poet's regulation of his material, but rather it seems emblematic of social pressures towards conformity, counter to the need 'for belief, to be good dogs'.

Cryptically, the opening of II, ii, 'Blocked. / (Make a song out of that; concretely) By whom?' (*P*, 78), is a meditative response to the poetess's question: 'That kind of blockage, exiling one's self from one's self — have you ever experienced it?' (*P*, 59-60). Paterson, at this point, makes his song from a series of blockages and their polarizations, the section's basic juxtaposition being that of the evangelist Klaus Ehrens's sermon counterpoised against Hamilton's fiscal schemes, the Hamiltonian economic fortification of business interests prevalent in the U.S.A. at least until the Great Crash of 1929.

Ehrens's figure is also contrasted with the effects of a 'massive church', the Church of European tradition, making serfs of its adherents and (as the drafts suggest) offering aesthetic formulations of 'love'. A man who has combined in his life active work for peace with the vision to create and sustain the Tennessee Valley Authority (opposite to the polluted Passaic) as a public corporation, David Lilienthal is considered against the Senate 'trying to block him'. Williams refers to the smear tactic of labelling people 'Communist', asking 'are the Communists any *worse* than the guilty bastards trying in that way to undermine us?' (*P*, 78). Besides deploring the economic monopolism of industrial capitalists, he charges them with the more central 'guilt' of undermining, polluting language itself. Lilienthal showed that industrial needs could combine with respect for nature.[8]

As Paterson continues walking, observing the multiplicity around him, there is music. Something of a St Francis figure[9] 'calling to the birds and trees', his attempt to speak to those around him is held off by the poetess's 'There are people — especially among women — who can speak only to one person' (*P*, 80). When his sermon begins, Ehrens, despite his passionate: 'But   . ! / You can't ignore the words of Our Lord Jesus/Christ who died on the Cross for us . . .' (*P*, 82-3), fails to capture the crowd's attention. He speaks on, revealing himself as, initially, a typical American 'success' story. Hamilton's realization of the need for federation and the establishment of good money credit is interwoven here with Ehrens's assessment of his own material success: 'It did *not* make me good' (*P*, 85). To reinforce the point a representative American, John P. Altgeld, is presented in a parody of patriotic song: 'America the golden! / with trick and money/damned'.

The sermon is interrupted by a lyric passage on the nature of beauty (*P*, 88-9), reverting to the epigraphic 'Rigor of beauty is the quest' (in the Yale Collection this material is included with drafts for Book I). Three forms of beauty are listed: the religious, the imaginative and the beauty of being as such. Any of these may be 'the beauty of holiness', or some balance of them — the whole fabric of life, perhaps, insofar as it can be kept intact from the 'lurking schismatists'.

In a draft page at Buffalo, Williams notes a plan for the poem (or perhaps II only): 'A design on the general structure of Chaucer's CANTERBURY TALES' (Chaucer being, according to the Preface to *Selected Essays*, p. xvii, one of the 'contemporaries of mind with whom I am constantly in touch — through the art of writing'). The linking device was to be 'the dreams of N. F. PATERSON', but stress is put on the paramount importance of the language, as structure is emphasized in the cancelled draft of a letter to Kenneth Burke included in the same file. Much of the substance was to consist of 'a series of digested letters' (particularly those of Lyle). Little direct trace of Chaucer is evident (see *P*, 208) and the Chaucerian model has not been specially adhered to, but the dream situation frames the poem, surfacing at times as it does here in the reversion ot first person, modulating from Ehrens to Paterson: 'And I began to feel better ... / — and leaned on the parapet, thinking' (*P*, 89). Now he has 'shifted his change' again by metamorphosis as the 'fresh budding tree', which not only rounds off the lyric on beauty but refers us back, first to the chokecherry (*P*, 77), which the drafts suggest was to feature in some way not brought out by the final text, and then to the long lyric beginning at *P*, 42. Thus the vague concept of 'holiness' is offered as one alternative, the tree's *newness* and rootedness as the other.

Ehrens's claim of Christ's contempt for money is succeeded by excerpts from a Social Credit leaflet, which Pound had sent Williams (Yale file of Pound-Williams correspondence). A typed copy at Buffalo is headed, in Williams's hand, 'Following the preacher's clownish talk', and offers the possibility that he saw the matter of the leaflet (*P*, 90, 91) as a *practical* alternative to the preacher's exhortations. Part of a second leaflet (*P*, 92), 'Tom Edison on the Money Subject', supplements it. Reviewing *Paterson II*, Robert Lowell saw Williams's use of prose passages as comparable with the didactic chapters of *Moby Dick*.[10]

Pound had more than once urged Williams to read one item on

the brief reading list of 'the Attack on Credit Monopoly', Brooks Adams's *The Law of Civilization and Decay* (1896 edition).[11] Adams put forward a theory that the differences between races were at bottom due to variable distribution of energy, while wealth was equivalent to stored energy. Usury of the common people, draining economic resources towards a small class, was a leading cause of debilitation of national vitalities. One side effect in this economic theory of history is that commerce is antagonistic to the imagination. The relation of such theories to both Pound and Williams is obvious enough (a listing of the Adams title in a notebook offers the possibility that Williams once had a copy). Pound also sent Williams reprints of Social Credit essays from the *New Age* (letter of 3 April 1934 — *Yale*).

These anti-monopolist Social Credit passages frame two paragraphs on the development of S.U.M. (Society for establishing Useful Manufactures) and a verse passage evoking defeat and disgust in the figure of the eagle, making himself 'small — to creep into the hinged egg'. Within five years S. U. M. failed in its intended purpose, as did Hamilton's dream of a 'federal city'. Edison's attack on usury (as perpetrated through the Federal Reserve Banks) is juxtaposed to Hamilton's ability, when S. U. M. was in financial difficulties, to raise a large loan at a low interest rate.

Next follows verse addressed to 'the eternal bride and / father' (*P*, 92) (God, in Buffalo draft) of which the true focus is Paterson's sense of the earth. The whole passage is as if Williams were stating 'God and the imagination are one': 'The Himalayas and prairies / of your features amaze and delight' (*P*, 93). This recognition of 'godness' in the world, connected as it is with Williams's interpenetrative faculty, implicitly is dependent on the favours and workings of imagination, through which the 'reduction to one' is achieved. Here Williams allies his localism to a conviction that experience of a number of places feeds only the 'multiplicity':

> knowing
> how futile would be the search
> for you in the multiplicity
> of your debacle. The world spreads
> for me like a flower opening — ....
>
> (*P*, 93)

Such passages show the true significance of his later phrase 'only the imagination is real'. In the present instance the cyclical nature of life and recurrent power of imagination are suggested simultaneously:

> wither and fall to the ground
> and rot and be drawn up
> into a flower again. But you
> never wither — but blossom
> all about me. In that I forget
> myself perpetually — in your
> composition and decomposition
> I find my . . .
> >   despair!
> >   (*P*, 93)

The notion of 'despair' here is a difficult one, but appears to be a statement of his *resignation* in the world. One facet of it is regret at the 'composition and decomposition' through mortality, which must be accepted as part of a whole process, another is 'despair' at not being able fully to realize the world in imagination. The experience, or emotion, closest to imagination is love (a position clear through Williams's late poems, but implicit as a positive in his work from the early 1940s). His celebration of the world has also a sexual connotation: 'The world spreads / for me like a flower opening . . . .' The whole passage should be balanced against I, ii:

> colder than stone   .
> >   a bud forever green,
> tight-curled upon the pavement, perfect
> in juice and substance but divorced, divorced
> from its fellows, fallen low —
> >   (*P*, 28)

Growth, fulfilment, cannot occur when bud is cut off from source. It must partake of the process of 'composition and decomposition'. Only in the sense that it does not achieve its cycle is it 'forever green', divorced from reality. Rejecting the mere artifact, this may be read as rebutting romantic implications such as those in Keats's 'Ode to a Grecian Urn'.

Once more the disturbing nagging of the poetess intervenes. Again she insists on the importance of self when compared with writing, but even the ultimately negative expression of her desire contains in it potential artistic process. Her phrase 'My own thoughts and ideas and problems which were turned into dry sand by your attitude' (*P*, 94) anticipates the symbol of the bottle in the fire in *Paterson III*, where metamorphosing fire is the dominant metaphor.

II, iii, opens with a tight lyric on the negative nature of woman, who none the less is the necessary ground of existence. Woman as such is a universal, part of the 'mathematics' from which the 'particulars' of experience (*P*, 13) are derived. Both 'mathematics' and 'particulars' confirm the cyclical nature of man's experience. A rhyming couplet (satirical in intent) leads into the famous verses 'The descent beckons'.[12] Much light may be afforded this difficult passage by referring to the notion of 'descent' at earlier points in Williams's work. One aspect of it is suggested by part of a paragraph in *Kora in Hell*:

> *In middle life the mind passes to a variegated October. This is the time youth in its faulty aspirations has set for the achievement of great summits. But having attained the mountain top one is not snatched into a cloud but the descent profers its blandishments quite as a matter of course.   (KH, 25)*

The third sentence quoted here reads as if it were a source for the opening lines of the *Paterson* passage. Relevant also in Williams's early work is the chapter of *In the American Grain* titled 'Descent'. There he shows that General Sam Houston is a significant figure in American history precisely because he 'took the descent once more, to the ground' (*IAG*, 213), just as Whitman 'had to come from under', having returned to source, to the beginning (see *P*, 11). Descent to the ground is for Williams essentially the same as immersion in the Passaic — at once return to source and self-abnegation. Memory itself is a kind of return; in its recoveries occurs an invention / discovery of 'new places'. Thus memory (as imagination) is 'a sort of renewal / even / an initiation' (*P*, 96). In being an 'accomplishment', memory partakes of imagination ('the whiteness of a clarity beyond the facts'), 'and no whiteness (lost) is so white as the memory / of whiteness'. The 'new awakening' (through imagination) is 'a reversal / of despair', but 'a descent follows / endless and indestructible' (*P*, 97).

Relevant here is a small earlier poem, 'The Descent' (*CEP*, 460):

> From disorder (a chaos)
> order grows
> — grows fruitful.
> The chaos feeds it. Chaos
> feeds the tree.
>
> (*CEP*, 460)

Just as the lyric ending on *P*, 89, referring to a 'fresh budding tree', may suggest the poem itself, in creation from the world's multiplicity, so here the tree stands for reality integrated and the poem's whole orientation is towards Stevens's 'A great disorder is an order'.[13] A *Paterson* joke: 'the pouring water! / The dogs and trees / conspire to invent / a world' (*P*, 97), epitomizes a creative act deriving from language (and note the sense of 'conspire' — 'breathe with', 'breathe together'); but because 'no poet has come', the dogs being just ordinary dogs, the language remains untransformed ('Bow, wow!').

Darwin's name, included with those of three economists (*P*, 98) may suggest another reading for 'The descent beckons / as the ascent beckoned', that is, to use Stevens's terms, that the 'great poem of earth' now beckons (asks to be written) as the poems of heaven did in the past. We may note that Williams more than once stresses that his father persuaded him, as a young man, to read *The Descent of Man* (*Autob.*, 15).

The 'descent' passage also deals overtly with love and particularly with the rediscovery of pure love in old age (a major theme of *Pictures from Brueghel*). Now as Faitoute/Paterson leaves the closing park his sense of the falls is of a great poem. His presence in the passage is multi-level and what emerges is a 'despair' at the divorce between poem and 'great beast': 'Love is no comforter, rather a nail in the / skull' (*P*, 99), while Faitoute

> shakes with the intensity
> of his listening

> Only the thought of the stream comforts him,
> its terrifying plunge, inviting marriage . . . .
>
> (*P*, 100)

She (here unidentified[14]) replies that 'stones' (the female, source, 'invented upon') do not invent, which a man does. Faitoute's responsive musing about 'the new' is interrupted by the poetess's accusatory pointing to the divorce between 'sensibility' and man's lot. Cold and angry in the 'weather', Faitoute now physically encounters the dwarf, figure of the poet and of man-as-he-is compared with man-as-he-could-be. Momentarily Faitoute is metamorphosed into the 'fresh budding tree' (*P*, 102), which will be blotted out unless the poet sings his songs quickly:

> He all but falls   .   .
> And She —
> Marry us! Marry us!

Such a marriage would be the achievement of full reality, the joining of man / woman into poem, the antithesis of divorce.[15] Williams had made his point in 'The Simplicity of Disorder' (1929): 'What is pure in marriage unless it be the actual?' (*SE*, 99). And in the present context: 'Be reconciled, poet, with your own world, it is / the only truth!' (*P*, 103). Refusing the marriage, fleeing the falls' roar, 'Faitoute ground his heel / hard down on the stone'. The weather report here[16] and the ensuing 'belly . . . cloud' verse passage are illuminated by reference to the suppressed lines concerning Ymir (see, p. 92) but these hints at possible fecundation cease, for an abrupt return to 'descent'; but the theme is now transformed, concerning self-destruction and disintegration as a means of achieving 'the sun kissed summits of love' (*P*, 104), and including Surrealist and allied approaches to language ('in to scribble').

Here is interpolated a lyric celebrating the 'full octave' of love, followed by a repetition of the 'belly . . . cloud . . .' simile, which may be collated with 'The Clouds, iv', at the close of which the clouds are 'the flesh itself (in which / the poet foretells his own death)' (*CLP*, 128). For Faitoute there is no consummation, however. The poetess now takes over the poem for eight pages of close print. Continuing to complain, she notes that she and her relationship with him 'could be turned by you into

literature, as something disconnected from life' (P, 106). By
attacking the poet's desire to make a poem out of her, C. attacks
an aspect of herself: but this is not all. Some of what she says is, of
itself, eminently sensible ('*Only* my writing (when I write) is myself
...', P, 106) — otherwise there would be no point in Williams's
using the material at such length. He is allowing that her charges
are based in truth, but she unconsciously admits similar charges
true of herself when she speaks of her aim 'to return to writing from
living' (P, 110), as though the two were antithetical. She also robs
the letter of much of its point by relenting at the end, weakening,
adding a covering note in which she once more resorts to
pleading.

Conflict is the crux of Book II. Simultaneously the poet is
inventing himself and inventing the world, that is to say
discovering, ordering and constructing both self and world. His
chief vulnerabilities are over-limited conceptions of those things
most important to him. His pursuit of the 'Beautiful Thing' at
this stage is fruitless, as is his search for the 'redeeming language'.
Both are unreal for a single, important reason — his distaste for
the actual 'local'. The poetess is right in accusing him of
separating writing from life, though it is a weakness of the poem
that her letter swamps the end of Book II. Nor is *he* complacent.
From here he continues the search for the language, for beauty,
and for himself.

Whittemore recounts that, when Williams was about to receive
the Loines Award, he wrote to both Stevens and Allen Tate
asking how he should dress for the occasion. Stevens advised him
to be himself, but Tate offered a prescription: 'Faded vine leaves
as a billet around the brow; a breech clout tied at the navel with
sea weed; the staff of Hermes, a caduceus, in the left hand, and
in the right a bunch of sour grapes.'[17] *Paterson II* was greeted by
the critics with rather less enthusiasm than its predecessor, but
Robert Lowell, who saw it as Williams's 'attempt to write the
American poem', remained generous in enthusiasm: '*Paterson* is
Whitman's America, grown pathetic and tragic, brutalized by
inequality, disorganized by industrial chaos, and faced with
annihilation. No poet has written of it with such a combination of
brilliance, sympathy, and experience, with such alertness and
energy.' With only the first two books available, *Paterson*
seemed to readers as penetrating as Lowell and Jarrell in the late
1940s to have immense potency and potential.

10 *Paterson III*

Paterson III is dominated by natural disasters[1] — cyclone, fire, flood — and individual murders and suicides. Centred on 'The Library' (the Danforth Memorial Library), III is prefaced by a quotation from Santayana's *The Last Puritan* reiterating *Paterson's* central metaphor, its gist that 'cities are a second body for the human mind'. Its opening song sets 'A fortune bigger than/ Avery could muster' (*P*, 117) against the pricelessness of the locust tree in flower. This tree embodies the theme of 'Beautiful Thing' which pervades the book. In tension with the parallel 'search for the redeeming language' and for love[2] is man's ambivalent response to beauty, his urge to possess and destroy it. Thus beauty is set over against the destructive elements.

The library first suggests itself as 'echoing the life' and therefore having some merit; but it is a mere echo of a roar. Books are the 'ghost of a wind' in a context full of the wind's roar, roar of the falls, of fire, of the mind, and even of silence (*P*, 119). Woven into the text, the repeated group of monosyllables 'so be it. So be it' (*P*, 120) asserts *things*, against fear, destruction, breathlessness. An isolated prose line noting the killing of 'the last wolf' (*P*, 119), itself almost certainly book-garnered, emphasizes destruction of a 'beautiful thing' (equal importance to both aspects, the beauty, the object) from fear of it. In the library, in old files of newspapers, may be found stored cyclone, fire and flood, ready for reactivation in the mind; but the mind 'starts back amazed from the reading . . / So be it' (*P*, 120).

Against such fear there can be 'knowledge / by way of despair', but the manner in which we live our lives is to destroy all that is not obviously useful, hence the destruction of Lambert's Castle.[3] Built by an immigrant mill-worker who became a silk manufacturer, the Castle was 'a Balmoral' (*P*, 122), 'rococo Victorian',[4] with stained-glass windows, ornate ceilings and gas chandeliers the height of which could be adjusted, since they were hung by machine-made telescoping brass tubes. Like

Williams's Joe Stecher, Lambert was an anti-union man. Having
spent a fortune on his dwelling he has been ruined by his intransigence in industrial relations.[5] These facts, social and economic,
are presented, simultaneously accepted and yet observed to be
'incomprehensible' (P, 121). They modulate into a direct
statement on 'the poem':

> The province of the poem is the world.
> When the sun rises, it rises in the poem
> and when it sets darkness comes down
> and the poem is dark
>
> (P, 122)

Facing both ways, taking part in the Stevens dialectic, these lines
allow the *same* degree of reality to poem and world. Both word
order and the connotations of 'province' allow ambiguous
reception, a possible version of the opening sentence being 'The
world is the province of the poem'. Similarly the double play of
'When the sun rises', etc. (and the double antithesis in the phonic
pater/sun), all concerns process, finding a related chord in
Stevens's:

> Placed, so, beyond the compass of change,
> Perceived in a final atmosphere;
>
> For a moment final . . . .
> (*Collected Poems*, 168, 'The Man with the Blue Guitar')

Neither Williams nor Stevens perceived the poem as an 'ideal'
entity, but it is by no means obvious that, as Glauco Cambon
suggests,[6] Williams 'cannot subscribe' to any theory of 'the
metaphysical autonomy' of poetry. We have, after all, such
statements as 'The poem alone focuses the world' (*SE*, 242), 'Who
are we anyhow? Just man. Rime is more' (*SE*, 262), and, of a somewhat different order, 'Poetry is a rival government' (*SE*, 199).

Roar of books tells Paterson nothing, but as his mind 'begins to
drift' he has some sense of the 'Beautiful Thing'. The library
contains 'Dead men's dreams, confined by these walls' (P, 123),
whereas Paterson is concerned with living dreams. The building
smells of 'stagnation and death', sheltering no redeeming
language, merely silence,[7] which brings only intimations of

Thalassa, the sea of death. The windows and outlets which might afford escape 'shriek / as furies' (*P*, 125). This obscure parenthesis is suggestive of Corydon and Phyllis (*P*, IV, i), or the poetess, or rocks and sea, perhaps even the Muse and Venus. As confrontation it is frequent in Williams's work. Here it is especially relevant to Paterson's struggle towards positive contact with both beauty and reality, as if two elements in him (which, combined, would bring fruition) are at war and cause continuing sterility or lack of constructiveness.

Then follows an excerpt describing a mid-seventeenth-century clash between Indians and white men, relating some details of Indian economics, Indians' mistreatment and persecution at white hands, and the death dance of two taunted, wounded and tortured Indians. These paragraphs touch upon several of Williams's deep concerns. Figures of native America, the Indians are wantonly and brutally destroyed. The incident also epitomizes the early settlers' lack of contact with their environment and lack of communication (shared language) between them and the native Indians.

An instance of alienation (divorce), this is followed by a brief account of a hasty, crudely arranged marriage (*P*, 126) and next a return to the motif of walking across the falls on a tightrope (included in drafts for Book II — *Yale*) and then by: 'The place sweats of staleness and of rot / a back-house stench . a / library stench.' The 'back-house stench' derives from the destructive stripping of the Indian's flesh, but also the library's staleness and corruption, though it has the potential to engender ('sweats'). It hints also of 'composition' (literariness, artificial arrangement), which is 'running away' as opposed to embracing the 'foulness', walking the tightrope of daily experience, 'the being taut, balanced between / eternities', living as Harry Leslie did, kindling a fire or dancing the Washerwoman's Frolic in mid-rope.

Now the 'Beautiful Thing' (in person, the young negro girl beating the rug) becomes involved in the 'reek of it' (of destruction). Paterson tries to win her to 'marriage' as a means of countering death:[8] 'But it is true, they fear / it more than death, beauty is feared / more than death' (*P*, 129). Only love, marriage of a man and a woman, the Joycean riddle, can stare death 'in the eye'. In the dry summer of no love there is 'no water among the stones', while the 'deathless song' to 'allay our thirsts' is marriage of rock and river, man, woman and the redeeming language of love.

An inner voice prompts self-doubt in Paterson, urging him that to attempt to separate the 'radiance' from the 'inert mass' is too difficult a task. In a resistant environment he is advised: 'Give up / the poem. Give up the shilly- / shally of art' (*P*, 132). None the less, there to be mined from the common experience is 'The radiant gist that / resists the final crystallization' (*P*, 133).

As common living comes at a cost, so also does full experience of the 'Beautiful Thing': 'Say I am the locus / where two women meet.' A node for the whole interwoven 'Beautiful Thing' poem, this links the 'innumerable women', the 'first wife' and the other wives, Old World and New, the grandmother Muse and 'Venus from the confused sea'. Among many 'flowers' Toulouse Lautrec (on his crippled legs) witnessed and recorded the dance, 'the tendons / untensed' (i.e. relaxed, but also immortal). 'Beautiful Thing' is to be discovered in any kind of circumstance, among all kinds of people and material. The whole role of the artist is to recognize it. At the end of III, i, Paterson is again the city, suffering the tornado; but he is also Paterson/Faitoute: 'Seeking' (*P*, 136) for whom 'Some things can be done as well as others'.

III, ii, taking the Paterson fire of 1902 as its central 'incident', is the physical and actual core of the poem, the focus presaged by the 'red-shouldered hawks' (III, i, *P*, 136), concerning the act of creation, the relationship between creation and destruction. A by-product of the grossness of living, the 'flame' is woman, but chiefly an agent of metamorphosis. Centring on the proposition 'to write, nine tenths of the problem / is to live' (*P*, 138), the opening poem holds that writing 'should be a relief'. Williams appears to subscribe to Freudian theory which he rejects elsewhere. The insight modulates into a series of colloquial responses to Paterson's role as writer, responses which are fatuously hobbyist. An account of an Indian fire ceremony, taken from Nelson,[9] follows; contriving to show at once the Indians' innate dignity and Nelson's detached amusement, it demonstrates again the 'divorce' among peoples through lack of shared language and customs. Equivalent to fire, in other circumstances the library books are objects of propitiation. In time of great danger the Indians huddle in their tepees, prostrate, offering tobacco to the fire to appease its hunger. Books and tobacco, each is source of unreal dreams. These passages culminate in a brief paragraph describing the start of the Paterson fire (*P*, 140).

A second briefer excerpt is preceded by a key passage, echoing the 'clearly' from the 'redbreast' passages of I, ii:

> Clearly, they say. Oh clearly! Clearly? What more clear than that of all things nothing is so unclear, between man and his writing, as to which is the man and which the thing and of them both which is the more to be valued.   (*P*, 140)

Offering tacit rejection of the merely logical, this also indicates Williams's repeated wish to assert the primacy and importance of art. 'What is man? Rime is more?' has the validity not so much of dogma as of vivid paradox. Behind it is obviously the sense of interpenetration, a mental accord with propositions such as Whitehead's 'we cannot tell with what molecules the body ends and the external world begins'.[10] Whitehead argues that there are *facts of nature* (Williams's *things*), that these are part of a *process* just as our observation of them is, that they are variously relevant and relative to any observer — it might be said that he would define experience as a series of 'momentary absolutes' (true, both of Williams and of Wallace Stevens). Elsewhere Whitehead observes that 'a man defined as an enduring percipient is a society', 'personal existence . . . is a society of occasions'. For both Whitehead and Williams, man is simultaneously conscious of himself *as* himself and of himself as part of a process. Since man could not be the first without being the second, clearly Williams's attitude, this rules out the conclusion that he ever conceived of the whole of experience as being mind-dependent. Yet because of this *relational* consciousness of man and thing, as their interpenetration is one possibility so another is the question of their relative values. Thus Randall Jarrell's conclusion from the 'redbreast' passage, that:

> The subject of *Paterson* is: How can you tell the truth about things? — that is, how can you find a language so close to the world that the world can be represented and understood in it?[11]

may be usefully amplified through Whitehead's observation that:

> Language was developed in response to the excitements of practical actions. It is concerned with the prominent facts . . . entering into experience by means of our sense organs.[12]

Williams would have claimed that the fullness of human existence
came about only through the correlation of the 'prominent facts'
with a language and measure appropriate to them. Even for a
people, existence depends on the achievement of a 'new' form
which is uniquely theirs.[13]

To return directly to the *Paterson* text, now is introduced 'an
old bottle / mauled' by the fire (*P*, 141), a central image of both
fusion and metamorphosis. Fusion here is a figure of merging of
male and female in procreation, and of the relation of artist to
materials, the bottle achieving 'a new glaze'. Williams is intent on
making an *action* from the processing of the bottle. One draft of
this passage[14] (*Yale*) includes the reiterated 'So be it', ultimately
omitted presumably because its insistence on stasis works against
the fluidity which is his focus of attention. His 'an investment of
grace in the sand / — or stone' (*P*, 143) includes the poetess as a
potential source of creativity (see *P*, 94). Not only the thing, but
the actual *making* is beautiful: 'The glass / splotched with
concentric rainbows / of cold fire' (*P*, 143). Artist and materials
are protagonists in a struggle which the artist ultimately
wins,[15] — 'Poet Beats Fire at its Own Game!' — the contact, similar
to that of man and woman, 'deflowered' and then 'reflowered'
(*P*, 143). (The poetess, C., bemoaning her creativity lost through
Paterson's indifference, has now been 'reflowered' by inclusion in
the poem *Paterson*.)

'Beautiful Thing' is now identified with the flames. In its
original context, 'Paterson: Episode 17' (*CEP*, 438), it is 'a
coloured girl beating a rug in the yard of the Episcopal rectory in
Rutherford' (*ND*, 17, 262) — thus an *action* towards an end, but
in itself an embodiment of beauty. Maid and bottle are examples
of 'the vulgarity of beauty' (i.e. its commonness which 'surpasses
all perfection') but they are also, as implied earlier, 'rainbows /
of cold fire': 'Beautiful thing / — intertwined with the fire. An
identity / surmounting the world' (*P*, 145). Just as the coloured
maid is beautiful, so (even more so) is her action, and so here is
the 'intertwining', the process of reshaping and glazing the bottle.
Language also is relevant in this way. Momentarily, in
celebration of the 'Beautiful Thing', the *fall* is reversed, process
completed, consummated:

> Rising with a whirling motion, the person
> passed into the flame, becomes the flame —

> the flame taking over the person
>
> (*P*, 146)

but the spontaneous roar, upsurge, cry is answered by silence (*P*, 147, and answered again superbly in Williams's great poem of love, 'Asphodel, that Greeny Flower', *PB*, 153ff.).

The library (SILENT) is set over against the vitality of the living person. 'Beautiful Thing'. As the person has risen in the 'upwind', 'submerged / in wonder, the fire become the person' (*P*, 147), so in contrast the 'pathetic library' 'must go down' (*P*, 148). Then the whole fire 'episode' is brought into focus (*P*, 148-9). Even though books are largely irrelevant and unnecessary, they are what we have, the remains of experience. They are all we can have, thus the paradox of Williams, ordering his own experience in a book, shaping a 'momentary absolute' from his own life, a 'white hot man become / a book'. Ironic extension of this is located in the semi-literate letter from D. J. B. ('Dolly' — *Yale* draft), the 'Beautiful Thing', whose effort to express herself finds its furthest reach in a postscript: 'Tell Raymond I said I bubetut hatche isus cashutute just a new way of talking kid . . . ' (*P*, 150).

To encounter her later, Doctor Paterson must go down (to Hades) where they meet 'in silence', a scene which dissolves into a tapestry (a motif which is later the basis of *Paterson V*). Complementing this is the encounter with the sick negro woman in the dirty basement (*P*, 151). They are not a contrast. In each is the 'radiant gist', the core of vital experience. The section closes with a long passage of the 'Beautiful Thing' lyric resolving into an explicit statement of love:

> I can't be half gentle enough,
> half tender enough
> toward you, toward you,
> inarticulate, not half loving enough
>
> (*P*, 154)

Appropriately this is directed towards a specific person and the universal sense of 'Beautiful Thing'.

In the Yale draft, III, iii is titled 'Flood' (another draft has 'Flood: Blood'). As with III, i its opening is directly concerned with the act and role of writing. Conviction that a 'chance word, upon paper, may destroy the world' (*P*, 155) is accompanied by the injunction: 'write carelessly so that nothing that is not green will survive', advice followed in the ensuing surrealistic passage ('Boney fish bearing lights / stalk the eyes') evoking the presence of the contemporary world, yet its transience, hinting backwards through an evolution. Instruction and illustration cast light once again on the link, for Williams, between form and process. He is not after realized entities but the 'vividness' of life itself.

The flood which follows the fire is like the flood of explication, emendation and commentary which follows original invention. Drowning even the harmless dogs, it is also the drowning flood of Noah, of the Homeric 'wine dark sea', 'the wine of death' (*P*,158).

A prose excerpt recounts the death of Pogatticut, Grand Sachem of the Delaware Indians, including the sacrificial death of a dog (and these dog incidents implement a motif noted earlier). The two dog killings, one pointless and one loving, make the same contrast as the whole of *In the American Grain*. Henry's reaction (*P*, 157) is the Puritan resentment of contact; Wyandach's sacrifice is a thanksgiving for loving contact. Yet both killings may exemplify the 'peace that comes of destruction' (*P*, 159), the 'peace' here being in their metamorphosis into the poem.

An account follows of the killing of a 'spectral cat' seen by Merselis Van Giesen, a lady of a prominent Paterson family. Paterson/Williams is using his source (Nelson) to show the limitations of earlier American society, but he is also momentarily casting doubt on the validity of his own poem. Asserting the facts, repeating them — ' ... assessed in 1807 for 62 acres of unimproved land, two horses and five cattle' (*P*, 161), making over part of the list into his own verse, he notes parenthetically '(that cures the fantasy)'. Referring to the belief in witches, re-presenting the same phrases made over, he is also *enacting* the removal of the fantasy. Invention, form, does this. As he had observed in 'The Poem as a Field of Action', 'the *subject matter* of the poem is always phantasy — what is wished for, realized in the "dream" of the poem — but ... the structure confronts something else' (*SE*, 281). What it confronts in part, as far the past is concerned, is the necessity for the artist to use it and not be used by it.

Mentioned immediately after the Van Giesen anecdote is *The Book of Lead*, which Thirlwall interprets as a reference to atom bombs. Alternatively, this may be one of the number of apparently unsystematic alchemical/mythological references throughout the poem. Lead is one version of the 'arcane substance' (*prima materia*, world-egg) of the ancient philosophers, associated with Saturn. In descent to the underworld the first gate was a leaden gate. According to Jung, Hermes can succeed in his search for Mercurius 'only through the rite of the ascent and descent, the "circular distillation", beginning with the black lead, with the darkness, coldness, and malignity of the malefic Saturn . . . '.[16]

With the flood the momentary rising has changed to a falling. Paterson too is falling, failing to communicate, failing in love, but with a degree of self-awareness: 'But somehow a man must lift himself / again' (*P*, 162). Prose description of a Prohibition days' dance follows, linking back to many actions, such as the dance as observed by Toulouse Lautrec, the old Italian woman in the park, Leslie going over the falls, the dying Indians dancing the *kinte kaye*.

All these dances are the endowment of form on chaos, but the differing dances appear to suggest that the particular form they take is inherent in the chaos embodied. All dances have in common the tact that they are a celebration.

Throughout this passage is opposition between seeing and doing. Paterson's doubt about his poem has extended to 'None wants our ayes' (*P*, 162), to an externalization in the poem itself: 'He feels he ought to *do* more' (*P*, 162), and the flat, 'I see things' (*P*, 163). Drafts of the reference to Puerto Plata in this passage (*P*, 163, *Yale*, 188/1) illustrate Williams's methods of elision. In the Yale manuscript a certain symbolic symmetry is attempted by the inclusion of a letter purportedly written to a ship sailing on Columbus Day, 1877. What we have, what 'things' he sees are flood ('no lullaby but a piston') continuing, undermining the railroad, smashing apart the text of the poem, its language, lining, paging (*P*, 164). He is driving against the completion of his own poem. Thus Paterson's world, Paterson himself, is on the point of disintegration. This juncture is presented physically in the text and also through a typical letter of Ezra Pound's, which is dated the day *after* Columbus Day. Pound wants to send Paterson back to the library and, at least in part, his advice is sound. Insisting on selectivity, he offers a brief reading list. Each item on it has profoundly influenced *The Cantos* either in thought or form. Williams, of course, rejected Pound's cultural eclecticism (of which Leo Frobenius is a source, or reference locus) but used in his own way the method Pound developed from it (juxta-position). Williams offers his own sources, geological, the stratifications of the American ground. His tabulation of substrata closes with a sentence (from the early pages of Nelson), which is his rejoinder to Pound: 'The fact that the rock salt of England, and of some of the other salt mines of Europe, is found in rocks of the same age as this, raises the question whether it may not also be found here' (*P*, 166).

One draft of the table concludes with the single local geographical reference 'Dublin spring!', which (besides con-necting Paterson with Joyce's Dublin) would have afforded the clue that the deep descent is to 'spring', rebirth, return to the beginning of a new civilization with new energy and a new-found language, the pattern indicated by Brooks Adams.

Momentarily there is a 'FULL STOP' of language (*P*, 167), and of seeing, and a possibility of affirmation. What sputters out instead is a hackneyed line of verse from Gray's 'Elegy', from the tradition Williams is refusing, and what is encountered is formless mud, 'a detritus . . . a choking lifelessness'. Merely blackened (opposite to 'white as a clarity . . . '), the stones are not invented upon, the sand is not fused into a bottle but is gluey. From this mud the problem is how 'to begin to find a shape'? Taking a jeering comment on the supposed paucity of American poetry, Williams in effect (and perhaps surprisingly) agrees with it, accepting it as basis for his often-repeated claim that what is needed is 'the new', which derives from the destruction of the old. The fragments are not 'shored against my ruins', but 'made piecemeal by decay' until 'a / digestion takes place' (*P*, 168).

A figure of his Muse, the cancerous, broken-jawed woman is here offered a song by the poet, but his mood for the moment at least is recalcitrant. In an apparent reference to Europe and Eliot, he contradicts the cyclical position with which he opened the poem; 'Who is it spoke of April? Some / insane engineer. There is no recurrence. / The past is dead' (*P*, 169).

This passage (*P*, 169), besides scoffing at Eliot, connects with *P*, 25-7. Paterson/Williams, dejected, turns away also from the one major poet who had shared his dismay at Eliot's triumph in the twenties, Hart Crane: 'Loosen the flesh / from the machine, build no more / bridges' (*P*, 169). Concerning the past as history, 'The past is dead', replaced by 'the testament of perpetual change', a recurrence of *the new*, the law of civilization and decay. Paterson, the poet (largely overt at this stage, more of commentary and less of action) now observes that 'the flood has done its work'. Repeated in new form, the injunction to write carelessly suggests also Williams's 'concrete indirection' in approach (presentation of concrete things without accompanying comment, like Stevens's 'a minimum of making in the mind'): 'Let the worlds / fall any way at all — that they may / hit love aslant' (*P*, 169). Just as he is rejecting the European past, Paterson/Williams hints at the betrayal of America's possibilities by Americans themselves, ironically naming a figure from Roman history to do so. For this cryptic reference to Vercingetorix (*P*, 170) he provides his own gloss:

> If there will ever come a prince to wake us from our modern utilitarian sleep, he may be from under a grey stone roof of Dijon, smelling of the grapes of the Cote d'Or where lived Vercingetorix, the last of the Gauls to hold out against Caesar. He was betrayed by his own tribesmates, as we all are in the end.   (*Autob.*, 210)

The broken-jawed woman becomes the old deaf woman who will mistake the canary's hiss for singing, a way of saying that the available language cannot fully cope with reality. Giving way to a prose account of African ritual, which connects with the African wives of Book I, the poem returns to the theme of 'divorce'. In this paragraph, as in the earlier, the women are involved with a tree, performing in song and gesture a fertility ritual. Its crux is 'Only married women, who have felt the fertility of men in their bodies, can know the secret of life' (*P*, 171).

The 'sweet woman' contrasts with the old woman (Muse) to whom Paterson has offered songs, the Venus figure, beautiful, but opposing the Muse: 'Either I abandon you / or give up writing' (*P*, 171).

Book III closes with a lyric in which the falls' roar becomes very immediate, 'the roar of the present'. All the *action* of the poem to this point has been Paterson's 'stream of consciousness', but these passages are, in some sense, an externalization of 'The descent beckons'. Paterson is explicit: 'a speech / is, of necessity, my sole concern' (*P*, 172), and from it he intends to make a replica which will counter the effect of 'the modern replicas'. Making a replica involves rejection of the past (tradition) and future (heaven, some kinds of ambition) in favour of that precise moment 'beside the sliding water'. The past has a special limited relevance, noted in the essay on Charles Sheeler, for the artist who 'is the watcher and surveyor of that world where the past is always occurring contemporaneously and the present always dead needing a miracle of resuscitation to revive it' (*SE*, 232).

As for '*la capella di S. Rocco*' (*P*, 172), 'the poet', Williams wrote to Reed Whittemore, 'is the Jesuit of his own mind, the end always justifies the means if he produce a good poem' (*SE*, 239). Should these views appear to be over-subjective, he is not so simple. Book III concludes 'this rhetoric is real' (to 'comb out the language' is as real as the man's combing his collie dog). He balances his own account in the Kenneth Burke essay, declaring that 'Writing is made of words, of nothing else. These have a contour and complexion imposed upon them by the weather, by the shapes of men's lives in places' (*SE*, 132). In such a context, of present fact, Paterson seeks his 'meaning', to 'lay it, white' beside the water, seeking through the facts 'a clarity' beyond them. Through the process of destruction and dejection which is Book III, in which the library, where he has retreated for cool and solace, turns out to be 'desolation', he has achieved a deep sense of the beauty of things, or rather the 'thingness' of beauty.

The visit to the library has exposed Paterson metaphorically to a series of elemental disasters. He survives them all, and especially the flood of words (we may recall that Paterson's first name is Noah), and escapes from the library into the real world. It is among people, and not books, that he must find the redeeming language.

11 *Paterson IV*

One version of Book IV begins 'Paterson or a slave to Passion' and is followed by vernacular 'details' of couples parting. Another note hints that here is to be discovered 'a miracle of resuscitation'. It reads 'A calm lies over the whole of this book — / an effete calm at the beginning but revived by a "transfusion" at the end. The river, the foulest glinter in the world, next to the Severn(?) but a river, a to and from river' (*Yale*, 189/3). IV, i is set mockingly as 'An Idyl',[1] including two traditional English pastoral figures, Corydon and Phyllis, Corydon being a lesbian whom Dr Paterson rivals for Phyllis's favours.[2] Phyllis, for her part, is unable to respond to any man sexually.

Phyllis comes from the Ramapos and was trained in Paterson as a masseuse. A dialogue between the two women, this section is interrupted by Phyllis's semi-literate letters to her father, which reveal both her crudeness and the only love-relationship of which she is capable. They show her 'failure to untangle the language' and the 'perverse confusions which follow'. Corydon, who links Paterson city with the politician Nicholas Murray Butler and 'his sister, the lame one', is herself a physical cripple.

Phyllis's father is a drunkard.[3] One set of drafts (*Yale*, 185) has the cryptic note 'Silenus — recurrence'. Later (in IV, ii) there are a number of references to Apollo, and the two successive sections may be built to some degree on the Dionysian/Apollonian opposition. References to drunkenness occur at various points throughout the complete poem, while Phyllis's father may well be 'Silenus', described by Edith Hamilton (whose work Williams consulted, according to Yale drafts, while he was making *Paterson*) as 'a jovial fat old man who usually rode an ass because he was too drunk to walk. He was associated with Bacchus. . . .'[4]

As Williams made clear (in letters to Marianne Moore and Robert Lowell, see *Selected Letters*), Corydon is much the more sensitive of the two women. Among other matters, this is true of her response to language, but her language has become disconnected from 'the shapes of men's lives in places', a fact conveyed in Williams's adroit play with the word 'silly', used both in its earlier, Elizabethan pastoral, sense and its current meaning. For Corydon, however, it is merely 'semantics, my dear' (*P*, 177). Even her proposed relationship with Phyllis is detached from reality ('Let's play games!', *P*, 187).

The introductory exchange between Phyllis and Paterson is nervy. Paterson is a 'married man', while Phyllis has a boy friend (a short poem which may be related to this context is 'Eternity', *CLP*, 36-8). All the relationships are abortive, with several references compounding Cupid's dart, the arrows of Artemis and the word 'shot' (*P*, 178, 187, 190). There are other repeated references to fertility symbols such as fish. Paterson's relationship with Phyllis has some affinities with the 'Beautiful Thing' section of Book III, even to 'take off your clothes' and the repeated suggestion that Phyllis's dress is sweaty (hinting fertility, fruitfulness).[5]

Corydon reads Phyllis a poem, the introduction to which is mock early Pound and the remainder a flat parody of Eliot, using his subway motif from *Four Quartets*, his connection with Dante's *Inferno*, Shakespeare and Milton, and culminating in a jibe at his use of *De Profundis* in 'Ash Wednesday'. Her poem's title also suggests a work by André Gide and further ramifications of the 'divorce' theme. Paterson is Corydon's 'rival', but Williams's own attitude to the lesbian is compassionate. He accepts her as part of his world and noted in a letter to Robert Lowell: ' . . . I started writing of her in a satiric mood — but she won me quite over. I ended by feeling admiration for her and real regret at her defeat' (*SL*, no. 193, p. 302).

Just as Phyllis's command of language is limited, so, too, is Corydon's, but in a different way. Hers is a 'literary' language, divorced from reality. The contact between the two women is restricted by Phyllis's lack of insight and by Corydon's special tastes. Similarly, the relationship between Phyllis and Paterson is hedged in on one side by his being a 'married man' and on the other by her having a 'boy friend', but ultimately because of the nature of their expectations of each other — what they want of each *other*.

In direct contrast is section IV, ii. The Yale draft notes read 'Curie: a different type of woman from the one just told. The "gist"', and 'The lecture on uranium (Curie), the splitting of the atom (first time explained to *me*) has a *literary* meaning — in the splitting of the foot (sprung meter of Hopkins) and consequently is connected thereby to human life or life' (*Yale*, also Buffalo autograph notebook, p. 48). Paterson/Williams takes his school-boy son to the Solarium to hear a lecture on atomic fission. In an aside he recalls Norman Douglas's stoical, or perhaps cynical, remark that the 'best thing a man can do for his son, when he is born, is to die' (*P*, 201). The point is more relevant than it may seem, since the whole section is rooted in Paterson's concern for his son's future.

Paterson suggests that the Solarium may be interpreted as a Temple to the sun, section IV, ii having Apollo as 'a kind of presiding deity'.[6] Although it is not carried a great deal further, the point is a useful one, connecting backward to *The Book of Lead* and forward to 'Carry Nation as Artemis'. On the evening of the lecture, 'The moon was in its first quarter' (*P*, 202) when Paterson's son, the future doctor, was born to his role. Apollo's son, Asklepios, was a doctor, the physicians' archetype, while Asklepios's mother, Coronis, the 'crow maiden', is associated with the new moon. Daughter of Fire, sister (or niece) of the murderer-rapist Ixion, Coronis was herself murdered by Artemis.

Alchemical/mythological allusions occur in *Paterson* apparently intermittently, but enrich the text's active possibilities. The items just mentioned, for example, may offer the 'unhatched sun' (*P*, 202)as Paterson's sun or even as the future world with a true language, or cast light on the description of the tapestry in Book III:

>   .   a docile queen, not bothered
> to stick her tongue out at the moon, indifferent,
> through loss, but   .
>   queenly,
> in bad luck, the luck of the stars, the black stars
>   (*P*, 152)

Against the fact of Madame Curie's discovery of radium (on which Williams's views had changed since his *Poetry* 'notes' of 1919), is set the Gantryish preaching of Billy Sunday; contrast also the park preacher, Klaus Ehrens. Sunday is hired by the 'bosses' (United Factory Owners' Association) to break this Paterson strike, circumventing the strikers 'by calling them to

God!' After his effort, Sunday is paid at the Hamilton Hotel.

A long letter from the young poet A. G. (Allen Ginsberg — the initials were originally A. P., suggesting Allen Paterson, 'son' of Paterson) is now interpolated. A. G., more positive and enthusiastic, fills the vacancy left by the disillusioned poetess. Paterson and A. G. are also a contrast. In this Apollonian section, Paterson's actions are clear and deliberate, while A. G. tells him 'I ran backstage to accost you, but changed my mind, after waving at you, and ran off again. Respectfully yours . . . ' (*P*, 206). A. G.'s 'enthusiasm' is at odds with the 'human objectivity' for which he is striving, but (even in this letter) his is a vital speech. Like Paterson, unlike C., he is searching for a 'redeeming language'. Later, Williams would rejoice in Ginsberg's survival as a poet.[7]

Similar in spirit is Madame Curie's search. She, too, is in contrast to the disillusioned poetess. Williams uses Pierre Curie's secondary role in it analogically, with Eve Curie as the Virgin bearing Christ (the Redeemer):

> But she is pregnant!
> Poor Joseph,
> The Italians say
>
> (*P*, 207)

He introduces Eve Curie in her own local setting, evoking the smells and sights of Paris. Paris, too, is 'a woman waiting to be filled' (*P*, 206) and the correspondence between Paris, Paterson, Madame Curie and A. G. is completed in the young poet's letter, where, speaking of himself, he claims that 'one actual citizen of your community has inherited your experience in his struggle to love and know his own world-city' (*P*, 205).

'Dissonance / . . . leads to discovery' (*P*, 207). Williams uses his concept of dissonance in a number of different ways. By citing the Curie experiments he indicates the conversion of mass into energy (metamorphosis). Such conversion had been predicted by Einstein, hence the scientist's fascination for Williams. As an outcome of extending the initial discovery physicists can now, with the aid of Mendelief's table of atomic weights (*P*, 210) change elements at will. Williams's way of describing the experimental process: ' — to dissect away / the block and leave / a separate metal' (*P*, 207), relates it to sculpture, but also to the artists's method of 'discovery' generally, and Williams's own experimental search for the 'new measure' (see *SL*, 242-3).

His attention shifts to the theme of love (*P*, 207), referring to Chaucer's 'Tale of Sir Thopas' as a parody of a type of English metrical romance which employed typically jingling rhyme and the language of cliché. Adapted from an actual one, the case report (*P*, 208) appears to be a private joke at the expense of the poetess, the 'intestinal disturbance' linking it back to the Sir Thopas passage, which could also conceivably be a judgment on the poetess. These two passages are an answer to the question 'Love, the sledge that smashes the atom?' (*P*, 208).

Returning to Madame Curie, Williams depicts the difficulties of her material situation (like Pound's, Villon's), and her actual discovery of radium, 'LUMINOUS!', the 'radiant gist', an inspirational discovery (versus 'knowledge the contaminant' — *P*, 209) comparable with Columbus's first landfall in the Western hemisphere. A passage from the Journal of Columbus's first voyage, already quoted in *In the American Grain*, is used again here, ending with the key phrase 'the most beautiful thing which I had ever known' (*P*, 209). Uranium, containing as it does the 'radiant gist', is 'a city in itself' (*P*, 209), but has also the characteristic of 'always breaking down . . . to lead', the *prima materia*.

A phrase (*P*, 210 top) continues the conversations of IV, i and is followed by the sexual cloud image taken up from earlier (*P*, 104):

> waiting for the sun to part the labia
> of shabby clouds . but a man (or
> a woman) achieved
>
> (*P*, 210)

Woman, 'the weaker vessel', is capable of 'mathematics' or 'murder', creating or destroying, 'Sappho vs Elektra!'. Eve Curie is Sappho, the creator. But our civilization has decayed to such an extent that Carrie Nation is our Artemis, protectress of the young, anti-contact.

Perhaps an ironic answer to Horace Greeley's 'Go West, young man!', the young woman photographer, having been to Denver 'to study chiaroscuro' (the white clarity and black lead which are life?) returns 'with the baby / openly' (*P*, 211), in this respect being counterpart to Coronis and the child Asklepios.

Various points in *Paterson* hint concern at the materialism of
the church. The break between mention of Abbess Hildegard
(apparently a reference to a painting or drawing; one draft has
'1462, at Bonn') and the '*Advertisement*' (*P*, 213) may have been
filled with a suppressed section among the Yale drafts, on 'FOR
SALE / This Desirable / Church Property / IDEAL / AS
BUSINESS SITE.' As it stands, the remainder of the section is a
Poundian attack on usury. Money is the 'brain tumor' of Paterson
(*P*, 214) (also the cancer of *P*, 210). The prevalent use of money
creates a situation in which the ship (the *Santa Maria*, for
example) is leaky.

> Money : Joke
> could be wiped out
> at stroke
> of pen
>   (*P*, 217)

A 'joke' because it is in practice a meaningless fiction. The
'surgeon' (financier) should not get all the benefit (credit), the
patient should. In this context, credit is the 'radiant gist',[8] the
radium luminous in its uranium, the wind which drives the ship
before it to safety and 'discovery', or, in Williams's version of
himself as summarized by Pound: 'IN/venshun. / O.KAY / In
venshun' (*P*, 218). Williams graphically epitomizes the problem:

> What is credit?   the Parthenon
> What is money?   the gold entrusted to
>   Phideas for the
>   statue of Pallas Athena,
>   that he 'put aside'
>   for private purposes
>   (*P*, 216)

His solution is the Poundian one, 'i.e. LOCAL control of local
purchasing / power' (*P*, 218), which fits exactly Williams's long
held view that the artist's work, in fact the whole of immediate,
valid human experience, depends upon a sense of the local, of
what is to hand.

The first two books of *Paterson IV* concentrate on what has been implicit in Williams's work from 'The Wanderer'. Creative energy has its source in the female, but (as the example of Madame Curie shows), the male is also necessary to the process of discovery, redemption or regeneration. Originally conceived as the poem's final section, IV, iii attempts to resolve the various themes woven through the whole work, and to centre on the poet's self-renewal. But it offers a number of paradoxes. In the opening conversation, She (the Mountain) says 'The past is for those who / lived in the past' (*P*, 219), but later the old man reminiscing extols the Paterson (city) of earlier days, a pastoral scene markedly different from the world of Corydon and Phyllis.

The sea is a sea of blood — living, murder, death and also the waters of birth and 'the sea of objectivity' (Buffalo notebook, p. 33) and memory. In addition, the sea as memory has double significance, for, in the old man's account of Paterson's past, memory is an enhancement, richer than the present. Besides this it is a confinement, a chaos from which we move to escape.

To implement his account of life's 'dissonances', Williams follows Nelson's version of the murder of a Dutch settler in his bed with a story told to him by 'an old friend, now gone' (Nathanael West) of 'a tall and rather beautiful young woman' (*P*, 221) encountered as a kind of epiphany, an incident recounted in a tone of generosity, 'credit', self-giving, of an epitomization of the Venus figure. This leads to the symbol of the ash-tray, 'a glazed / Venerian scallop . . . . A sea-shell' (*P*, 221). The glazing links back to the bottle in the fire, while the motto on the ash-tray, '*La Vertue / est toute dans l'effort*' is not to be taken as common moralizing, but refers to the effort of *making*, living, process. At one level, the ash-tray may be read as a metaphor for the poem. Or, rather, what is implied in the motto and particular shape of the ash-tray, implications amplified in the short prose paragraph 'Kill the explicit sentence . . . ' (*P*, 222), another oblique statement of Williams's interest in 'the bloody loam and not the finished product', in the action of making rather than the made object. The motto may even be read as an extension of Sam Patch's curious aphorism 'Some things can be done as well as others' (*P*, 25).

A memory of one of Paterson's 'innumerable women' includes a variation in the definition of virtue:

Virtue, she would say
                    (her version of it)
      is a stout old bird,
                         unpredictable
                              (*P*, 223)

— an important attribute of process. Therefore of itself the 'brain
is weak', unable to 'focus the world' or fertilize man's 'marriage' to
it. A sense of the physical world is much more real than mere
knowledge. Recollections of many women friends are preceded by
the expressed desire for unity, to 'hold together wives in one wife',
park, rock, women, wife merge:

              All these
      and more — shining, struggling flies
      caught in the meshes of Her hair
                         (*P*, 225)

Historical Paterson and the women are, however, no more than
reminiscences. In Yale drafts (185) the women are counterpointed against a crestomathy of flowers, which follows a brief
account of the discovery of the grave of Peter van Winkle, the
dwarf. Elsewhere (*Yale*, 189/6) this account is followed by
Whitman's:

We level that lift, to pass and continue beyond . . .[9]
Ages, precedents, poems, have long been accumulating in-
      directed materials,
America brings builders, and brings its own styles.

Yellow is next invoked (*P*, 226), as the colour of the sun, the
radiant gist and the 'stain of love', and against these is set the
serpent, the river of time, whose drink is sand (compacting the
clouds — belly, the river sand, the dry sand in the bottle — these
together may clarify the headnote, 'the clouds resolved into a
sandy sluice' — *P*, 10). This beautiful passage gives way to a brief
'song' celebrating an approaching birth (one draft referred to
Williams's grandchild, Suzie) and also the sexual union of its
procreators: 'And here's to the peak / from which the seed was
hurled!' (*P*, 226).

From *P*, 226 to *P*, 232 (mainly the old man recalling an earlier Paterson) the text is based on a nine-page typescript at Yale, paragraph 2 of which reads:

A little story of Paterson: as told by an old man — The city of Paterson owes much of its importance to its historical associations. So to the past this little volume is dedicated. Although it is not written simply to give facts, it does give the correct facts about what it says.

The very fluidity of this account suggests there is an unreality about, juxtaposed as it is with the young A. G.'s 'inadequate' telling of his own attempt to realize the present Paterson, and with two accounts of past murders — the Goodell murder (*P*, 229) to set against the approaching birth, and John Johnson's murdering for money of the aged Van Winkle couple.

A. G.'s promise is of life, to continue the search in which Paterson himself has been engaged, while the murders bring to the forefront an immediate concern at the time the poem was being written, that of war. In an earlier passage, concerning David Lilienthal, Williams has connected war with the capitalists. Now, in a telling reversal, he cries 'War! / a poverty of resource' (*P*, 233), dismissing it as a positive way of solving man's problems, 'guts on the black sands of Iwo' convincing no one.

What Guimond describes as Paterson's languid examination of previous images brings us at last to the sea. Ultimately the sea is chaos, carrying both weeds and seeds, wrack and words, and 'I warn you, the sea is *not* our home' (*P*, 235). This negative is a denial of the *final* descent in the falling process which has taken Paterson out to the Passaic estuary. The outcome is not death, rather a new birth or a rebirth, but the point is disputed, voices at argument.

Among the chaos of the sea, however, the Venus figure may be realized:

> Seed
> of Venus, you will return . to
> a girl standing upon a tilted shell, rose
> pink
>
> (*P*, 236)

This figure against Thalassa:

> the blood dark sea!
> nicked by the light alone, diamonded
> by the light.

The Venus is metamorphosed into the original image of lame-
dog man, which is Paterson, reborn and emerging from his dream
of the falls. Scattering seed, rubbing 'the dry sand off', he heads
inland followed by the dog (his thoughts, his enduring self, his
'faithful bitch' Muse) 'toward Camden where Walt Whitman,
much traduced, lived the latter years of his life' (*Autob.*, 392).

A dissonance closes the poem (rather, the poem as originally
planned). The prose excerpt of John Johnson, an Englishman,
hanged for murder amid a 'sea' of people is deliberately
juxtaposed to the closing lines, which 'sing'. These are an
enactment of Johnson's end, 'the blast' of the last trump, the drop
through the trapdoor; but Paterson has, an Odysseus, risen from
the waves, born again to the ever-present now, the final
somersault into birth. An earlier contents summary makes
explicit what is implied here. In this (*Yale*) plan Book IV is titled
'The River' and a seasonal schema has for book IV 'Winter. The
conserver of life, solver — forgetfulness — conserver and
progenitor (summer imagined)'. As 'the beginning is assuredly /
the end', so the end itself coincides with a birth, and so the poem
has no 'final' end, but merely stops. Paterson, which is 'ANY /
EVERY PLACE' (*Yale*, 185) is also every man, always returning
home and starting out, but at this moment, as Williams had said
of Poe and Daniel Boone in *In the American Grain*, 'faced inland
to originality' (*IAG*, 226).

Methodologically, *Paterson I-IV* is a considerable distance from Williams's Imagist and Objectivist views of 'the
poem'. As we have seen, he had experimented with the melding
of prose and verse, breaking down the traditional distinction
between the two, from early in his career.

His actual Imagist practice, aiming for 'vividness' in the
recording of his discoveries, retreated before the necessities of
Paterson. A crucial difference between *Paterson* and the early
short poems of, say, *Al Que Quiere!* is that *Paterson* is not merely
a 'discovery' on a large scale (as so many of the earlier poems,

'Between Walls', for example, are small-scale 'discoveries'). *Paterson* is a *search*. Emphasis has shifted, therefore, from recognition to quest. The epic poem began from a *need*, urgently recognized by the poet. Themes, epiphanies, parables — all are held together in a sense of onward verbal thrust, a process. *Paterson* has moments of strength, others of weakness — deriving from its very status as a poem. Logically, it is a culmination of Williams's sense of the poem as an experience, an enactment, almost as if it were self-creating.

Referring to its prose excerpts and adaptations, we may add that Williams's sense of the 'thing' broadened immeasurably as he was working on the poem. Each word (of prose and verse) is a 'thing' in its own right, a step in the search. Each excerpt — varying in specific quality, so that the most factual, e.g. the tabulation of substrata (*P*, 166) may be most suggestive to the imagination — is also present as a 'thing', duly weighed. Williams's working habit was to gather material over a long period, then to work it together as a poem (see *SL*, 234-5, to Horace Gregory). Behind this is the assumption that everything is material for the poem, to be selected and arranged. What has changed is the selective criterion. Where once the material would have been first chosen, then pared back — for its 'vividness' *per se* — for *Paterson* larger considerations, thematic, redemptive, the need for an 'alternative government', have forced a breaking-down of barriers, between poet and poem (so that 'inter-penetration' has occurred on a vast scale), and between poem and world.

12 *Paterson V*

Williams apparently intended the original *Paterson* as a unity. A major difficulty in so accepting it is the way in which the poetess's letter monopolizes at length the end of *Paterson II*. Many critics (Randall Jarrell and Marianne Moore among them) have found each successive book less satisfactory than its predecessor. Some of these critics perceive in *Paterson V* a lifting of the poem, but even Williams himself was forced to see, with its publication, that for a poem like *Paterson*, 'there can be no end to such a story' (*P*, 7) in the terms he had laid down for himself in Books I-IV. As this statement shows, he saw a qualitative difference between Book V and the earlier books.

Paterson V is set not by the Passaic River but by the Hudson. Having turned back towards Camden, Paterson found himself at the Cloisters, overlooking the New Jersey Palisades, contemplating the Unicorn Tapestries. His attention to these, a flower of late mediaeval Europe, may seem an abandonment of concern with the local, but since in fact the tapestries are located at a branch of New York's Metropolitan Museum of Art, this is not strictly so. They are but a short distance from Paterson.

In his note to the complete *Paterson* Williams remarked 'I had to take the world of Paterson into a new dimension if I wanted to give it imaginative validity' (*P*, 7-8).[1] Important in the poem as a whole is its concern with the separation between life and art, or learning. Williams seeks to discover a fusion. Book V is his clearest celebration of the imagination. Formally we may regard this book as enclosing or containing the earlier four (a sixth might have either fitted into the container or made a further container). There is some evidence that Williams may have planned to go further even while he was working on Book IV. Some lines in *Yale* 189/6 read:

> the clustered violet without
> odor — and without residual meaning

> the clarity, sacrificing nothing — like
> a woman who is beautiful without
> affectation — the clarity, retain the
> clarity: which is a mind made up.

these lines may be related to points in the poem expressing desire for clarity in man's relation to thing (*P*, 32, *P*, 140). Contrasting with 'the din of fracturing thought' we here have 'a mind made up'. Pencilled at the end of these lines is the phrase: 'The Fifth Act and Book'. Elsewhere in the same set of drafts is written 'Maybe even a 5th book of *facts. / Recollection.*'

With reference to the odorless flower, early versions of 'Of Asphodel, that Greeny Flower' were apparently intended as *Paterson V*, which was to have no prose but 'to embody whatever I have learned of form (with variants)' (*Yale*, 190/1). A provisional title for Book V was 'The River of Heaven', and a complete page of autograph draft reads:

> Of asphodel. without / color, a sort of buttercup. ragged but a / flower — a / stringy, odorless ghost / a sort of mental / flower, a sort of / buttercup. Ranunculosiae / a rumour of a flower / like a priest in / hell / like a lecturer on the / Lord, a Thomist / . Blossoms in those fields.

This summary, and much of the other material, suggests death-preoccupation, but also a sense of an attempt to encompass what has gone before. If the fifth was to be a book of 'facts' then these facts were to be 'a sort of mental flower'.

From one point of view this accounts for the dedication to Lautrec's memory (the painter is mentioned briefly in Book III, i). Like Brueghel, who could discover the 'radiant gist' amid grossness, Lautrec was like Williams also, in this and in their common fascination by women. Williams is to make of the 'whore and the virgin an identity' (*P*, 245), while Lautrec notoriously sought and found beauty among the whores of Paris. Both men evidently felt it important to recognize that humanity was not confined to the virtuous.

Williams explained to Thirlwall, 'When the river ended in the sea I had no place to go but back in life ... I had to take the spirit of the River up in the air' (*ND*, 17, 290). His opening lines imitate a bird's flight, directing a specific reading (as he told

Stanley Koehler).² The casting off point is 'Paterson / its rocks and streams' on a 'cloudy morning' — weather with feminine associations throughout the poem. He reasserts his key position: 'Not prophecy! NOT prophecy! / but the thing itself!' (*P*, 242) in favour of what Hillis Miller calls 'a subtle theory of poetry which rejects both the mirror and lamp, both the classical theory of art as imitation, and the romantic theory of art as transformation'?

Himself as Don Perlimplin, Lorca's 'aged bridegroom', Paterson/Williams opens a complex meditation on erotic love, art and human morality. His figure for the human soul is the unicorn of the tapestries. At The Cloisters are six of these tapestries and the remnants of a seventh, dating from the late fifteenth and very early sixteenth centuries, the first and seventh being later than the others.⁴

Characteristically, the unicorn (which appears in early Indian and Near East folklore) is a swift, powerful animal, the mediaeval belief being that it could be caught only by a virgin. When she confronted him the unicorn would lay his head in her lap and be taken by the hunter. Allegorizing the Incarnation, this legend also became associated with courtly love. The seventh tapestry in the series, showing the unicorn alone, symbolizes Christ incarnate (the enclosed garden symbolizes both the Virgin and the Incarnation), but, in Rorimer's words, 'Since the unicorn is leashed with a golden chain, symbol of marriage, to a tree bearing pomegranates, symbols of fertility, this tapestry is also to be interpreted as the consummation of marriage' (*P*, 38).

In *Paterson V* Williams comes nearest to the overt Poundian method, effectively combining local and mythical.⁵ He allows himself to draw his full range of experience towards his own *locus* and, indeed, remarks in the relevant drafts that 'all places remain the same: all are "Paterson" to me if I make them so ... whether Hong Kong or the past: their details are interchangeable if I have the eyes for it' (*Yale*, 190/1). Thus he expands himself when he refers back to his thirty-year-old translation of Philippe Soupault's *The Last Nights of Paris*,⁶ a work relevant in a number of ways: Soupault's Dadaist method, intense interest in certain aspects of America (sports, fashions, jazz, movies), his picture of the decline of European society including a sympathetic evoking of *fin de siècle* whores and prostitutes. Against Paris's decline is set: 'A WORLD OF ART / THAT THROUGH THE YEARS HAS ... SURVIVED!' (*P*, 244). Its art makes the museum real, art itself being '*la réalité*'. The letter which follows, from a woman writer friend and contrasting with the poetess's complaints, tells of the flower-laden Pennsylvania countryside. In its joyousness, the letter is a bouquet for the poet, sharing his own sense of place, echoing the opening lines of 'The descent beckons': 'a place is made of memories as well as the world around it' (*P*, 245).

A single line follows which focuses the poem as a whole and is central to Williams's whole career: 'The whore and the virgin, an identity.' The Venus figure, in its apparent contradictions, its 'disguises', is located as the core of Williams's response to the world, both 'Beautiful Thing' and 'your virgin purpose, / the language' (*P*, 219), and also the Pink Church. Venus, all men's whore and yet the virgin in whose lap the unicorn lays his head, is the ordering faculty and so the Muse seen from one aspect.

Now the 'walking' motif is resumed, here related to Audubon, in whom art and nature (imagination and chaos) are reconciled, figured in the 'horned beast among the trees / in the moonlight' (*P*, 245–6), perhaps a glimpsed unicorn. Throughout these passages Williams uses the metamorphic technique to great effect, fusing actual accurate observation of flowers with tapestry's 'millefleurs background', which is itself the grounding of the narrative of the tapestries in multitudinous actuality.

At this point occur the words 'circled' and 'sphere', an undertone of Book V, suggesting the world's multiplicity, the shadowings of subconsciousness and, later specifically, cyclical renewal. All is to be encompassed by 'indirection', presentation of objects without explicit comment, allied to a particular sense of locality and reality: 'Here / is not there, / and will never be' (*P*, 246). Parallel to this, 'the artist / has no peer'. A legendary beast 'in a field crowded with small flowers', the unicorn is also a figure of the artist, both being regal.

The unicorn, in the seventh tapestry, is both dead and reincarnated. Thus he states Williams's implied belief in the cycle, but the fact of death is not denied, for 'Death / has no peer' and 'death is a hole / in which we are all buried' (*P*, 246). Finely ambiguous, Williams states his belief that death, after all, has a peer, a hole in the bottom of the hole:

> It is the imagination
> which cannot be fathomed.

> It is through this hole
> we escape
>
> (*P*, 247)

Interpolating Ginsberg's letter here allows reiteration of Williams's own non-parochial sense of locality: 'In any case Beauty is where I hang my hat. And reality. And America . . . I mean to say Paterson is not a task like Milton going down to hell, it's a flower to the mind too' (*P*, 247). Ginsberg and his mentor have the same idea, looking to 'big sad poppa' Paterson for a new language, whose (in a phrase of Lyle's) 'grammar is inherent structurally in the universe'. Contrary to any suggestion that Williams finally came to perceive all experience as mind-dependent, the precise interaction between universe and observer is one in which the latter invents, but also discovers, this being the precise nature of: 'Pollock's blobs of paint squeezed out / with design!' (*P*, 248). Chance and design together, the unknown and the known, another subtle figuring of virgin and whore, and the question and answer, 'which / most endures? the world / of the imagination most endures' (*P*, 248). The 'world of the imagination' is not merely the unknown, but the concatenation of the two, 'squeezed out . . . pure from the tube'. Thus it is necessary to 'WALK in the world', to have direct contact with it. Speeding through it or over it in car or aeroplane, this is not true contact. Still less so is to attempt to see it 'from the moon', out of any kind of real contact. There must be 'a "present" / world', but to complete it 'a secret world, / a sphere, a snake with its tail in / its mouth' (*P*, 249). Besides figuring the other aspect of the world of imagination, the symbolic snake, tail in mouth, both destroys itself and nourishes itself by feeding on its own body. It is therefore cyclical, 'rolls backward into the past'.

Next is an excerpt from a prose piece by a young poet,[7] Williams's disciple, describing events in a South American whorehouse, one of the whores seen against a white door, ' . . . snow, the virgin, O bride' (*P*, 250), a chaotic language set against a refrain of the word 'FOUR' (the alchemical quaternity, for order, completeness). The passage's design closes on a repetition of the colour white, lifting the whole experience into the world of imagination and then the circling snake figure is repeated, transformed: 'A lady with the tail of her dress / on her arm' (apparently a detail from the damaged fifth tapestry), emphasis also on her 'round / head'. The tapestry King (Francis I of France) is also Paterson 'the king-self', creator king, both in imagination and erotically: 'The lady's brow is serene / to the sound of a huntsman's horn.'[8]

Book V, i closes in a compounding of erotic love and imagination, where the satyr's role (that is, the artist's) is to guard Venus in the water. Casting our minds back to the fate of the aged Don Perlimplin, the poet finishes with an item of frank sexual advice, 'Loose your love to flow / while you are yet young' (*P*, 252), but the phrasing contains his larger urgency, of the need to experience love, and to express it.

Sappho provides the opening antithesis of Book V, ii. A professorial pronouncement which makes her seem vapid is set against a 'broken' (Poundian) translation of four Sapphic stanzas telling of the creatiive fire and sexual, generative sweat, giving way to a typical Poundian *pronunciamento* on economics, towards which Williams's attitude is by no means unequivocal, placing it as he does between Sappho and her 'modern replica'.

Pound's insistence on 'something as simple as 2 plus 2 makes four' (*P*, 254) echoes the refrain in the passage about the Rio whorehouse, therefore contrasting with it. The sum may also be read as his rejection of part of himself, pointed if we recall Dostoievsky's *Notes from Underground*, his insistence on having two and two equal five and his description of the rational sum as 'a piece of insolence'. Pursuing his method of 'indirection', Williams allows Pound's tone and vocabulary to make their own impression.

Paterson/Williams longs to relate to (or name, or conceive) the 'woman in our town' figure of his Muse: 'It is all for you' (*P*, 257); but the 'you' includes (Audubon's) birds and the jazzman Mezz Mezzrow, from whose *Really the Blues* a paragraph is taken, momentarily fixing on the unreal, racial white/black opposition (the 'Beautiful Thing' sequence having shown already its unreality for Williams himself), holding that if black and white could find a common language (Rapp, rap — talk) — 'you could dig the coloured man's real message and get in there with him, like Rapp' (*P*, 257), wholeness would be achieved. Mezzrow himself effected reconciliation through the art of a coloured woman (Bessie Smith). Art is seen as a satyr's dance, with an element of the child, but 'not the work / of a child' (*P*,

259). Even 'the shark that snaps / at his own trailing guts' (*P*, 234), an inversion of the snake symbol, becomes a figure of the artist, in one of his creations, 'fish / swallowing / their own entrails' (*P*, 259). This three-tiered line passage resolves into a series of epiphanic moments, first the emergence from a chrysalis, then moments of mythology, of art figuring love, and all these reduced in scale by a factual account of a heroic Jew murdered by the Nazis. Yet in some sense the shot Jew and Beethoven's music are given equal value by being there together in the poem.

The moment of tragic grandeur offered by the massacre of the Jews in the pit is played down by means of the 'fashionable grocery list' offered to interviewer Mike Wallace as a poem and defended as rhythm. It is no accident that the E. E. Cummings poem cited contains a series of movements vastly important in *Paterson* (presumably part of the reason why Williams uses the whole passage) — fall, leaps, float, tumble, drift, whirl — not to mention the cat! (*P*, 261). True, Williams in the interview professed not to 'understand' the poem, to 'reject it as a poem', but that is in the interview. His use of it in *Paterson* is indirection, not rejection. A *thing*, like his own 'grocery list', it stresses the important *quidditas*, a piece of reality given value by its location.

Book V, iii turns to another painter, Brueghel, to a Nativity, with Virgin and Baby (linking with Book IV, Curie), some emphasis being placed on Joseph, the foster-father, pitied by the Italians earlier in the poem and here his fellows' 'butt', cause of their 'amazement'. Throughout this passage Williams is seeing the Muse as mother of art, with the artist as foster-father. Making a rapid shift he considers the shoddiness of modern 'morality' and the paucity of modern government (through Dahlberg's letter (*P*, 267)).

Older, Paterson although 'the dog of his thoughts / has shrunk' (*P*, 268), ponders his memories. His imagination is also a 'flight of birds, all together', a tapestry 'woven / in his mind' centred on the artist-satyr.[9] The shrinking consists in his feeling that 'the river has returned to its beginnings' (*P*, 271). A reconciliation, always potential, has been accomplished, summed up in a phrase (slightly modified) from 'The Wanderer': 'and "I knew all (or enough) / it became me"' (*P*, 271).

He confronts the idealist possibility:

> — shall we speak of love
>   seen only in a mirror
>   — no replica?
>   (*P*, 272)

He rejects this, again stressing the need for both mirror and touch:

> — every married man carries in his head
>   the beloved and sacred image
>   of a virgin
> whom he has whored

Thus the 'marriage' theme as presented earlier is modified, for here the whoring of the virgin implies the virility of the married man (Paterson). For 'King-self' Paterson 'Anywhere is everywhere' (*P*, 273), implying all possible metamorphoses, including the 'young man / sharing the female world' (*P*, 276). Some drafts (*Yale*, 190/3) include a five-stanza poem addressed to Sappho and concerning the artist's self-love, which modulates into a memory of his English grandmother (the 'china doorknob' an echo from *KH*, p.11).

Finally, Williams chooses not to adopt Lyle's aphorism from Protagoras that 'man is the measure of all things', but takes instead an important modification of it — man as measurer, choosing his measure in the dance of life. As Williams had written many years earlier, the poem, the artist's creation, is 'a new object, a play, a dance which is not a mirror up to nature' (*SA*, 91). Dance and ground, with the latter uncertain in quality, changing its nature; and the dance ultimately signifying complete marriage of substance and form, a balance between chaos and the deathly rigidity of fixed form. The 'inimitable particles of dissimilarity' are recognized in the dance which is our 'hidden desire' (*SE*, 16, Prologue *KH*) and it is for this that the 'poet transforms himself into a satyr and goes in pursuit of a white skinned dryad' (*KH*, 50).

Deliberately moving to a new location in Book V, poet as eagle has indeed cast off 'rebelliously . . . from its crag', viewing all earlier antithesis, as it were, from above. Book IV ended in a counterpointing of dissonances, but in the contemplative fifth book Williams has not been confined by his earlier adherence to the *thing*. Moving into his 'new dimension' has afforded resolutions, even though it becomes clear (if only through the existing fragment of Book VI) that *Paterson* is, of its very nature, open-ended.

The wholeness of the poem rests in its thorough-going engagement to reality, its commitment to process rather than completeness.

13 'The Odorless Flower'

The great interest of the last fifteen years or so of Williams's life is to be found in his preoccupation with *measure*, and in his immense achievements in the poem after he had apparently finished *Paterson* in 1951. *The Desert Music and Other Poems* (1954) and *Journey to Love* (1955), the two books which preceded *Paterson V*, consist almost entirely of poems in the three-tiered line, the measure he believed he had always been searching for (but which he modified in various ways for much of the work in his final book, *Pictures from Brueghel* (1962).

His late involvement in two related concepts, measure and 'the variable foot' is anticipated in a sentence from *Kora in Hell*, 'A thing known passes out of the mind into the muscles' (*KH*, 71), the basis of his often repeated claim that structure, not subject-matter, is the poet's contact with reality, the one way in which he can modify it. 'Structure' is the presentation of reality with the aid of invention (and/or discovery). In his essay 'The Poem as a Field of Action' (worked on at the same time as *Paterson III* and *IV*), he observes 'Now we have come to the question of the origin of our discoveries: Where else can what we are seeking arise from but speech? From speech, from American speech . . . ' (*SE*, 289). He had expressed the same idea many years earlier in remarking that 'Pound's line is the movement of his thought', which is its measure. Elsewhere he wrote 'The only reality we can know is MEASURE' (*SE*, 283), which is itself relative.

Its relativeness is evident in his concept of the 'variable foot', the working of which he described quite clearly to Richard Eberhart in a letter in 1954, citing poems from *The Desert Music*:

By measure I mean musical pace. . . .
By its *music* shall the best of modern verse be known and the *resources* of the music. The refinement of the poem, its subtlety, is not to be known by the elevation of the words but —

the words don't so much matter — by the resources of the ×
music.

To give you an example from my own work — not that I
know anything about what I have myself written:

(count): — not that I ever count when writing
         but, at best, the lines must be
         capable of being counted, that is
         to say, *measured* — (believe it or
         not). — At that I may, half consciously,
         even count the measure under my
         breath as I write. —

(approximate example)
    (1) The smell of heat is boxwood
        (2) when rousing us
            (3) a movement of the air
    (4) stirs our thoughts
        (5) that had no life in them
            (6) to a life, a life in which
(or)
    (1) Mother of God! Our Lady!
        (2) the heart
            (3) is an unruly master
    (4) Forgive us our sins
        (5) as we
            (6) forgive
    (7) those who have sinned against

Count a single beat to each numeral . . . . Over the whole
poem it gives a pattern to the meter that can be felt as a new
measure. It gives resources to the ear which result in a language
which we hear spoken about us every day. (*SL*, no. 211,
pp. 326–7)

This and other pronouncements, such as the late long essay on
'measure',[1] show that there is little difference between the
'variable foot' and Charles Olson's conception of a 'breath unit' or
'cadence unit'.[2] In each case the measure has two characteristics:
(a) it is a unit of natural speech, and (b) the unit as such is
dependent on the individual speaker at least as much as on the
requirement of making communicable sense. It follows that an

American poet, using the American idiom, will have American speech-rhythms. Poets such as Gary Snyder have gone further, to suggest that the measure of a poem depends on the dominant psycho-physical activity of its maker at the time when it is made. For Williams (and others, such as Zukofsky, Creeley) this is almost the whole explanation of measure, but not quite. Williams himself mentioned to Eberhart the connection with music, and 'music' in the poem is the continuing *relation* between the poet and the world about him. Syntactical groupings apart, Williams's other chief requirement for measure is 'vividness', direct unfalsifying contact with each object in the world. True measure depends on it.[3]

In his essay 'On Measure — Statement for Cid Corman' in *Selected Essays*, Williams makes a direct connection between measure and morality, as when he says 'The very grounds of our beliefs have altered. We do not live that way any more; nothing in our lives, at bottom, is ordered according to that measure ... ' (*SE*, 337). Hence his rejection of traditional measure, and forms such as the sonnet, use of which appeared to him either foolish or even reprehensible.

Reprinting 'The descent beckons' from *Paterson II* as the opening poem of *The Desert Music and Other Poems* ('The Descent'), he did so because he thought of it as 'my solution to the problem of modern verse' (*ND* 17, 178). Obscured in *Paterson* because of the very nature of that poem, 'The Descent' is a characteristic example of Williams's late tendency towards dis-cursiveness, first pervasively evident in some of the less successful poems of *The Wedge*, though we should note here the justness of Breslin's evaluation of the late style as 'an easy, measured grace, a tone of relaxed assurance, tenderness and benignity of feeling, a manner that is openly discursive and personal' (*P*, 203).

By this late stage Williams's devotion to *things* has receded to become part of a larger approach, a discussion of life, expression of a view of life in which love is central and necessary: 'Love without shadows stirs now / beginning to awaken / as night / advances' (*PB*, 74, *DM*). The change from the early 1950s onward is in part due to the simple fact that he had become old and ill, and as a result his physical surroundings were more restricted. As fits his own theory of measure, his late line is less rapid, more contemplative, sometimes even (the point is Kingsley Weatherhead's) 'faltering'.

Addressed to his daughters-in-law, 'To Daphne and Virginia' (*PB*, 75, *DM*), a poem which he cited to Eberhart, reasserts Williams's view that 'the poem alone focuses the world' (*SE*, 242). Asking the women to be patient that he talks to them in a poem, he claims that: 'There is no other / fit medium. / The mind / lives there.' He adds, later: 'A new world / is only a new mind.' To read this as Williams making the world over in his own image would be to misjudge it. What counts is the *focus*. He stresses what he has always known, that each person's contact with reality is peculiarly his own. Making this quite explicit, he combines a natural fact with a figure of speech (which may also be called a 'psychological fact'), simultaneously subscribing to the world of phenomena and revitalizing the figure:

> We are not chickadees
>   on a bare limb
>   with a worm in the mouth.
> The worm is in our brains . . . .

Meditating on the stresses of sexual love, the irrational urge to destroy love (and perhaps marriage, too), he is troubled a little by recollection of sexuality and even the tinge of it he feels still, for these younger women. Yet there is a 'healing odor' abroad, in which he can write a poem. Part of the same world is a pair of robins nesting and, an analogy for himself, 'a heavy goose / who waddles, slopping / noisily in the mud of / his pool' (*PB*, 79, *DM*).

'The Orchestra' (*PB*, 80, *DM*) also concerns love, suffering, making poems. From a cacophony, the orchestra progresses, through a twittering to a design. As he regards each instrument separately, so also the poet is conscious of all sorts and conditions of people — old, children, sick, dying — 'together, unattuned / seeking a common tone', which is love. Sought by means of the ordering principle (i.e. the orchestra), this common tone is also the 'design', which is to be carried through despite the 'wrong note', expressed in a prose quotation: 'Man has survived hitherto because he was too ignorant to know how to realize his wishes. Now that he can realize them, he must either change or perish' (*PB*, 82, *DM*). Here ignorance is in direct contrast with man's innocence, the ground of his love, the means by which he can change his wishes rather than perish.

The other poem quoted to Eberhart, 'For Eleanor and Bill Monahan' (*PB*, 83, *DM*), is also a meditation on love and old age, no longer 'a flight of small cheeping birds':

> Now,
> in the winter of the year,
> the birds who know how
> to escape suffering
> by flight
> are gone. Man alone
> is that creature who
> cannot escape suffering
> by flight

Here the poet is both man and woman, not inclusively as at the end of *Paterson IV*, but dependently, so that his wife has become an essential part of his very existence. The poem's 'she' could as well be his Muse, the 'flower' to whom he clings in fear, in old age, offering up this prayer to Mary, apotheosis of his Venus, 'the female principle of the world'.

Similarly age, his pain, allows him to identify with the injured, dying dog ('To a Dog Injured in the Street' — *PB*, 86, *DM*). He feels the finality of his own situation, as he does that of the dog, resulting in his ultimate detachment regarding the world's fate, which had been one of his nearest concerns. He ponders Keats, master-poet of his youth, slightly misquoting him (to rid the context of any air of pretentiousness) and his friend René Char, all of whose suffering is concentrated into poems of 'sedgy rivers, of daffodils and tulips'. Williams's own pain reminds him of his kicking a puppy in childhood, and of the dead rabbit 'on the outspread palm / of a hunter's hand', memories almost too strong for 'the power of beauty / to right all wrongs'. Yet memory serves to focus beauty, his ultimate belief, assuaging his cry.

Now, for him, 'Memory / is liver than sight'. Dominant of the 'two worlds' (the other 'the rose in bloom'), it serves mainly as a substitute for action, but even so is a continuation of process. Looking back, he is able to affirm that the fact of living, of having lived, is in itself the 'virtue'. As he puts it in 'Deep Religious Faith':

> All that which makes the pear ripen

> or the poet's line
>   come true!
> Invention is the heart of it.
>   (*PB*, 95, *DM*)

Invention is his main effort as a poet, for without it 'the paralytic is confirmed / in his paralysis'.

'The Yellow Flower' (*PB*, 89, *DM*) is deliberately kept out of full focus, so that in it we may gain from all the richness of Williams's earlier treatment of flowers — the direct, flower as woman, flower as poem. Here also the flower's crookedness is his own pain and sickness. From a mustard flower it becomes the 'odorless flower' of *Paterson V*: 'some recognized / and unearthly flower'. His central question here is of life's purpose: 'But why the torture and the escape through the flower?'. Able to see clearly his own mortality, the 'ruin' of 'all that I hold / dear', he has

> through the eyes
>   and through the lips
> and tongue the power
>   to free myself
>   and speak of it
>   (*PB*, 91, *DM*)

But why does 'the tortured body of my flower' exist? Answered by implication, he observes that the 'crooked and obscure' flower is also 'sacred' because it exists 'for me to naturalize / and acclimate / and choose it for my own'. This sense of sacredness is amplified in 'The Host' (*PB*, 92, *DM*): 'It is all / (since eat we must) / made sacred by our common need.'

A more explicit, conventional religious sense, a quality of these late poems, is also stated here: 'There is nothing to eat, / seek it where you will, / but of the body of the Lord.' The context shows that this is anything but a subscription to orthodoxy. These lines precede a statement which has become controversial : 'Only the imagination / is real', which, to Roy Harvey Pearce for example, purveys some form of 'idealism'.[4] In fact, yielded to the imagination as the Lord's body are the 'blessed plants / and the sea'. Through the force of these the imagination 'becomes real'. The world has 'otherness', made real to the perceiver by being transformed in his imagination, as various products of plants and sea make the host which, however, attains its complete nature only in the imaginations of the religious. In 'The Pink Locust' (*PB*, 140, *JL*), taking a famous Gertrude Stein proposition, Williams states the case from a different viewpoint: 'A rose *is* a rose / and the poem equals it / if it be well made.' Remaining unconvinced by the host produced in priestly imaginations, Williams is more interested in the priest with whom he might 'carry on a conversation'. Close enough to Stevens, he ends the poem by suggesting that he *as poet* could have offered them 'the food' of real present imaginings, as Mr T does in achieving his *entrechat* (*PB*, 101, *DM*, 'The Artist').

The artist in 'The Mental Hospital Garden' (*PB*, 97, *DM*) is St Francis of Assisi, and the garden a metaphor for the restrictions of a life in which the imagination is limited or distorted. Another theme woven into the poem is that of 'bawdy' love; but the active distinction between this bawdy love and 'Holy love' is not kept clear throughout. Love (of whichever sort) is both terrifying and revelatory. Bawdy love is the 'first folly', after which one may discover 'in the full sunlight' the summer realization of Holy love.

In the general context of his poems written throughout the 1950s, Williams, as he wrote to Louis Martz, had his own winter realization. Suffering confinement and restriction through illness, none the less he told Martz (*SL*, 298-9) he was afforded time for reading and reflection, through which he concluded that perhaps his over-vigorous rejection of the past had been a blunder. These ideas are at the back of his new style of elegant ruminative wisdom, and the qualitative change, perhaps not unexpected in old age, of perceiving things under the aspect of eternity rather than in their singularity.

In the long title poem 'The Desert Music'[5] (*PB*, 108-20) Williams's concerns are akin to those in *Paterson V*. 'The dance' in the poem centres on a decrepit cripple who sleeps on the international bridge between Juarez and El Paso. His physical presence suggests both life ('Eggshaped') and death, the life-cycle. What is to be said about the area inhabited by this creature, the border between human and inhuman, life and death? By what means can anything be said:

> Only the counted poem, to an exact measure:
> to imitate, not to copy nature, not
> to copy nature

> NOT, prostrate, to copy nature
> but a dance! to dance
> (*PB*, 109)

Conscious of the Aristotelian concept here (a matter discussed with Cid Corman over these very lines; Corman's letter was at one stage apparently to be included in *Paterson V* — see Yale drafts), Williams insists on the subtle distinction between 'representation' and the 're-presentation', the latter implying an action of the imagination rather than mere copying of nature. The dance is the act of re-presenting. Its music is the poem and, while the dance continues, the desert itself.

Opposed to the dance (of life) is the law, whose product is a corpse. Poem, poet and locus are all simultaneously subject and object: 'an agony of self-realization / bound into a whole / by that which surrounds us'. Fully encountered, the desert is that otherness which could become fertile if it were watered by the poem. The poet's desire is to give himself to the scene, identify with it, its 'Texas rain' and begging children. Also the poem is exactly identified with the actions in it, even to the initial impulse of retraction.

Entering the strip joint, the protagonist observes its dancer: 'She's no Mexican. Some worn-out trouper from / the States'; but he feels 'I like her. She fits / the music'. She has her own dance, her own music, but:

> There is another music. The bright-colored candy
> of her nakedness lifts her unexpectedly
> to partake of its tune
>
> (*PB*, 116)

This other music is the power and measure of the poem, lifting the local dancer and her place to another level of expression. Once again whore and virgin are identified:

> Andromeda of those rocks,
> the virgin of her mind   .   those unearthly
> greens and reds
> in her mockery of virtue
> she becomes unaccountably virtuous.

In the poem's reality she is transformed from a worn-out trouper, yet the poet wonders at his urge to celebrate 'an old whore in / a cheap Mexican joint', and at 'so sweet a tune, built of such slime'.

This situation is 'the world writ small', while the poem itself represents the Eternal Virgin set over against it. Yet the poem is *in* the world, 'there to be written', both elements, slime and poem, having a common source. Williams is rejecting the possibility that the dance here is lifting the anti-poetic to a higher level. Rather slime and poem are simultaneous, even co-terminous, just as unexpected qualities in the whore lift her. The lifting is at once in the situation and in the poet's imagination, a focus, 'relief from that changeless, endless / inescapable and insistent music' (*PB*, 119).

Cyclical movement is enacted in the return to the figure on the bridge. The theme's birth aspect is made explicit. The music of reality is the 'bag' surrounding the child in the womb, and also the poem, born in the affirmation, 'I *am* a poet I / am. I am' (with its Cartesian echo). At the birth moment 'the dance begins' and 'The verb detaches itself / seeking to become articulate.'

Structurally, this poem poses an interesting problem. Not employing the three-tiered line, Williams returns to a texture more like that of the main body of *Paterson*. Here his factual details correspond to the prose passages of his epic (though the one time he uses prose is to put a question which is a compromise between fact and meditation — see *PB*, 115). Long as it is, he regarded this as less 'important' than the other poems in *The Desert Music* because of his technical revision (*IWWP*, 89). His approach here, to some extent, allows a split between his 'facts' and his 'ideas'. The three-tiered line, which lends itself structurally to the oblique forward movement of meditation is not here to assist, so his responses to the facts encountered, made of a 'cloth' not unlike the facts themselves, seem self-conscious. Yet, if all details are not 'lifted' to a unity, the central metaphor of virgin/whore–poem/world does succeed.

Technically the poems of *Journey to Love* (1955) are closely related to those of the 1954 volume, the preoccupations much the same, culminating in the masterly 'Asphodel, that Greeny Flower'. In 'The Ivy Crown' (*PB*, 124, *JL*) Williams continues to meditate on the contrast between: 'whatever the heart / fumbles in the dark / to assert / toward the end of May' and the summer roses, which say for him, 'I love you / or I do not live / at all', causing his realization that 'You cannot live / and keep free of / briars'. Children's love is careless and carelessly cast aside, but the love of age is compounded of will (thorns accepted) and imagination: 'We will it so / and so it is / past all accident.'

Some briefer poems in this volume have an epiphanic quality, the negro woman waddling along with a bunch of marigolds, the Swiss church glimpsed on a calendar, the sergeant at Belleau wood shouting, 'Come on! Do you want to live / forever?' Such poems are 'To a Man Dying on is Feet', 'A Smiling Dane' and a number of others, but the poem which dominates the collection is 'Asphodel, that Greeny Flower'. Here not only the line but use of metaphor and image are so integral as to be the 'movement' of Williams's thought. Used both symbolically and objectively, the asphodel is death, the foreboding of death and descent to the underworld. As elsewhere 'Time is a green orchid' (*CEP*, 190), the asphodel is 'green and wooden'. Setting off the poet's meditation, the flower has been part of his consciousness since:

> When I was a boy
> > I kept a book
> > > to which, from time
> to time,
> > I added pressed flowers
> > > until, after a time
> I had a good collection.
> > The asphodel,
> > > forebodingly,
> among them.
> > > > (*PB*, 155, *JL*)

This passage of itself serves to show the control, both of line and emotion, Williams had over his material. Another early reference enhances the context: 'One has emotions about the strangest things . . . heads bowed over the green-flowered asphodel' (*KH*, 32, there is a comparable reference in *A Voyage to Pagany*, p. 87). Young, there was that death-consciousness, now he looks back upon 'a life filled, / if you will, / with flowers', a reference both to the quality of what he has shared with his wife and, with irony, to his own lifelong interest in women. Association allows him to move back and forth among various preoccupations: the nature of his love for his wife, his response to youth so that 'The whole world / became my garden!' (*PB*, 156), his sense of the actual sea, of the sea as metaphor for life's inclusiveness, as source of life, and the nature of consciousness. Quite naturally he moves to ponder 'I have learned much in my life / from books', another source from which he has discovered the nature of life, love's force exemplified in 'Helen's public fault', told in the *Iliad*.

'The sea alone / with its multiplicity / holds any hope' (*PB*, 158, *JL*): personal crisis, involving poet and 'you', is a storm on the sea, but also the storm in the mind (imagination) to be cured only by the will. The will is the mode and ultimate form of their love, so 'the will becomes again / a garden', which reverberates from lines at the end of 'The Orchestra':

> I love you. My heart
> is innocent. And this
> the first day of the world!

In his response to the world, looking back, he discerns an all-embracingness, a love of love, which he has also recognized in her. Love's message, he tells her, is to be found in the poem. He brings 'news' of love (reminding the reader of Pound's definition of a poem as 'news that remains news'). Difficult as it is 'to get the news from poems', men die for lack of it. With this claim Williams closes Book I, having presented the flower(s) of experience as two kinds of love — *eros* and *caritas* — now pleading for and offering the latter.

Book II declares that 'the particulars / of place and condition' have at last become unclear enough to appear 'wavering through water' (*PB*, 162). Particularized recognition is not the same as understanding. This realization leads to the conclusion that to understand 'our time' one cannot go to recent Western history, but must search 'in earlier, wilder / and darker epochs ...'. He recollects the responses of an artist chiefly interested in 'the abstractions of Hindu painting' (*PB*, 163), who liked his poem, therefore clarifying for him his sense of his own work.

Next his mind turns to a shared experience of the Jungfrau, then to an encounter with gipsies in the hills above Granada. Part of our presence in the world, our relation to it, he perceives, depends on how we relate to other people: 'The deaths I suffered / began in the heads / about me' (*PB*, 164, *JL*). Partly through relating to others he had discovered his own necessity, the poem — but the poem must do more than merely reflect 'the glint of waves'.

Thinking of the sea, multiplicity, change, he now turns to another preoccupation of the last two decades of his life: the bomb, which is also, in form and figure, a flower, a destructive flower. Against the bomb, insistent death, he posits love and the poem (in its lyric and epic possibilities):

> Death is no answer,
> no answer —
> to a blind old man
> whose bones
> have the movement
> of the sea,
> a sexless old man
> for whom it is a sea
> of which his verses
> are made up.
> There is no power
> so great as love
> which is a sea,
> which is a garden —
> as enduring
> as the verses
> of that blind old man
> destined
> to live forever.
>
> (*PB*, 166, *JL*)

Opposition between clear speech and silence, so important in *Paterson*, is also an aspect of the present poem. At this point silence is embodied in the Communist fellow-travellers, the Rosenbergs, executed for spying, going to the electric chair 'incommunicado'. Set over against this are the discoveries of Darwin and Columbus:

> It was a flower
> upon which April
> had descended from the skies!
> How bitter
> a disappointment
> . . .

a new measure!
Soon lost.
(*PB*, 167, *JL*)

As a result, 'We come to our deaths / in silence. / The bomb
speaks', the bomb now figuring as every kind of suppression or
exploitation. Here Williams's tone becomes quite distinctly that
of Whitman: 'Every drill / driven into the earth / for oil enters
my side / also' (*PB*, 168, *JL*). This modulates into contrast
between wanton destructiveness and the artist's creativity, so that
Book II also concludes in affirmation of the poem.

Book III opens by asserting that the true character of love is
caritas, including forgiveness. In this respect it is the spring flower
returning after winter's harshness, or (looked at in another way)
like the asphodel it can blossom in unlikely places. A barrier to
love is self-pride, epitomized in memories of prideful horses in
sculpture and painting, 'pictures / of crude force' (*PB*, 171),
culminating in an epiphany of power, an incident at a railroad
station:

a fast freight
thundered through
kicking up the dust.
My friend,
a distinguished artist,
turned with me
to protect his eyes:
That's what we'd all like to be, Bill,
he said

(*PB*, 171, *JL*)

Meeting another man, a stranger, in the subway, the poet
observes and describes in detail the man's shabby flair, his
intelligent presence, then suddenly realizes 'I am looking / into
my father's / face!' (*PB*, 173). Having the urge to speak with the
subway stranger he does not do so, feeling the occasion 'a flower /
whose savor had been lost', or 'some exotic orchid / that Herman
Melville had admired / in the / Hawaiian jungle' (*PB*, 174), or as
strange to him as the draftsmanship of some Pyrenees cave artist.
Nevertheless the encounter is some sort of epiphany, rewarding
the poet with a sense, 'a picture / of all men'.

Observing his wife's 'kindness' to the winter flowers, he feels encouraged that she will be kind also to him. He expects of her a forgiveness, a largeness of spirit, which he sees otherwise as characteristic of the artist. Intuitively, he is aware that the flowers know their 'proper season' for pride, while men are cupidinous unless they be 'the flowers of the race' (*PB*, 176). Recalling more shared experience of their younger life, he now offers his wife 'a last flower', each 'fact of the thing itself' being also a flower, as are the works of the imagination, 'Which proves / that love / rules them all' (*PB*, 178). Keeping in pattern, Book III also ends with a statement on the poem, now seen as dominated by love.

The 'Coda' metaphor of thunder and lightning brings together all Williams's concerns:

> In the huge gap
>> between the flash
> and the thunderstroke
>> spring has come in
>>> or a deep snow fallen.
> Call it old age.
>> (*PB*, 178, *JL*)

Old age and the spring season are in some quasi-mystical sense allied. The 'thunderstroke' is also the bomb, but 'the heat will not overtake the light. / That's sure. / That gelds the bomb . . .'.

Repeating his claim that 'only the imagination is real', he later qualifies, giving an equal place to love:

> But love and the imagination
>> are of a piece,
>>> swift as the light
> to avoid destruction.
>> (*PB*, 180, *JL*)

Even eternity is held in the poet's imagination. He can declare:

> If a man die
>> it is because death
>>> has first
> possessed his imagination,

if he 'refuse' this death, the worst that can befall him is the death
of love. Love and imagination combined in us enable us to 'watch
time's flight / as we might watch / summer lightning'.
Reconciled to physical death, he celebrates the light, which is
also a ceremonial, turning to 'Mediaeval pageantry', raiment of
priests and savage chieftains, pomp and circumstance of
weddings. He thinks of a snatch of Spenser (used by Eliot
ironically) which is for him a point of celebration. Now he is
ending his song. His memory turns back through a whole lifetime
to his own wedding. The odour of that 'sweet-scented flower'
convinces him that he can accept death:

> Asphodel
> > has no odor
> > > save to the imagination
> > but it too
> > > celebrates the light
> > > > (*PB*, 182, *JL*)

but it is the 'odor / as from our wedding', which finally affords
him a sense of affirmation, suffusing his whole world.

In the poems of his last book, *Pictures from Brueghel*, Williams
uses the three-tiered line, but departs from it at will. He also
treats the 'variable foot' variously, even including a demonstration of some humour, 'Some Simple Measures in the
American Idiom and the Variable Foot' (*PB*, 47). A number of
the poems show that the concept goes beyond the relatively
simple idea of a 'breath unit' towards emphasis (sense):

> knees
> lithely built
> in their summer clothes
> show them
> predisposed toward flight
> or the dance
> > (*PB*, 50)

In

> What I got out of women

was difficult
to assess Flossie

the third line makes nonsense of a purely breath-controlled 'variable foot', making more point as an attempt at ambiguity. Other poems (an example is the first one in the book) offer similar difficulties, so it is evident that the scope of Williams's new measure goes beyond speech phrases to a more abstract music, which *includes* speech rhythms but also unexpected departures from them. For example, the lines, 'In a red winter hat blue / eyes smiling' have a distinction and concreteness which is lacking in the more predictable alternative: 'In a red winter hat / blue eyes smiling.'

The title sequence, 'Pictures from Brueghel', simultaneously *presents*, as poem, the world, the dance of life which Williams and Brueghel share, and is a series of exemplary descriptions of the contents of Brueghel's canvases. These poems do not falsify their subject paintings by infusing their presentation with tones or ideas having nothing to do with Brueghel. Where, once or twice, Williams does comment his remarks are part of the poem's action. Rather than falsifying Brueghel they serve to illuminate Williams. In the third poem, for example, 'The Hunters in the Snow', he concludes the detailed concreteness of the hunt picture:

> Brueghel the painter
> concerned with it all has chosen
>
> a winter-struck bush for his
> foreground to
> complete the picture.   (*PB*, 5)

Williams is recognizing a fellow perceiver of 'things others never notice'. He may not merely fix on the detail, but resolve his poem with it, as in 'V   Peasant Wedding':

> a trestle made of an
>
> unhinged barn door by two
> helpers one in a red
> coat a spoon in his hatband
>   (*PB*, 7)

To highlight the deliberate sparseness of Williams's method, it is well worth comparing 'IV The Adoration of the Kings' with Auden's 'Musée des Beaux Arts'. Williams is 'the chronicler', Auden allows himself a more or less overt moral perspective. Williams's interest is, as always, in the 'bloody loam', and so in 'VI Haymaking' he concentrates precisely on this quality in Brueghel, mastery of detail and the need for it. 'IX The Parable of the Blind' demonstrates how this sense of detail is the sense of a world, and how Brueghel's relationship with his world is inevitably concerned with form. For example, the gaiety and warmth of many Brueghel paintings is expressed both in choice of subject but also in the colour and organization of the paint.

The concerns of *Pictures from Brueghel* are very much those of Williams's whole career: beauty, process, the poem. He can move freely from object to subjectivity, into personal concern or reflection and out again, without losing detachment. At moments his fascination by the spoken word is readily apparent. Evident also is a certain natural polarization, between poems concerned with children (chiefly his grandchildren) and those preoccupied with old age and death.

'Elaine' (first of '3 Stances' — *PB*, 18) is a muted contrast between the observer, passive, old, but affectionate, and a young girl poised to move on to a new stage of her existence. Like the other two sections of the poem, this renders an action which is its own comment on the children, their grandfather's sense of them, and his sense of the world. Permitting himself a 'wish' at the end of the whole poem he does not, and does not need to, intrude further. Successfully here Williams has made his line organization, syntax and punctuation carry the nuances of comment.

A more directly reflective group of short poems is 'Suzy' (*PB*, 20–1). Openly asserting the contrast between 'a girl your age' and 'an old man', he allows his personal emotion, his sense of loss, of the actual tragedy of human life, to dominate the second and third poems of the sequence. Nor is he afraid to use a language inviting sentimentalism ('trembling', 'timorous', 'protectively', 'cherishes'). He does so successfully by control of tone and line.

A corresponding group of small poems, to Paul, interests itself in the boy's pastime of catching blackfish. His catch affords the boy satisfactions of gutting and eating it. Such typical activity is 'that language you / will understand' (*PB*, 22), but an additional experience is gained, more private because more individual,

momentary contact with the beauty of the fish's 'glistening /
body':

> however you
> divide
> and share
> that blackfish heft
> and shine
> is your own
>   (*PB*, 23)

Such satisfaction results not merely because the fish must be
intrinsically beautiful, to anyone. It is a product of the boy's
being involved in the action.

Everwhere in this last book, even when his mind is gripped by
death, Williams remains acutely conscious of the world's beauty,
although he sees it as 'no more than a sop' in the face of death.
Beauty seems to him often the crucial expression of a person, as
the 'blue stoneware' is of the unnamed man at the back of 'The
Stone Crock' (*PB*, 28). It has for him in his surroundings the old
Imagist quality:

> winter
>
> woods hang out the snow as if
> it were gay
> curtains
>   (*PB*, 24)

or the iris

> a blue as
> of the sea
> struck
> startling us from among
> those trumpeting
> petals
>   (*PB*, 30)

or Flossie's garden roses, kept on ice (*PB*, 45).

This acute awareness of beauty, the need for it, is a sense of joy, a grounding of ultimate celebration — the poignant, tentative joy of 'Asphodel, that Greeny Flower', or the small, joyful 'satisfaction' of 'Portrait of a Woman in Her Bath', who, although, 'no/ Venus', is life itself, to which he responds vitally, so that

> The sun in
>
> glad of a fellow to
> marvel at
> the birds and the flowers
> look in
>
> (*PB*, 46)[6]

Here Williams uses a domestic incident to lead his mind to the world outside the restricted environment of his last years. Naturally this is a period of many poems of old age, such as 'The Woodthrush', 'To a Woodpecker', 'Suzy', the 'Song' on the Carolina swamp (*PB*, 25), 'The High Bridge Above the Tagus River', 'The Snow Begins' and 'The Rewaking'. Closed in though he is, the fear of death manifest in *Journey to Love* has all but gone from these last poems, although in 'The Woodthrush' he speaks of his 'tragic / winter thoughts', and laments elsewhere:

> but I have forgot beauty
> that is no more than a sop
> when our time
>
> is spent and infirmities
> bring us to
> eat out of the same bowl!
>
> (*PB*, 25)

Yet the death lamentations of 'To a Woodpecker' become the 'gay curtains' of snow on branches. In a mood of acceptance, snow's softness becomes the figure for death:

> before
>
> this benefice all the garden's
> wounds are healed
> white, white, white as death.

Against death, for an old man, there are dreams and memory, 'a kind / of accomplishment', or as in 'The High Bridge Above the Tagus River', the dogs (linked perhaps with 'the dog' of Paterson's thoughts) which in his youth seemed of 'savage appearance', in old age 'walk in the old man's dreams and still walk / in his dreams, peacefully continuing in his verse / forever' (*PB*, 53). Finally, 'The Rewaking' (*PB*, 70), which concludes this last collection, sees love ('your love') as the source of a new spring, a new beginning: 'by / your love the very sun / itself is revived'.

Few moments in these late poems need suffer the burden of exegesis. Almost everywhere they are achieved by simplicities and sure tone. By and large they are a triumphant flowering of Williams's genius, justifying his ultimate reliance on the ear for a discovery of music and on 'things' rather than intellectual subtleties for giving body and presence to the poems. Thus he is able to declare, naturally and truly:

> All men by their nature give praise.
>   It is all
>   they can do.
>
> The very devils
>   by their flight give praise.
>   What is death
> beside this?
>   (*PB*, 62)

This praise is the poem, focus of the world — no substitute reality but a parallel plenitude:

> The rose fades
> and is renewed again
> by its seed, naturally
> but where
> save in the poem
> shall it go
> to suffer no diminution
> of its splendor
>   (*PB*, 39)

Supremely, the poem is the instance when 'the mind dances with itself' (*PB*, 32), but it is not completeness, for 'there are always two / yourself and the other'. The dance of life is something we participate in because we live, but we should also make it 'our own', the only thing 'sure'. In 'the storm / that holds us, / plays with us and discards us' we dance as well as we know how. The dance's gaiety, the gaiety of things as they are, of what we can know, is expressed in the movement and action of the dance-poem, 'Calypsos':

> Love the sun
> comes
> up in
>
> the morning
> and
> in
>
> the evening
> zippy zappy
> it goes
>   (*PB*, 57)

Zest, concreteness, imagination, this is the height of the dance of life, so Gagarin's triumph as the first man in space is an ecstasy, with an eternal quality: 'heel and toe he felt / as if he had / been dancing' (*PB*, 69). Thus everywhere in the book, awareness of 'tragic winter', but also of the dance of living, of words, of creatures, the bird planing to a stop 'miraculously' before the poet's very eyes, the 'coiffeured / and perfumed old men', Daumier-like figures, gossiping about 'the news from / Russia or a view of / the reverse surface of / the moon' until 'the ear and the eye lie / down together in the same bed' (*PB*, 15). At the core of all this: 'beauty is a shell / from the sea / where she rules triumphant / until love has had its way with her'.

The great universal Williams sought, timeless, was a 'life that is here and now'. His belief was that only the artist could apprehend the *new*, the present *thing*, in all its 'vividness', only he could invent 'today'. It is in this sense of full realization that, for him, the 'only world that exists is the world of the senses. The world of the artist' (*SE*, 196).

14 Conclusion

For criticism, the important question is: what criteria are we to apply in judging Williams's poems? Many American poets, of the past two decades in particular, have signified their approval of his work either by imitating it or advancing it. Critical difficulty is encountered not so much in characterizing his discoveries concerning 'the poem' as in deciding which among his typical poems are successful, and good, poems, and why this is so.

At the beginning of his career, and by now the point has been made often enough, Williams's poems were highly literary, modelled on approved masters in the English tradition, both in diction and measure. When he broke away from this stale sense of poetry, it was first through the influence of Pound and Imagism. As he suggests in the Preface to *Kora in Hell*, Williams, at this period, escaped from a common mental attitude of the literary poet — considering, or thinking about, one thing in terms of another. Simile, analogy and metaphor he rejected as inappropriate to his sense of 'the poem', preferring to assert the necessity of keeping one's eye on the object, recognizing the 'true value', 'that peculiarity which gives an object a character by itself' (*SE*, 11), discovering 'in things those inimitable particles of dissimilarity to all other things which are the peculiar perfections of the thing in question' (*SE*, 16). Such insistence on the specific individuality of the object, as opposed to its likeness and relation to other objects, is distinctly American, as is the aim for 'vividness' rather than propriety.

Seeing clearly was, for him, the great virtue, as it was for his painter friends Demuth and Sheeler. Throughout Williams's career we encounter the isolation of the moment of clear perception or experience as if it were hard won from the ever-encroaching flux. In a constant state of alertness the artist makes his discoveries, but he is also active, and morally so, a selector, who 'must keep his eye without fault on those things he values, to which officials refuse to give the proper names'

(*SE*, 231). Genuine contact is made through concentration on the object with great intensity, to 'lift it' to the imagination. An object lifted to the imagination yields up its 'radiant gist'. Sometimes this is simply discovered, while at others (given that the field of energy does not stop at the skin or outer envelope of the human being), the process is completed by the poet by means of invention or structuring. In poems such as 'The Red Wheelbarrow', Williams draws our attention simultaneously to the world out there and to our relationship with it, which must be fresh, now. Here is one significance of his assertion that 'Nothing is good save the new' (*SE*, 21), which is far from claiming that a thing is inevitably good *merely because* it is new.

'Nothing is good save the new' because what is important is here and now, our immediate experience. In the face of centuries of traditional poetic form, which had run into the nineteenth-century mire of 'moral homily' (seeing the poem as aiming for perfection in long-established verse-forms along with the expression of edifying or uplifting material), Williams had the insight to see that the significance of the poem is not in its subject-matter (which is nearly always 'phantasy' or 'dream'), but, as he asserts over and over again in many different ways, in its form.[1] Given his deep convictions on the need for contact and that 'the local is the only universal' it is natural that he should have rejected traditional forms and measure, since these are not local, nor have Americans direct access to their sources. Where to look, then, for new form?

Seen in this way, Williams's position is both perceptive and sensible. A poem is made with words and possesses whatever reality it may have through 'the shapes of men's lives in places'. What more natural than to use the language of those men? When, in his 1948 essay 'The Poem as a Field of Action', Williams, looking back, observed that 'Imagism was not structural: that was the reason for its disappearance' (*SE*, 283), he meant that it did not derive purely from the speech-patterns of its day. Having recognized the vital link between poetry and speech, he then had to work for most of a lifetime before achieving a sound technical base (the variable foot), which could incorporate the American idiom on all occasions without strain. Even while he was working towards this there appears to have been a subsidiary approach to measure in his work, related to syllable-counting, some Pythagorean musical conception (for which there is only slight occasional evidence, but enough to confuse a tracking of the main line of development).

Only the tradition-bound will by now find it hard to accept Williams's innovations in the line. From *Al Que Quiere!* on, he largely escaped the tyranny of quantitative measure, employing instead a measure based on phrasing. A difficulty in making categorical assertions about Williams's measure (and therefore codifying it) is that his practice varies somewhat. Occasionally it is purely 'musical'. In this early, Imagist period it depended considerably on the syntax and phrasing of written statement. Very often, at its strongest throughout his career, it related to speech. Sometimes (as in 'Struggle of Wings', for example) it can be criticized as too long, or heavy; but even length is no sure criterion, as witness some writing in 'The Clouds' (*CLP*, 124). Generally, however, it can be said that the longer line is most successful when deployed to create a forward verbal flow. Much of the work in *Collected Later Poems* ('The Mind's Games', for example, or 'Aigeltinger') is not easy to classify in terms of the line. Almost all of it is natural in flow, which saves it from the charge of being 'chopped-up prose', but a great deal of it is not far removed from prose. Sometimes (as in 'Aigeltinger') one suspects a deliberate tinkering with quantitative measure. Ultimately our bases for judging Williams's line must be broad ones: its energy in the specific instance, its 'naturalness' (which, almost inevitably, depends on the spoken word).

Naturalness as a criterion may remind us of another statement in the Prologue to *Kora in Hell*: 'By the brokenness of his composition the poet makes himself master of a certain weapon which he could possess himself of in no other way. The speed of the emotions is sometimes such that thrashing about in a thin exaltation or despair many matters are touched but not held, more often broken by the contact' (*SE*, 14). We may think of poems as various as 'Della Primavera Trasportata al Morale' (*CEP*, 57) and 'Perpetuum Mobile: the City' (*CEP*, 384), which have this quality, but they are held together by a definite relation to speech rhythms. For Williams, 'brokenness' and naturalness are of a piece. Where he fails, according to his own aims, is in such a poem as 'The Yachts', close as it obviously is to quantitative measure, even to the extent that its closing lines depend on a regularly established rhythm for making their 'dying fall' effect.

Traditional prosody is fixed, while for Williams measure in the poem is always relative. He never insisted on establishing a new set of rules, beyond observing the (for him) undeniable relationship between American measure and American speech. 'The only reality we can know is MEASURE' (*SE*, 283), but different worlds call for diffeent measures, each consonant with its own time and place. Any critic would seem to be in the position of recognizing and adumbrating the prosodic rules established by Williams, but there are (ultimately) no rules, except in the most general sense. Having limited ourselves to observing that Williams is in the American (as opposed to the English) tradition, we must note the further restriction that each man's 'line' is, implicitly, his own (hence Williams's explanation of his own short line: 'I didn't go in for long lines because of my nervous nature. I couldn't. The rhythmic pace was the pace of speech . . .' — *IWWP*, 15).

Williams's basic short line was established in *Al Que Quiere!* Poem after poem in that volume, some quiet some less so, shows surprising tautness and strength of line. Much depends on the energy in the specific line, used with great range and subtlety:

> When I was younger
> it was plain to me
> I must make something of myself.
> Older now . . . .

Here, and in numerous other instances, the line disposition entirely suits the action of the poem (an obvious example here is the muting of line 4). Beyond this everything depends on the articulation of lines throughout. Hence, the poem is 'a field of action', and hence Williams's recognition of the rightness of Olson's theory of composition by field, rather than through accumulating well-turned lines.

Part of the outcome of this new sense of measure as 'relative'[2] is a new respect for the individual word, accepting it freshly not as a label but as an alternative reality, an object in its own right. The word is a 'thing-in-itself', but it derives energy (usually in the form of 'meaning') through contact with other words. Much can be understood concerning Williams's use of the line if we recognize the range of his sentence structures. Vividness is gained very often by employment of the present tense, but he can (through syntactical arrangement) create a sense of immediacy without it:

> Then I raised my head
> and stared out over
> the blue February waste
> to the blue bank of hill
> with stars on it
> in strings and festoons —
> but above that:
> one opaque
> stone of a cloud
> ('Winter Sunset', *CEP*, 127)

Frequently Williams's poems begin with a question or an exclamation or exhortation, all indicating his eagerness, wonder, curiosity, and usually transmuting his excitement into the energy of the poem. Typically, throughout his career his language is simple and, despite subtle sentence variation, clearly and directly organized. In much of his verse of the late 1930s, early 1940s, which makes *Collected Later Poems* disappointing compared with *Collected Earlier Poems,* he allows himself discursive sentence structures, employing pause, parenthesis and qualification to a greater extent that he had earlier. Seen in the perspective of his whole development, it may be that much of the work of that period is preparatory for *Paterson,* an effort to extend his means deliberately in the direction of discursiveness, which bore fruit not so much in *Paterson* as in the assured, relaxed statement of many poems in *The Desert Music* and *Journey to Love.* Meantime, to the extent that he forgot Pound's dictum that the good writer 'uses the smallest possible number of words',[3] Williams's work of that period lost distinction.

To summarize thus far, the attributes of the true poem, according to Williams, are that: it recognizes the *uniqueness* of each thing or object in experience; the poet's task is to perceive this uniqueness with as great a clarity as possible and to render it as a poem with as much 'vividness' as he can command; to pursue this task he must be in deeply attentive contact with his immediate environment and he must have the imaginative insight to recognize the object or detail which will be key to the universal in the local; 'what actually impinges on the senses must be rendered as it appears' (*SE*, 119), but the poet gives it structure without in any way interfering with its essential nature, so it is simultaneously a discovery (in itself) and an invention (by his relating it to all else, through rendering it in words). The true poem must be 'new' because our experience is always new, even though it is always in danger of being dominated by the past. As each age has its own brand of experience, so also it will have a typical prosody and a characteristic type of poem, but inside that each individual makes his own poems, never by an outdated means or measure, according to his own imagination and internal rhythms, but inevitably influenced by the 'weather' and speech of his environment.

Technically, each poem will create its own shape, having the general characteristics of simplicity, clarity and naturalness, succeeding according to the strength and/or appropriateness of energy discharge over its whole field.

Like Pound, Williams employs the technique of juxtaposition, but where Pound juxtaposes literary or cultural 'echoes' or apparent correspondences, Williams (until *Paterson*) tends to place together things-in-themselves. Even his juxtapositions in *Paterson* are treated so, not intended to suggest analogies, but to present the quality of American experience direct and without interference. Sometimes his juxtaposed objects possess 'one-thousandth part of a quality in common', but often they deliberately (or carelessly) clash. Therefore, in some sense, juxtaposition is 'suggestive', but the reader is not necessarily led through a thought process, almost certainly to a flash of recognition which is an energy-discharge linking the juxtaposed items. Not that Williams is against activity of the intelligence. Traditional metaphor means the positive presence of the writer, in the text, directing his reader, contrary to Williams's belief that the artist should be 'remote from the field' and that art is created through 'concrete indirections' (*SL*, 24).

Not the artist's autobiography, but the quality of his experience is important. To prevent his experience from being trammelled by convention it must be 'open' and not preconceived. A sense of form must be allied to a willingness to descend to the 'formless ground'. Williams's advice to 'write carelessly' is not really at odds with his insistence on accuracy of observation and rendering. What must be avoided is 'thought about' the object or experience, and (again from Williams's point of view) before *Paterson* evidence of deliberate thought in the *details* of a poem (like over-attention to 'subject-matter') would constitute a weakness in that poem. Perception and the imaginative disposition of perceptions, these are primary to the poem. Verbal and causal connectives, any verbal arrangement which is based on the structure of thought, these adulterate the poem, diminishing its purity and effectiveness. Apart from escaping the tyranny of quantitative measure, this must have been Williams's pre-eminent consideration in his search for, and development of, the variable foot.

All these criteria, and others, are positive and reasonable. Nothing can bridge the hiatus between Williams's intentions and those critics who cannot accept his major requirement — the rejection of quantitative measure for contemporary American poetry. However, almost everywhere the variable foot and composition by field have been accepted at least as legitimate, valuable extensions of the poetic means. Given this, Williams's own requirements for the poem offer adequate tools by which to assess his work, up to the mid-1940s.

Paterson poses fresh problems for the critic. What are to be his evaluative criteria for it? One is the valuable notion of the metamorphic poem implicit in the work, put forward by Sister M. Bernetta Quinn.[4] Williams's own 'theory' of 'interpenetration' accords well with the metamorphic technique. His use of 'raw material' in the form of a variety of prose passages is of a piece both with his rejection of the 'anti-poetic' and his belief in the thing-in-itself.

To consider Williams's poetic development progressively is to wonder, at times, if he was sidetracked by Imagism and Objectivism. Although 'not structural', Imagism certainly persuaded him of the value of intense concentration upon the object. Objectivism may have intensified this in two ways: by emphasis on the removal of self from the poem and by (consequently) drawing the attention to the speech or music in which the objective experiences presented themselves (such an influence is evident today in fine poet craftsmen, from Lorine Niedecker — an associate of the original Objectivists, whose work is too little known — to Paul Blackburn and many of the contributors to Cid Corman's *Origin*).

Both Imagism and Objectivism are in the same theoretical line as Poe's insistence on the poem as a striving for a single effect. In its very name each of these 'movements' suggests a concentration on noun or thing as opposed to 'an easy lateral sliding' through a statement of abstractions easily divorced from reality. His insistence on the value of the thing-in-itself is important in Williams, but even more important in his sense of process. More than many of his associates he was conscious of the antithesis between, so to speak, Heraclitus and Parmenides. As we have seen, there are the tight 'imagist' poems and the poems which flow 'carelessly'. Perhaps the crucial clue in the *Paterson* headnotes is 'by multiplication a reduction to one' (*P*, 10). Implying, as it does, movement, activity, this categorically shifts the emphasis of Williams's poem from thing to process, a passing through. His central means is in the metamorphoses of Paterson himself/itself. How are we to judge the value or success of this means? If the nature of Paterson, the man–city, becomes very clear at any one point in the poem, would not this be distracting? Would it not limit the range of possible response? Quest, perpetual change, fluidity, instability — these are characteristic of *Paterson*, giving it vitality. All objects in the poem are instantaneously there and are instantly gone. They are *here and now*. *Paterson I–IV* is a search for order. As originally conceived, the poem is search only, process only, and the failure of Paterson, the man-city, is comparable with that of, say, Père Sebastian Rasles in *In the American Grain*, a failure which has its own kind of success, in recognizing that '*La Vertue est toute dans l'effort*'. Notably, *Paterson V*, which concerns itself with the tapestry, the relationship of art to life and Williams's lifelong Kora–Venus preoccupation, has a greater immediate clarity, concentration upon the object, and a more obviously discursive point.

The earlier books of *Paterson* are sustained, paradoxically, as much by the fragments of 'experience' or 'thing' as they are by the necessarily fluid central metaphor. Curiously, metamorphosis *invites* discourse, while the 'gathering up' of its own weight has, at times, an effect opposite to the 'taking up of slack'. If one has any reservation about *Paterson V*, it is that the appeal to art, to imagination, is obvious rather than new, or penetrating, or decisive. Yet as a 'resolution', it confirms the tendency of Williams's whole career and is very much of a piece with all the work of his last phase.

Williams's late concentration on the imagination, his alignment of imagination and love, his self-searching, these are not narcissism. Rather his belief in the imagination is similar to his lifelong sense of the local. Emphasis is not on *his* locality, or imagination, because they are *his*. Imagination works from material in one's own experience (whoever one may happen to be). That experience differs from one phase to another, so constant reference to it is simply carrying devotion to 'the new' to its ultimate conclusion.

From his Objectivist period onward all Williams's work implies a sense of the self other than the merely autobiographical or egotistical. In 1947 he observed: 'The objective in writing is to reveal. . . . The difference between the revealer and others is that he reveals HIMSELF, not you' (*SE*, 269). Again, this stems from a realization that, just as the place a person can truly know is his own locality, so the only self he can truly know is his own. Avoidance of falsification, pretence, is at back of this and of the finally developed sense of imagination. In the long run, love is the important emotion in human experience. What keeps man alive (or kills him, for that matter) is his own imagination and how it relates to the world. Imagination has the power of transforming or maintaining the world, and is the chief metamorphic agent:

> But love and the imagination
> are of a piece,
>   swift as the light
> to avoid destruction.
>
> (*PB*, 179)

Williams's latest work is generally discursive in comparison with his pre-*Paterson* poems. Interestingly, this is due at least in part to his metrical experimentation. The stepping of the three-tiered line, which he had used first in 'The descent beckons' (*Paterson II*), has the effect of casting aside the static, fixed-object presentation of many earlier poems. To suggest that Williams was never discursive in his earlier work would be inaccurate. Even though expressed negatively ('No ideas but in things!'), Williams's awareness of the 'idea' in poetry is about as long as his career. His late development of 'the variable foot' allowed him to be discursive without abandoning the cadence and rapidity of natural speech. The order of speech, of prose statement, has replaced a repetitive, metronomic pattern, as the *expected* element in Williams's line. By and large, the line units are dictated by speech, but they have a flexibility and offer a range of possible discovery far exceeding those of traditional meter. Looking for criteria to judge 'the variable foot' we may suggest: (a) is it natural, true to speech? (b) are the variations vital and interesting? For Williams the anti-poetic would be aping of traditional literary forms or copying the speech and/or measure of others.

As an innovator, Williams shared many of his positions with Pound, but he may in the long run prove to be more influential. Pound to a much greater degree applied himself to, and found his material in, art and literature. Williams, likewise interested in simultaneity and interaction rather than causality, suggests his own far different sense of experience in chapter 54 of the *Autobiography*. He refers to the exciting secrets of the 'underground stream' of human experience itself, unselected. Attending closely to it, 'there is no better way to get an intimation of what is going on in the world' (*Autob.*, 360). His whole objective, as it ultimately became clear to him, is to lift the 'inarticulate' up to imagination. A sense of the common people as prime source of life, shared in the early years with Eliot, seems never to have left Williams, despite a discouragement made plain at least as late as *Paterson II*.

A 'lifetime of careful listening' to the speech arising from his daily tasks and contacts, convinced him that poem and life, also, are one — and that each person is trying to communicate to the world the poem of himself. In many works, but particularly in *Kora in Hell*, *In the American Grain*, *Collected Earlier Poems*, *Paterson* and the late poems, he demonstrated the informing need for imagination, having realized early that 'The imagination transcends the thing itself' (*KH*, 24). An explorer and discoverer, always conscious of the handful of men who had contributed positively to the shaping of the American spirit, he takes his place alongside them.

Notes

NOTES TO CHAPTER ONE: THE RIVER

1. See also Emily Mitchell Wallace, *A Bibliography of William Carlos Williams* (Middletown, Conn.: Wesleyan University Press, 1968) Introductory note, pp. xix-xx. [Hereafter cited as *Wallace*.]
2. Unpublished notes relating to *IWWP* in American Literature Collection, Yale University Library.
3. J. Hillis Miller, *Poets of Reality: Six Twentieth-Century Writers* (Cambridge, Mass.: Belknap Press of Harvard University Press, 1966) p. 287.
4. Rod Townley, *The Early Poetry of William Carlos Williams* (Ithaca, N. Y.: Cornell University Press, 1975) p. 42. Stuart Peterfreund, 'Keats's Influence on William Carlos Williams', *William Carlos Williams Newsletter*, vol. III, no 1 (Spring 1977) pp. 8–13, runs counter to the usual argument that Williams's earliest career as a poet was a struggle between the influences of Keats and Whitman, which resulted in Williams moving away from Keats and towards his own true voice. Peterfreund shows Keatsian influence up to and including *Paterson*. According to Weaver, 'In March 1908 Ezra Pound, who was passing through Rutherford on his way to Europe, saw Williams' long Keatsian poem "Philip and Oradie", and pronounced it "great" — Mike Weaver, *William Carlos Williams: the American Background* (Cambridge: Cambridge University Press, 1971) p. 7. Or so Williams wrote to his brother Edgar on 18 March 1908 (Yale).
5. *The Letters of Ezra Pound 1907-1941*, ed. D.D. Paige (New York: Harcourt, Brace & World, 1950; Harvest Books edn, 1967) p. 3. Quotes taken from the paperback edition.
6. Ibid., pp. 7–8.
7. James E. Breslin suggests that 'As a young writer, Williams first thought he was Keats, later thought he was Pound, but then through a 1913 reading of *Leaves of Grass*, discovered he was William Carlos Williams' — 'William Carlos Williams and the Whitman Tradition', *Literary Criticism and Historical Understanding* (selected papers from the English Institute), ed. Philip Damon (New York: Columbia University Press, 1967) p. 153. In *IWWP* Williams gives the impression of having read *Leaves of Grass* a decade or so earlier. Mr Breslin reads 'The Wanderer' as a poem much influenced by Whitman and perhaps tends to undervalue Pound's relationship to Williams.
8. Pound's 'Introductory Note' to *The Tempers* is reproduced in *IWWP*, pp. 12-13.
9. Pound, *Literary Essays* (London: Faber & Faber, 1954) p. 9.

10. *The Egoist*, vol. I, no. 6 (16 March 1914) pp. 109-11. (See *Wallace* C4.)
11. A page of Williams ms. is reproduced in *Massachusetts Review* (Winter 1962) p. 307, with the comment: 'A manuscript page of WCWs earliest extant verse, 1908. . . . It is actually in the possession of John C. Thirlwall.' Presumably this is the 'Philip and Oradie' referred to by Weaver, op. cit., p. 7.
12. James Guimond, *The Art of William Carlos Williams: a Discovery and Possession of America* (Urbana: University of Illinois Press, 1968) p. 15.
13. Patrick Renshaw, *The Wobblies: The Story of Syndicalism in the United States* (New York: Doubleday, 1967) pp. 122-8. The strike eventually failed, but not before involving 25,000 workers. Some lines from this section of the poem made Eda Lou Walton think 'The Wanderer' a recent poem when she reviewed *CCP in The New Masses* (29 November 1938).
14. *Poets of Reality*, p. 297.
15. Lucien Stryk and Takashi Ikemoto (eds and trans.), *Zen: Poems, Prayers, Sermons, Anecdotes, Interviews* (New York: Doubleday, 1965) p. ix. See also Joseph N. Riddel, *The Inverted Bell: Modernism and the Counter-Poetics of William Carlos Williams* (Baton Rouge: Louisiana State University Press, 1974) pp. 61-2.
16. *Poets of Reality*, p. 287.
17. *Transfigured Night* (New York: Macmillan, 1946) p. xi. (See *Wallace* B49.)
18. Tony Tanner, *The Reign of Wonder: Naivety and Reality in American Literature* (Cambridge: Cambridge University Press, 1965). Williams is considered only very briefly, but the book as a whole details the framework, as far back as Emerson, in which Williams's work must be set.
19. Gertrude Stein, *Lectures in America* (New York: Random House, 1935) p. 196. Quoted by Tanner, op. cit., p. 193.
20. Sherman Paul, *'The Music of Survival: a Biography of a Poem by William Carlos Williams* (Urbana: University of Illinois, 1968), in an interesting discussion of dance in Williams, regards this rather attenuated poem, in the shape 'of a pirouette', as successful.
21. Bram Dijkstra, *The Hieroglyphics of a New Speech: Cubism, Stieglitz, and the Early Poetry of William Carlos Williams* (Princeton, N.J.: Princeton University Press, 1969) p. 52.
22. Guimond, op. cit., p. 42, considers the poem 'remarkably like Demuth's "white architecture" series'.
23. This poem is quite closely related to Williams's short story 'A Descendant of Kings'.
24. See *SE*, p. 303.
25. *Poets of Reality*, p. 288.
26. Not included in *AQQ*. First published in *Others*, vol. III, no. i (July 1916) p. 30. (See *Wallace* C11.)
27. *William Carlos Williams: a Collection of Critical Essays*, ed. J. Hillis Miller (Englewood Cliffs, N.J.: Prentice-Hall, 1966). p. 48.

NOTES TO CHAPTER TWO: DESCENT AND CONTACT

1. Pound dedicated *Ripostes* to Williams, quoting from Propertius: '*Quos ego*

Persephonae maxima dona feram'. Weaver suggests that the title itself came directly from Pound (Weaver, op. cit., p. 6).

2. *Literary Essays*, p. 397.

3. *A Novelette and Other Prose* (Toulon: To Publishers, 1932) pp. 20f. (cited hereafter as *A Novelette*).

4. *SE*, p. 125. Reed Whittemore, in his biography of Williams, calls *Kora in Hell* his 'winter book', and suggests that its main impetus was the 'dark stealings' of Williams's sex life. Whittemore's book is puzzling because so often its tone is just *wrong* if the writer intends to treat his subject seriously and as worthy of respect. The phrase 'winter book' is appropriate, though, if we read it as describing what is antithetical to Venus, and the birth of spring. See Reed Whittemore, *William Carlos Williams: Poet from Jersey* (Boston, Mass.: Houghton Mifflin, 1975) pp. 122–4, 156–9.

5. The terms are T.E. Hulme's. Much of Williams's subsequent thinking on the poem (a term he preferred to 'poetry') concurs with Hulme's in *Speculations* (London: Routledge, 1924) and *Further Speculations* (Minneapolis: University of Minnesota Press, 1955). See also A. Kingsley Weatherhead, *The Edge of the Image* (Seattle: University of Washington Press, 1967) pp. 29–31.

6. For the publishing history of *Kora in Hell*, see Joseph Evans Slate, 'Kora in Opacity: Williams' Improvisations', *Journal of Modern Literature*, vol. I, no. 4 (May 1971) pp. 463–76.

7. *The Letters of Ezra Pound*, p. 124 (compare variant version in *SE*, p. 8). Williams's description of deflection from 'the thing' as 'an easy lateral sliding' may be related to Hulme's remark on the language of poetry: 'It always endeavours to arrest you, and to make you continuously see a physical thing, to prevent you gliding through an abstract process' (*Speculations*, p. 134). 'Romanticism and Classicism', the essay in which this occurs, was, of course, written long before 1924.

8. Expressing ideas pervasive in his work, these phrases occur in Marshall McLuhan's *Verbi-Voco-Visual Explorations* (New York: Something Else Press, 1967).

9. *A Novelette*, p. 25.

10. In a useful essay, which offers some measure of summary interpretation, Sherman Paul objects to the kind of explication by association which inevitably relates *Kora in Hell* to *Les Illuminations*. See Sherman Paul, 'A Sketchbook of the Artist in his Thirty-Fourth Year: William Carlos Williams' *Kora in Hell: Improvisations*', in *The Shaken Realist*, ed. Melvin J. Friedman and John B. Vickery (Baton Rouge: Louisiana State University Press, 1970) pp. 21–44. On the dance in *Kora in Hell*, see Linda W. Wagner, *The Prose of William Carlos Williams* (Middletown, Conn.: Wesleyan University Press, 1970) pp. 20–3.

11. *Speculations*, p. 146. Also, Mike Weaver, in several succinct pages of background, draws attention to Williams's specific mention in the 'Prologue' of Kandinsky's *Concerning the Spiritual in Art*, which was introduced to English readers by the painter Marsden Hartley shortly before he met Williams. The concept of the 'Improvisation', 'a largely unconscious, spontaneous expression of inner character, non-material in nature', comes directly from Kandinsky. See Weaver, op. cit., 37–9.

12. Karl Shapiro, *In Defense of Ignorance* (New York: Random House, 1960; paperback edn, 1965) p. 154. Quotes come from paperback edition.
13. 'Notes from a Talk on Poetry', *Poetry*, vol. XIV (July 1919) pp. 211–16.
14. John Dewey, 'Americanism and Localism', *The Dial*, vol. LXVIII (June 1920) pp. 684–8.
15. *Sour Grapes* (Boston, Mass.: Four Seas, 1921). The State University of New York at Buffalo (SUNYAB) has a typescript of 'March' edited by H.D., with wholesale excisions. Williams followed many of her suggestions, but did not delect section V.
16. *SL*, no. 32, pp. 46, 47.
17. Bram Dijkstra, op. cit., pp. 162–7, provides illuminating comments on the link between the flower poems in *Sour Grapes* and the paintings of Williams's friend Charles Demuth. Demuth's painting may well have contributed at this point to the continued loosening of William's verse technique.
18. Neil Myers, 'Sentimentalism in the Early Poetry of William Carlos Williams', *American Literature*, vol. 37 (1965–6) p. 462.
19. *Poets of Reality*, p. 349.

NOTES TO CHAPTER THREE: 'SPRING AND ALL'

1. *Spring and All* (Dijon: Contact Publishing Co., 1923); also included in *Imaginations*.
2. Dijkstra, op. cit., pp. 130–7; Rosenfeld actually wrote at length about *Spring and All* in *Port of New York*, first published in 1924 (New York: Harcourt, Brace & World).
3. The most readily available complete text of *Spring and All* is William Carlos Williams, *Imaginations*, ed. Webster Schott (New York: New Directions, 1970; paperback edn, 1971). Page references in the text are to the paperback edition.
4. Dijkstra, op. cit., p. 169.
5. Alan Ostrom, *The Poetic World of William Carlos Williams* (Carbondale and Edwardsville: Southern Illinois University Press, 1966) p. 126.
6. *Manikin*, no. 2 (New York, 1923). (See *Wallace* A8.)
7. Wagner, *The Prose of William Carlos Williams* pp. 32–46.
8. *Poetry*, vol. XXIII (November 1923) pp. 103–5.
9. Daniel Henry Kahnweiler, *Juan Gris: His Life and Work*, trans. by Douglas Cooper (New York: Harry N. Abrams, 1946) p. 194. See Rob Fure, 'The Design of Experience: William Carlos Williams and Juan Gris', *William Carlos Williams Newsletter*, vol. IV, no. 2 (Fall 1978) pp. 10–19.
10. See John Senior, *The Way Down and Out: the Occult in Symbolist Literature* (Ithaca, N.Y.: Cornell University Press, 1959), especially the introduction, for perceptive discussion of this aspect of modern literature.
11. Kiki figures in a number of memoirs of the period, including Williams's *Autobiography* (New York: Random House, 1951) and Robert McAlmon's *Being Geniuses Together* (London: Secker & Warburg, 1938; rev. edn Garden City, N.Y.: Doubleday, 1968).
12. Virgil Jordan, 'Patterns', *Contact*, IV (1922). As published, it is a summary

or abridgement by either Williams or McAlmon, to which Jordan added a note '. . . unintelligible, since everything is left out but a few bones . . .'.

NOTES TO CHAPTER FOUR: WORDS AND HISTORY

1. *The Great American Novel* (Paris: Three Mountains Press, 1923). References are to the text included in *Imaginations*.
2. William Carlos Williams, 'In Praise of Marriage' (a review of Kenneth Rexroth's *The Phoenix and the Tortoise*), *Quarterly Review of Literature*, vol. II, no. 2 (1944) p. 147.
3. Kenneth Rexroth, *Assays* (Norfolk, Conn.: New Directions, 1961); see esp. 'The Influence of French Poetry on American', p. 153.
4. 'An Approach to the Poem', *English Institute Essays: 1947* (New York, 1948) p. 52.
5. *SL*, no. 94, p. 131.
6. Senior, op. cit., here refers to George W. Russell (AE), but the words apply precisely to Williams, especially in view of his insistence that 'imitation' is re-creation rather than copying. Senior quotes AE's *The Candle of Vision* (London: Macmillan, 1931) p. 120: 'The roots of human speech are the sound correspondences of powers which in their combination and interaction make up the universe.'
7. An excellent and respectful introduction to *The Great American Novel* is that by R.P. Blackmur in his edition of *American Short Novels* (New York: Thomas Y. Crowell, 1960) pp. 307–43. Also useful are Hugh Kenner's 'A Note on *The Great American Novel*' in his *Gnomon* (New York: McDowell Obolensky, 1958), and chapter 4 of Wagner, *The Prose of William Carlos Williams*.
8. *In the American Grain* (New York: Albert and Charles Boni, 1925) (see *Wallace* A9). The edition cited here is the 1939 edition, printed offset reduced from the original sheets and published in Norfolk, Connecticut, by the New Directions Publishing Co. The pages of Horace Gregory's introduction are not numbered. The connection between *IAG* and D.H. Lawrence's *Studies* is made by Guimond, op. cit., and others. Dijkstra links it to the Stieglitz group. Breslin, in his *William Carlos Williams: an American Artist* (New York: Oxford University Press, 1970), sees resemblances with Van Wyck Brooks's *America's Coming of Age* (1915), Waldo Frank's *Our America* (1923) as well as D. H. Lawrence, and Lewis Mumford's *The Golden Day* (1926).
9. Donald Davie, 'The Legacy of Fenimore Cooper', *Essays in Criticism*, vol. 9, no. 3 (1959) p. 223.
10. Edward Dahlberg, *Alms for Oblivion* (Minneapolis: University of Minnesota Press, 1964) p. 73.
11. D.H. Lawrence, 'American Heroes', *Nation*, no. 112 (14 April 1926) pp. 413–14.
12. Although he names a different source (*The Long Island Book*) for the Red Eric piece, Williams used for the two opening essays and some others the volumes of *Original Narratives of Early American History*, American Historical Association (New York: Charles Scribner's Sons), the Red Eric

and Columbus material coming from vol. I, *The Northmen, Columbus and Cabot* (1906).

13. Based on *Spanish Explorers in the Southern United States* (*Original Narratives in Early American History*, vol. 11, particularly 'The Narrative of the Expedition Hernando De Soto, by the Gentleman of Elvas', ch. 7f. Dating in Williams's essay differs from source throughout, by a margin of nine years. Of this *IAG* essay Williams noted: 'The chapter on De Soto was used by Hart Crane in "The Bridge"' (*IWWP*, 43). Breslin's account of *IAG*, one of the most illuminating, points out a major tendency, shared with Waldo Frank and the others, 'in these polemical works to see American history as developing out of a Freudian conflict between repression and liberation' (Breslin, op. cit., p. 88). Breslin also values Williams's sense of an American mythology and his recreation of American legendary heroes in such a way as to allow each to speak in his own voice: '... *In the American Grain* grows out of the tension between Williams's reverence for literal, individuating detail and his desire to discover mythic recurrences ...'.

14. Alan Holder, '*In the American Grain*: William Carlos Williams on the American Past', *American Quarterly*, vol. XIX, no. 3 (Fall 1967) pp. 499-515, esp. p. 509.

15. *SL*, no. 177, p. 276.

16. Benjamin T. Spencer, 'Doctor Williams' American Grain', *Tennessee Studies in Literature*, vol. VIII (1963) p. 6, suggests that *IAG* posits three 'Americas': (a) 'a kind of Platonic idea'; (b) 'a covert America intuited by poets like Poe and Whitman'; (c) 'an existential America'. According to Spencer, Williams thought Raleigh's sense of America was of the type (a).

17. Thomas Morton, *The New English Canaan*, ed. C.F. Adams, Jr. (Boston, Mass., 1883). Williams names the editor 'A.C. Adams'.

18. Apparently in response to references to her in *Autob*. Bryher in her own autobiography *The Heart to Artemis* (New York: Harcourt, Brace & World, 1962), says of Williams on this visit, 'his apparent hatred of his native land startled even us' (p. 218). Undoubtedly pro-American, Williams never hesitated to voice harsh criticism of his own country.

19. See especially Breslin, op. cit., pp. 117-21.

20. One shared by Hart Crane, who wrote to Waldo Frank on 21 November 1926 that *In the American Grain* was 'most important' and the view of Poe in it similar to that '*symbolized*' in 'The Tunnel' section of *The Bridge*. As noted in my *William Carlos Williams: the Critical Heritage*, Williams and Crane never met, but they began a literary connection in 1916 when Williams accepted some of Crane's poems for *Others*. Their literary relationship is fully explored in Joseph Evans Slate, 'William Carlos Williams, Hart Crane, and "The Virtue of History"', *Texas Studies in Language and Literature*, vol. VI (Winter 1965) pp. 486-511, which includes a detailed comparison of *In the American Grain* and *The Bridge*. In his introduction to *In the American Grain*, Horace Gregory finds a good handful of traces have carried over from that book into *The Bridge*.

21. *A Voyage to Pagany* (New York: Macaulay, 1928) (hereafter cited as *VP*).

22. Morley Callaghan, 'America Rediscovered', *New York Herald Tribune Books*, 7 October 1928, p. 4.

1. Whittemore, op. cit., p. 209.
2. Vivienne Koch, *William Carlos Williams* (Norfolk, Conn.: New Directions, 1950) p. 58.
3. 'You do not *copy* nature, you make something which is an *imitation* of nature — read your Aristotle again' (*SE*, 303).
4. *Contact* (1921) I, ii, 'Comment', unpaged.
5. See John C. Thirlwall, 'William Carlos Williams' *Paterson*: the Search for a Redeeming Language — A Personal Epic in Five Parts', *New Directions*, no. 17 (1961) p. 265ff.
6. Louis Zukofsky, 'American Poetry 1920-1930', *The Symposium*, vol. II (1931) p. 81. Reprinted in *Prepositions* (London: Rapp & Carroll, 1967) pp. 129-43.
7. *SL*, no. 73, p. 101. The original at Yale is not in itself a letter. Notes written on a punch-holed notebook sheet, it is dated 5 July 1928, and accompanied by a covering note not included in *SL*.
8. *An 'Objectivists' Anthology*, ed. Louis Zukofsky (Toulon: To Publishers, 1932). See *Prepositions*, op. cit., p. 21.
9. *Poetry*, vol. XXXIX (February 1931), an 'Objective' issue edited by Zukofsky.
10. Louis Zukofsky, *A*. The complete 24-part text of *A* has recently (1978) been published by University of California Press. 'A6' dates from 1930, the year in which Chatto & Windus published a retrospective *Imagist Anthology*.
11. Also in *Encyclopedia of Poetry and Poetics*, ed. Alex Preminger (Princeton, N.J.: Princeton University Press, 1965) p. 582. See *Autob.*, pp. 264-5.
12. A parallel of some interest occurs in the periodical *This Quarter*, vol. I, no. 2 (1925) in a poem by Robert Roe, a now forgotten poet who contributed also to *Poetry* and *transition*. Roe's poem, 'Meanings', reads in part:

> If you ask me for meanings
> I cannot give you any.
> I can only give you things.
> Everything its own meaning.

13. *transition* no. 19-20 (June 1930) p. 19.
14. *An 'Objectivists' Anthology*, '"Recencies" in Poetry', p. 22.
15. Ibid., p. 204.
16. *CP 21-31*, Preface, p. 2. At least one critic has interpreted this in the opposite way. Paul Mariani, in his succinct account of the book's critical reception says: 'the judgment of Williams as the classical imagist broadened (thanks to Wallace Stevens) to include the view of Williams as "antipoetic" romantic. It was a category which subsequent critics pursued with unrelenting zeal for twenty years . . .' — *William Carlos Williams: the Poet and his Critics* (Chicago: American Library Association, 1975) p. 39. Certainly, Mariani is correct about the effect of Stevens's remarks. Stevens himself, on the other hand, may be seen as using the term to characterize Williams's attempted anti-romanticism. In other words, Stevens's actual

view of Williams may have been nearer to that expressed by the Objectivist, Carl Rakosi.

17. *Little Review* (final number), vol. XII, no. 2 (May 1929) p. 88.
18. William Carlos Williams, *The Embodiment of Knowledge* (New York: New Directions, 1974). Five essays at the end of the book date from much earlier, from Williams's earliest career.
19. Riddel, op. cit., p. 126n. See also p. 258 and 258n.
20. Townley, op. cit., pp. 160-3.
21. Paul Mariani, review of *The Embodiment of Knowledge* in *William Carlos Williams Newsletter*, vol. I, no. 1 (Fall 1975) pp. 9-12.

NOTES TO CHAPTER SIX: INTO THE THIRTIES

1. Fernand Léger, 'The Esthetics of the Machine', *Little Review*, vol. IX, nos 3 and 4 (1923-4) pp. 45-9; 55-8; and 'A New Realism — the Object', *Little Review*, vol. XI, no. 2 (Winter 1926) pp. 7-8.
2. *The Wedge* (Cummington, Mass.: The Cummington Press, 1944) Introduction.
3. 'The New Poetical Economy', *Poetry*, vol. XLIV (4 July 1934) p. 221.
4. See *IWWP*, p. 56; *Wallace* C50; Guimond, op. cit., pp. 96-7.
5. Linda Welshimer Wagner, *The Poems of William Carlos Williams: A Critical Study* (Middletown, Conn.: Wesleyan University Press) p. 26.
6. Parker Tyler, 'The Poet of *Paterson* Book One', *Briarcliff Quarterly*, vol. III (October 1946) pp. 168-75.
7. Letter to Thomas Edward Francis, 4 January 1961 (Yale Collection).
8. 'Symposium on Writing', *The Golden Goose*, series 3, no. 2 (Autumn 1951) p. 94.
9. A remark by Neil Myers is worth noting, in that it suggests the poem may not, after all, be untypical. Myers sees one development in Williams's poetry after *Spring and All* as 'developing "measured" looseness and flow of structure and intense emotionality of theme — in long, expansive poems like *An Elegy for D.H. Lawrence* ...' — see Myers, 'William Carlos Williams' *Spring and All*', *Modern Language Quarterly*, vol. 26, no. 2 (June 1965) pp. 285-301. It is quoted here from *William Carlos Williams: a Critical Anthology*, ed. Charles Tomlinson (Harmondsworth, Middx: Penguin Books, 1972) p. 231.
10. *New Directions in Poetry and Prose* (Norfolk, Conn.: New Directions, 1936). Reprinted as appendix to Wagner (see note 5 above).
11. John L. Thirlwall, 'Two Cities: Paris and Paterson', *Massachusetts Review*, vol. III, no. 2 (Winter 1962) p. 285.
12. *The Complete Collected Poems of William Carlos Williams 1906-1938* (Norfolk, Conn.: New Directions, 1938). Horton's review appeared in the *New Republic* (21 December 1938) pp. 156-8.
13. Horace Gregory, *New York Herald Tribune Books*, 5 February 1939; Yvor Winters, 'Poetry of Feeling', *Kenyon Review*, vol. I (Winter 1939) pp. 104-7. The remaining reviews are either summarized in Mariani, or are included in my *William Carlos Williams: the Critical Heritage*.
14. A.N. Whitehead, *Adventures of Ideas* (New York: Macmillan) p. 355.

These words are quoted by Charles Olson, *A Bibliography for Ed Dorn* (San Francisco: Four Seasons Foundation, 1964) p. 9. See also Williams's poem 'The Pink Church' (*CLP* 157):

> O Dewey! (John)
> O James! (William)
> O Whitehead
>
> — above and beyond
> your teaching stands
> the Pink Church ...

15. Carol C. Donley, '"A little touch of / Einstein in the night": Williams' Early Exposure to Themes of Relativity', *William Carlos Williams Newsletter*, vol. IV no. 1 (Spring 1978) pp. 10-13, gives a detailed context for the writing of this poem.
16. *White Mule* (Norfolk, Conn.: New Directions, 1937).
17. *Life Along the Passaic River* (Norfolk, Conn.: New Directions, 1938).
18. *Many Loves and Other Plays* (Norfolk, Conn.: New Directions, 1961) pp. 1-104.
19. Guimond, op. cit., p. 107.

NOTES TO CHAPTER SEVEN: POEM AS MACHINE

1. For details see Bibliography.
2. *SE*, pp. 196-218, closing paragraphs (misplaced) p. 230. First published in *Twice a Year*, no. 2 (Spring-Summer 1939) pp. 53-78. William's weather is not unlike that of Stevens, climate of opinion/feeling, cultural ethos.
3. Introduction to *The Wedge* is in *SE*, pp. 255-7, and also in *CLP*, pp. 3-5.
4. Stanzas reversed in Buffalo ms, giving a more logical sequence, but less power.
5. 'Two New Books by Kenneth Rexroth', *Poetry*, vol. XC, no. 3 (June 1957) esp. pp. 187, 189.
6. Ernest Fenollosa, *The Chinese Written Character as a Medium for Poetry*, ed. Ezra Pound (San Francisco: City Lights n.d.) p. 16.
7. *Pictures from Brueghel and Other Poems* (Norfolk, Conn.: New Directions 1962), including *The Desert Music* and *Journey to Love* (New York: Random House, 1954 and 1955).
8. Randall Jarrell, 'Poetry in War and Peace', *Partisan Review*, vol. 12, no. 1 (1945) pp. 122-3.
9. Unsigned review, 'An American Poet', *Times Literary Supplement*, no. 2 564 (23 March 1951) p. 178.
10. David Daiches, in *Yale Review*, vol. 41, no. 1 (Autumn 1951) pp. 153-5.
11. Gorham B. Munson, *Destinations: A Canvass of American Literature since 1900* (New York: J.H. Sears, 1928) p. 125.
12. Unpublished letter of 6 April 1943, at Buffalo.
13. In the Buffalo ms. all but the first stanza has pencilled notations of letter count (hand undetermined).

14. Buffalo has a number of drafts of this poem, one of which Wagner, *The Poems of William Carlos Williams*, p. 54, compares with the final version, providing a fine specimen of Williams's working methods.
15. William Carlos Williams, *Two Poems* and William Zorach, *Two Drawings*, pamphlet no. 1 (New York: The Stovepipe Press, 1937).
16. *The Pink Church* (Columbus, Ohio: Golden Goose Press, 1949).

NOTES TO CHAPTER EIGHT: 'PATERSON': THE FIRST STAGES

1. *The Dial*, vol. LXXXII, no. 2 (February 1927) pp. 91–3.
2. An unpublished letter to Viola Baxter Jordan dated 11 June 1914 contains a passing remark on 'Handsome Mr Towne — or any other city . . .' (*Yale*).
3. Included in the annual *New Directions* (1937).
4. Peterfreund, op. cit.
5. Buffalo typescript headed 'NOTES FOR A LYRIC DRAMA' reads:

> These are studies to be used in plays — if they can be written — or operas — if the music can be found. Love is the theme through most of them, more or less formally treated. As contrasted with that there are bits of conve[r]sation studied for the rhythmic regularity of the words according to current colloquial conversation — more or less.
> [N]o particular play is intended. All that is intended is to try out the language for its sound. It's [*sic*] appeal to the ear is object enough in most cases —
> Or something else — it doesn't matter; something unforseen [*sic*]. the pleasure is in the abandon of the writing to its — to the sensitivities of the ear and the imagination, playing. Therefore, a play.

An important amplification of this (*Buffalo*) is included as Appendix II to Thirlwall's essay in *New Directions*, no. 17, pp. 305–6. See also *SL*, no. 161, p. 251 to Kenneth Burke in 1947, and *SL*, no. 215, pp. 333–4 to Henry Wells, especially para. 4, which includes a possible definition of what it is to 'write carelessly'.
6. *SL*, no. 13, pp. 23–4.
7. Louis Zukofsky, *A1–12* (London, 1967) 'A6', p. 36.
8. *Paterson, Book I* (New York, 1946); *Wallace* A24.
9. *Paterson, I–V* (New York: New Directions, 1963). Useful summaries of Book I–IV are contained in Thirlwall's long essay in *New Directions*, no. 17 (Appendix I, pp. 299–304).
10. Randall Jarrell, 'The Poet and his Public' *Partisan Review*, vol. XIII (Sep–Oct 1946) pp. 493–8. Reprinted in *Poetry and the Age* (New York: Vintage Books 1953) pp. 208–12.
11. See 'Choral: The Pink Church'. Whitehead is mentioned at least twice in drafts related to *P IV* (*Yale*, 189/3). See also letters to Kenneth Burke and Horace Gregory on Dewey (*SL*, nos 95, p. 145, and 138, p. 224) and *Autob.*, p. 391.
12. Sister M. Bernetta Quinn, *The Metamorphic Tradition in Modern Poetry* (New Brunswick, N.J.: Rutgers University Press, 1955) ch.3: 'William

Carlos Williams: a Testament of Perpetual Change'.
13. Ibid., p. 90.
14. Ibid, p. 90, and Thirlwall, *New Directions*, no. 17, p. 275, who connects
    this with the spelling 'Patterson' ('patters on', chatterer; also the name of a
    town in New York State where Hart Crane worked on 'The Bridge') used in
    An Early Martyr. The following passage occurs in Lyle's letter dated 30
    November 1938: 'Schiller defines a per-son as continuity. Person (L.
    Peersona [*sic*] . . . mask. Per, through plus L. sonare to sound'. On 11
    December 1940, Lyle wrote: 'Paterson . . . which is good as a CITY OF
    THE SUN' (*Yale*).
15. A cancelled passage in *Yale* 186/3 supports this, expressing the cyclical view
    implicit in Williams's echo of Whitman/Eliot (*P*, 11, bottom; also relevant,
    the closing paragraph of 'Descent', *IAG*, 215.) The draft reads:

> — today is tomorrow is yesterday
> is time reversed, circuitous.

16. 'Notes from a Talk on Poetry', op. cit., pp. 211-16.
17. T.E. Hulme, *Speculations*, op. cit.; p. 146.
18. See Patrick Renshaw, op. cit., p. 112: 'Known as the "Lyons of America",
    Paterson was a silk-weaving city.' Thus, from its very opening *Paterson* is
    related to the strike of 1913, and the workers. This deleted passage is also a
    reminder of the scene in *The Great Gatsby* in which Daisy weeps over
    Gatsby's silk shirts, token of his American success.
19. Denise Levertov, *The Jacob's Ladder* (New York: New Directions, 1961)
    p. 44.
20. David Lyle letter of 1 December 1938, expanded 9 April 1939 (*Yale*, p. 6).
    In the late 1930s and early 1940s Williams associated, and corresponded,
    with David Lyle. At one stage he intended to adapt many of Lyle's letters
    for use in *Paterson*. Perusal of a Yale file of the letters reveals definite
    kinship between the tone and method of *Paterson* and Lyle's epistolary
    manner. Broadly interested in sociology, philosophy, economics and
    mathematics, Lyle tends to use his findings in these fields somewhat
    unsystematically, though keeping in mind certain of his own central
    attitudes.
21. And see Mary Ellen Solt, 'William Carlos Williams: Idiom and Structure',
    Massachusetts Review, vol. III, no. 2 (Winter 1962) pp. 304-18, esp. p. 316.
22. Thirlwall, *New Directions*, no. 17, p. 267.
23. The name 'Pischak' is given various forms, this one occurring in 'Notes in
    Diary Form' (*SE*). In his earlier work Williams habitually associated *woman*
    and *city*. In 'The Flower' (*CEP*, 236) the city is the flower, but also woman.
    One title considered for *Autobiography* was *Root, Branch and Flower* (*SL*,
    no. 188, p. 295.)
24. Jung, in his *Mysterium Coniunctionis* (London: Routledge & Kegan Paul,
    1963; English trans. by R.F.C. Hull) cites a source which claims that the first
    men were made from the sweat of Ymir (p. 40, nn. 228, 229). Several
    instances are given of sweat as a generative source.
25. R.S. Lynd and Helen Merrell Lynd, *Middletown: a Study in Contemporary
    American Culture* (New York: Harcourt, Brace, 1929), and *Middletown in*

Transition: a Study in Cultural Conflicts (New York: Harcourt, Brace, 1937). In a letter to the present writer date 10 November 1967, Mrs Florence H. Williams notes that: 'Muncie is a small city in Indiana that was chosen in a nation wide contest every year — as outstanding on various grounds. The cleanest, the most attractive, — etc., etc. — there are various classes. . . . I think Bill just liked the sound of the name Mumsie!'

26. Exact source not located, but a number of close resemblances, e.g. *National Geographic*, vol. XVII (1906) p. 344, and vol. XLIX (June 1926) p. 716: 'The "Better Halves" of a Mangebetou Chief, Lined Up in Order of Preference.' Crouched as if seated on a log, the youngest at the top, they resemble a growing tree.

27. Noah Davis, *The Narrative of a Coloured Man* (Boston, 1859). Part of another draft (*Yale*, 185) reads: 'Group Poem: Sunday School Class yell . . . in the year of Grace, 1933'. One should note Williams's remark to Marianne Moore, 'Heaven seems frankly impossible' (*SL*, 147). Walter Scott Peterson, *An Approach to Paterson* (New Haven, Conn.: Yale University Press, 1967), suggests a connection with Biblical Noah and with Noah Webster, master of the American idiom.

28. Joseph Evans Slate, 'William Carlos Williams, Hart Crane, and "The Virtue of History"' op. cit., shows that this prose passage is adapted from Charles P. Longwell's *Historic Totowa Falls and Vicinity in Art Literature Events* (Paterson, N.J.: The Call Printing and Publishing Co., 1942) pp. 36–40. Slate discusses Williams's recognition of a connection between his own work and Crane's.

29. See Quinn, *The Metamorphic Tradition*, p. 99, on 'source' and 'genesis', also for the text of Patch's brief speech, quoted from Jenny Marsh Parker, *Rochester: a Story Historical* (Rochester, N.Y.: Scranton, Wetmore and Co., 1884).

30. *Poetry and the Age*, p. 208.

31. In a notebook draft of *Paterson III* (Buffalo) there are variants of this motif: 'the aversion of scientific men to learning something new' (attributed to Freud) and as Anatole France put it, in Freud's time, '*Les Savants ne sont pas curieux*'. Williams remarked to Harvey Breit: 'But isn't poetry, at its most significant, the very antithesis of the academy?' (*SL*, no. 130, p. 194).

32. See Cary Nelson, '"Suffused-Encircling Shapes of Mind": Inhabited Space in Williams', *Journal of Modern Literature* (May 1971) pp. 549-64, on the significance of flowers and flowering.

33. A number of small, private or semi-private jokes are hidden in the *Paterson* text. For this letter in the first edition of *Paterson I*, Williams used the initials T.J., possibly echoing Pound's 'Canto XXXI', where a number of Jefferson's letters are quoted, Jefferson himself referred to throughout as 'T.J.'.

34. Breslin, op. cit., p. 184, sensing the joy in these passages, reads them as a joke, as part of Paterson's refusal to take himself seriously in any one dimension.

35. A parenthesis on p. 40 of Buffalo notebook, which contains drafts for *Paterson III* and *IV*, reads: '(Pound's story of my being interested in the loam whereas he wanted the finished product)'.

36. Buffalo draft sheet: 'End with the monastery in the country as compen-

sation or corellative [*sic*] of (to?) the city and its draggle.' Benjamin Sankey, *A Companion to William Carlos Williams's 'Paterson'* (Berkeley: University of California Press, 1971) p. 66, connects this with a passage from *Autob.* p. 119, or Williams's reactions after visiting the Comédie Francaise.

37. This complements the passage from Edith Hamilton which Wagner, Weatherhead and others have applied to Williams, to the effect that the Greeks believed in simplicity, clarity and the beauty of common things. See Edith Hamilton, *The Greek Way to Western Civilization* (New York: W.W. Norton, 1948) pp. 40-51.

NOTES TO CHAPTER NINE: 'PATERSON II'

1. *Paterson (Book Two)* (Norfolk, Conn.: New Directions, 1948).
2. Thoreau, *Complete Works*, vol. X (Boston and New York: Houghton Mifflin, Riverside Press, 1906) p. 351, quoted in Tanner, op. cit., pp. 47-8.
3. Yale drafts show that, while working on *Paterson*, Williams read, or at least consulted, Henry Bamford Parkes, *The American Experience* (New York, 1947). Source of this exchange may be found in Parkes's ch. 3 (New York: Vintage Books paperback edn., 1959) p. 49. The original source, quoted by parkes, is Benjamin Franklin's 'Information to those who would remove to America' (1782). Williams adapts it to suggest criticism of America, possibly by an expatriate American.
4. Quinn, *The Metamorphic Tradition*, p. 93, and William Nelson, *History of the City of Paterson and the County of Passaic*, vol. II (Paterson, N.J. Press, Printing and Publishing Co., 1901), pp. 499-500.
5. '. . . Hamilton, at a New York dinner, replied to some democratic sentiment by striking his hand sharply on the table and saying, "Your people, sir — your people is a great *beast*!"' — Henry Adams, *History of the United States of America during the First Administration of Thomas Jefferson*, vol. I (New York, 1890) p. 85.
6. Edgar F. Racey, 'Pound and Williams: The Poet as Renewer', *Bucknell Review*, vol. XI (March 1963) pp. 21-30.
7. Sankey, op. cit., p. 88.
8. Buffalo draft locates the particular church in Spain, seen (it is not clear by whom) 'going by bus from Arenas de San Pedro . . . to Avila'.

    Williams is not so much attacking industry as such. His target is uncontrolled private enterprise. Lilienthal had regarded the Tennessee Valley Authority both as an experiment in decentralization and as against private monopoly. Subsequently, during the period when the U.S.A. was the only country with an operable A-bomb, he was first Chairman of the Atomic Energy Commission.

    Williams remarked in a letter to Srinivas Rayaprol that, 'after all a bomb isn't unique and has existed in our wishes for centuries' (*SL*, no. 181, p. 282).
9. Buffalo draft: 'The birds and the trees listened or didn't / listen — not even the dog. Understand by that what was meant when it said St Francis spoke to the creature, going (?) about him'.

10. Robert Lowell, *Nation* (19 June 1948) p. 692.
11. Brooks Adams, *The Law of Civilization and Decay*, 2nd edn (London: Macmillan, 1896). This was the specific edition Pound recommended to Williams.
12. Writing to Thomas Edward Francis in 1961 (unpublished letter, *Yale*), Williams said: 'This poem from the viewpoint of the complete art is the finest I have ever made since my discovery of the American idiom and the variable foot. That ends the theoretical controversy as to the structural poem . . .' (dated typed sheet 1/461). See also *Paris Review*, vol. 32 (Summer − Fall 1964) pp. 117, 118, 119, 120, and *IWWP*, pp. 80-2.
13. Wallace Stevens, *Collected Poems* (New York: Alfred A. Knopf, 1955) p. 215.
14. 'She' is related to the figure in the De Soto essay (*IAG*, see above).
15. Note in *Yale* 186/1:

> The poet's weapon is metaphore [*sic*] his strength is marriage. Marry us, the stream cries. Marry us, give us blood. We are cold, we are prone, we crawls [*sic*] and have prickles − give us the wormth [*sic*] of your invention we are prone. Honor us with metaphore [*sic*] closely fastened to our interness − or else! Marry, marry, marry, marry! the water pours down. She was married with empty words and at the magic sound of my stream threw herself upon the bed − a pitiful gesture of a tuned mind − lost among the words:
>   Invent, discover or nothing clear will surmount the drumming in your head. Nothing clear. There is nothing clear, He fled! pursued by the roar!

To this is added the pencil note 'End of Part II'.
16. Compare Lynd and Lynd, *Middletown: a Study*, p. 252.
17. Whittemore, op. cit., p. 294.

NOTES TO CHAPTER TEN: 'PATERSON III'

1. Lyle's letter of 30 November 1938: 'To be . . . healthy and whole . . . depends on what we can truly believe of a superhistorial . . . or Atman . . . or great (ether) wind . . . and the various immovable spaces, immovable ethers . . . nets or webs or Middletowns of material . . . or thotstuff';
    Other points in the letter: mention of Lawrence's 'dark otherness', of the hurricane wreckage of a telephone system in north-east USA, and of what can be achieved by walking, dancing.
2. 'Book III / the theme is love tenderness' (*Yale* draft).
3. 'Lambert castle, the lookout and pleasure spot where the Ryerson girls used to go for their great parties − fresh from painting school: now the public convenience center: where the preacher has pulled a few benches together for Sunday service' (*Yale*, 185). See also *P*, 21.
4. George Zabriskie, 'The Geography of *Paterson*', *Perspective*, vol. VI, no. 4 (Autumn 1953) p. 212.
5. Lambert appears to contribute to the character of Joe Stecher in *In the*

Money, while Gurlie's name may well derive from Elizabeth Gurley Flynn of the International Workers of the World (mentioned *P*, 122).

6. Glauco Gambon, *The Inclusive Flame: Studies in Modern American Poetry* (Bloomington, Ind.: Indiana University Press, 1965) p. 203.

7. While Williams was working on *Paterson III* Lyle wrote to him of a book salesman who had said: 'There is dead silence all over this country' (2 April 1948; *Yale*).

8. Jung (ch. 8, n.24), p. 40, n.229 — 'they conceive in the baths' (*P*, 128, 129).

9. Nelson, op. cit., pp. 37–8.

10. Whitehead, op. cit., pp. 290, 271.

11. Jarrell, *Poetry and the Age*, p. 207.

12. Whitehead, op. cit., p. 209.

13. See, for example, 'An Approach to the Poem', *English Institute Essays, 1947* (New York, 1948).

14. The passage beginning with the last two lines on *P*, 142.

15. See *KH*, p. 11, italicized paragraph.

16. Jung, op. cit., p. 227.

NOTES TO CHAPTER ELEVEN: 'PATERSON IV'

1. 'The Form, an idyl of Theocritus, a perverted but still recognizable "happy" picture of the past, is there' (*SL*, no. 195, p. 305). Breslin, op. cit., p. 201, characterizes this idyll as taking us 'down into some of the poem's most hellish experiences'.

2. Thirlwall suggests Phyllis is Dolores Mary Pischak (*New Directions*, no. 17, p. 267). Jarrell, in his damning review objects to the literariness of the Corydon–Phyllis episode in a supposedly anti-literary work (*Poetry and the Age*, pp. 236–40).

3. Shapiro, op. cit., p. 149, suggests that Williams's definition of 'divine' is near 'drunken'.

4. Edith Hamilton, *Mythology* (Boston, Mass.: Mentor Books, 1942) p. 41.

5. *P*, 193; Jung, op. cit., p. 40, n.229.

6. Peterson, op. cit., p. 193.

7. Allen Ginsberg, *Howl and Other Poems* (San Francisco: City Lights Books, 1956) Introduction, pp. 7–8.

8. In Buffalo rough draft of a talk, 'The Attack on Credit Monopoly', Williams speaks of credit control as 'the gist of the economics of the power age'. Williams's attitude is largely that of Walters's advertisement (*P*, 213), for government control rather than private exploitation. He proposes Social Credit as a guard against Labour or Fascism. His brief analysis of the pro-social to anti-social trend of completely uncontrolled individualism is similar to Hermann Levy's in *Economic Liberalism* (London: Macmillan, 1913).

9. Sankey, op. cit., p. 201, notes Williams's apparent intention, at some stage, to feature Whitman in this section of *Paterson*. He quotes a passage from Williams's essay on *Leaves of Grass*, which pictures Whitman on the New Jersey shore listening to the 'new language'.

NOTES TO CHAPTER TWELVE: 'PATERSON V'

1. Excerpted from a letter to Robert McGregor of New Directions, dated 16 May 1958, paras 2 and 3. The 'new dimension' is, in an important way, aesthetic and it is worth noting that drafts of *Paterson I–IV* contain much more directly concerning art than do the unpublished texts.
2. *Paris Review*, vol. 32, (Summer–Fall 1964) p. 127. The identical shaping had been used in a periodical of the twenties with which Williams was familiar. Tony Palmer's 'Crinky Coeur' contains the lines:

— swagger aslant slew of wind.

   In the same issue of *This Quarter*, vol. I (1925) no. 2, 'Immigrant', a poem by Eugene Jolas, is made with a three-tiered line.
3. Miller, *Poets of Reality*, op. cit., pp. 309, 310.
4. James J. Rorimer, *The Unicorn Tapestries at the Cloisters* (New York: Metropolitan Museum of Art, 4th edn, rev., 1962).
5. Louis L. Martz, *The Poem of the Mind: Essays on Poetry English and American* (New York: Oxford University Press, 1966) p. 156.
6. Philippe Soupault, *Les Dernières Nuits de Paris*, translated by William Carlos Williams as *The Last Nights of Paris*, with an introduction by Matthew Josephson (New York: Macaulay, 1929).
7. Gilbert Sorrentino, 'Bordertown' (Yale Williams mss.)
8. In American, 'horn' has not the sexual significance it has in English, but these lines correspond to an unquoted phrase of Sorrentino's: 'woman's face serene in the anal violation'.
9. Hidden in this passage may be a reference to the fact that in his early St Elizabeth days Pound needed medical attention for his big toe over a considerable period.

NOTES TO CHAPTER THIRTEEN: 'THE ODORLESS FLOWER'

1. 'Measure', *Spectrum* vol. III, no. 3 (Fall 1959) pp. 152–3.
2. Charles Olson, *Projective Verse* (Brooklyn N.Y.: Totem Press, 1959); reprinted in Olson's more readily available *Selected Writings* (New York: New Directions, 1966) and partially in *Autob*.
3. In America, the physiological approach to versification dates back as far as Oliver Wendell Holmes's essay, 'The Physiology of Versification'. See Michael Weaver, 'Measure and its Propaganda', *Cambridge Annual*, 1964, p. 16.
4. Roy Harvey Pearce, *The Continuity of American Poetry* (Princeton, N.J.:

Princeton University Press, 1961) esp. pp. 344-8.

5. See Sherman Paul, *The Music of Survival*, op. cit., a book-length study of the poem.

6. Wagner, *The Poems of William Carlos Williams*, pp. 128-9, has an excellent discussion of this poem's structure. Note also the activation of 'the flowers', both backward and forward through the text.

NOTES TO CHAPTER FOURTEEN: CONCLUSION

1. 'The So-Called So-Called', *Patroon*, vol. I, no. 1 (May 1937) p. 1.

2. '... prosodic values should rightly be seen as only relatively true ...', *Poetry*, vol. XLIV, no. 4 (July 1934) pp. 221-2.

3. *Literary Essays*, p. 50.

4. Quinn, *The Metamorphic Tradition*, Introduction.

Select Bibliography

1. *Primary*

Wallace, Emily Mitchell, *A Bibliography of William Carlos Williams* (Middletown, Conn.: Wesleyan University Press, 1968).

Williams, William Carlos, *The Embodiment of Knowledge*, ed. Ron Loewinsohn (New York: New Directions, 1975).

———, *Imaginations*, ed. Webster Schott (New York: New Directions, 1971).

———, *A Recognizable Image: William Carlos Williams on Art and Artists*, ed. Bram Dijkstra (New York: New Directions, 1979).

2. *Secondary*

Adams, Brooks, *The Law of Civilization and Decay*, 2nd edn (London: Macmillan, 1896).

Breslin, James E., *William Carlos Williams: an American Artist* (New York: Oxford University Press, 1970).

Burke, Kenneth, 'Heaven's First Law', *Dial*, vol. LXXII (February 1922) pp. 197-200; reprinted in *William Carlos Williams: a Collection of Critical Essays*, ed. J. Hillis Miller.

———, 'The Methods of William Carlos Williams', *Dial*, vol. LXXXII (February 1927) pp. 94-8.

———, 'William Carlos Williams, 1883-1963', *New York Review of Books* (Spring-Summer 1963) pp. 45-7; reprinted in *William Carlos Williams: a Collection of Critical Essays*, ed. J. Hillis Miller.

Conarroe, Joel Osborne, *William Carlos Williams' 'Paterson': Language and Landscape* (Philadelphia: University of Pennsylvania Press, 1970).

Dewey, John, 'Americanism and Localism', *Dial*, vol. LXVIII (June 1920) pp. 684-8.

Dijkstra, Bram, *The Hieroglyphics of a New Speech: Cubism, Stieglitz, and the Early Poetry of William Carlos Williams* (Princeton, N.J.: Princeton University Press, 1969).

Doyle, Charles (ed.), *William Carlos Williams: the Critical Heritage* (London: Routledge & Kegan Paul, 1980).

Fields, Kenneth, 'The Free Verse of Yvor Winters and William Carlos Williams', *Southern Review*, vol. III (Summer 1967) pp. 764-7.

Guimond, James, *The Art of William Carlos Williams: a Discovery and Possession of America* (Urbana: University of Illinois Press, 1968).

Holder, Alan, 'In the American Grain: William Carlos Williams on the American Past', *American Quarterly*, vol. XIX, no. 3 (Fall 1967) pp. 499-515.

Kenner, Hugh, 'Columbus' Log Book', *Poetry*, vol. XCII (June 1958) pp. 174-8.

———, *A Homemade World: the American Modernist Writers* (New York: Alfred A. Knopf, 1975).

——, *The Pound Era* (Berkeley and Los Angeleş: University of California Press, 1971).

Koch, Vivienne, *William Carlos Williams* (Norfolk, Conn.: New Directions, 1950).

Léger, Fernand, 'The Esthetics of the Machine', *Little Review*, vol. IX, nos 3 and 4 (1923–4) pp. 45–9, 55–8.

——, 'A New Realism — the Object', *Little Review*, vol. XI, no. 2 (Winter 1926) pp. 7–8.

Litz, A. Walton, 'William Carlos Williams', *The Literary Heritage of New Jersey*, ed. Nathaniel Burt, Lawrence B. Holland and A. Walton Litz (New Brunswick, N.J.: Rutgers University Press, 1964) pp. 83–130.

Lynd, Robert S. and Lynd, Helen Merrell, *Middletown: a Study in Contemporary American Culture* (New York: Harcourt, Brace, 1929).

——, *Middletown in Transition: a Study in Cultural Conflicts* (New York: Harcourt, Brace, 1937).

McAlmon, Robert, *Being Geniuses Together* (London: Secker & Warburg, 1938); rev. edn and with supplementary chapters by Kay Boyle (Garden City, N.Y.: Doubleday, 1968).

Mariani, Paul, *William Carlos Williams: the Poet and his Critics* (Chicago: American Library Association, 1975).

Martz, Louis L., '*Paterson*: a Plan for Action', *Journal of Modern Literature*, vol. I, no. 4 (May 1971) pp. 513–22.

——, *The Poem of the Mind: Essays on Poetry, English and American* (New York: Oxford University Press, 1966) chs VII and VIII.

Mazzaro, Jerome, *William Carlos Williams: the Later Poems* (Ithaca, N.Y.: Cornell University Press, 1973).

Miller, J. Hillis, *Poets of Reality: Six Twentieth-Century Writers* (Cambridge, Mass.: Belknap Press of Harvard University Press, 1966).

—— (ed.), *William Carlos Williams: a Collection of Critical Essays* (Englewood Cliffs, N.J.: Prentice-Hall, 1966).

——, 'Williams' *Spring and All* and the Progress of Poetry', *Daedalus*, vol. 99 (Spring 1970) pp. 405–34.

Moore, Marianne, 'Three Essays on Williams', in J. Hillis Miller (ed.), *William Carlos Williams: a Collection of Critical Essays*, pp. 37–46; reprinted from *Contact* (first series), *Dial* (March 1927) and *Poetry* (May 1934).

Mottram, Eric, 'The Making of Paterson', *Stand*, vol. 7, no. 3 (1965) pp. 17–34.

Munson, Gorham B., *Destinations: a Canvass of American Literature since 1900* (New York: J.H. Sears, 1928).

Myers, Neil, 'William Carlos Williams' *Spring and All*', *Modern Language Quarterly*, vol. 26, no. 2 (June 1965) pp. 285–301.

Nelson, Cary, 'Suffused-Encircling Shapes of Mind: Inhabited Space in Williams', *Journal of Modern Literature*, vol. I, no. 4 (May 1971) pp. 549–64.

Nelson, William and Shriner, Charles A., *A History of Paterson and its Environs* (Paterson, N.J.: The Press Printing and Publishing Co., 1901).

Nelson, William and Shriner, Charles A., *A History of Paterson and its Environs* (New York: Lewis Historical Publishing Co., 1920) 2 vols.

Olson, Charles, *Projective Verse* (Brooklyn, N.Y.: Totem Press, 1959); reprinted from *Poetry New York* (1950) and reprinted in Olson's *Selected Writings* (New York: New Directions, 1966).

Original Narratives of Early American History, reproduced under the auspices of the American Historical Association, gen. ed. J.F. Jameson (New York: Charles Scribner's Sons) 18 vols. See especially vol. I (1906), vol. II (1907), vol. IV (1907); also vols XV and XVII.

Ostrom, Alan, *The Poetic World of William Carlos Williams* (Carbondale and Edwardsville: Southern Illinois University Press, 1966).

Parkes, Henry Bamford, *The American Experience* (New York: Vintage Books, 1959).

Paul, Sherman, *The Music of Survival: a Biography of a Poem by William Carlos Williams* (Urbana: University of Illinois, 1968).

_____, 'A Sketch-book of the Artist in his Thirty-fourth Year: William Carlos Williams' *Kora in Hell: Improvisations*', in *The Shaken Realist*, ed. Melvin J. Friedman and John B. Vickery (Baton Rouge: Louisiana State University Press, 1970) pp. 21-44.

Peterfreund, Stuart, 'Keats's Influence on William Carlos Williams', *William Carlos Williams Newsletter*, vol. III, no. 1 (Spring 1977) pp. 8-14.

Peterson, Walter Scott, *An Approach to Paterson* (New Haven, Conn.: Yale University Press, 1967).

Quinn, Sister M. Bernetta, *The Metamorphic Tradition in Modern Poetry* (New Brunswick, N.J.: Rutgers University Press, 1955).

_____, '*Paterson*: Listening to Landscape', in *Modern American Poetry : Essays in Criticism*, ed. Jerome Mazzaro (New York: McKay, 1970) pp. 116-54.

_____, '*Paterson*: Landscape and Dream', *Journal of Modern Literature*, vol. I, no. 4 (May 1971) pp. 523-48.

Rexroth, Kenneth, 'The Influence of French Poetry on American' and 'A Public Letter for William Carlos Williams' Seventy-fifth Birthday', *Assays* (Norfolk, Conn.: New Directions, 1961) pp. 143-74, 202-5.

Riddel, Joseph N., *The Inverted Bell: Modernism and the Counter-Poetics of William Carlos Williams* (Baton Rouge: Louisiana State University Press, 1974).

Rorimer, James J., *The Unicorn Tapestries at the Cloisters* (New York: Metropolitan Museum of Art, 4th edn, rev. 1962).

Rosenthal, M.L., *A William Carlos Williams Reader* (New York: New Directions, 1967).

Sankey, Benjamin, *A Companion to William Carlos Williams's 'Paterson'* (Berkeley: University of California Press, 1971).

Senior, John, *The Way Down and Out: the Occult in Symbolist Literature* (Ithaca, N.Y.: Cornell University Press, 1959).

Shapiro, Karl, *In Defense of Ignorance* (New York: Random House, 1965).

_____, *To Abolish Children and Other Essays* (Chicago: Quadrangle, 1968).

Slate, Joseph Evans, 'William Carlos Williams, Hart Crane, and "The Virtue of History"', *Texas Studies in Language and Literature*, vol. VI (Winter 1965) pp. 486-511.

_____, 'Kora in Opacity: Williams' Improvisations', *Journal of Modern Literature*, vol. I, no. 4 (May 1971) pp. 463-76.

Sutton, Walter, *American Free Verse: the Modern Revolution in Poetry* (New York: New Directions, 1973) pp. 118-51.

Tanner, Tony, *The Reign of Wonder: Naivety and Reality in American Literature* (Cambridge: Cambridge University Press, 1965).

Taupin, René, *L'Influence du Symbolisme Français sur la Poésie Américaine* (Paris: H. Champion, 1929).

Thirlwall, John C. (ed.), 'The Lost Poems of William Carlos Williams', *New Directions*, no. 16 (1957) pp. 3-45.

——, 'William Carlos Williams' "*Paterson*": the Search for a Redeeming Language — a Personal Epic in Five Parts', *New Directions*, no. 17 (1961) pp. 252-310.

Tomlinson, Charles, 'Dr. Williams' Practice', *Encounter*, November 1967, pp. 66-70.

—— (ed.), *William Carlos Williams: a Critical Anthology* (Harmondsworth: Penguin, 1972).

Townley, Rod, *The Early Poetry of William Carlos Williams* (Ithaca, N.Y.: Cornell University Press, 1975).

Wagner, Linda Welshimer, *The Poems of William Carlos Williams: a Critical Study* (Middletown, Conn.: Wesleyan University Press, 1964).

——, *The Prose of William Carlos Williams: a Critical Study* (Middletown, Conn.: Wesleyan University Press, 1970).

Weatherhead, A. Kingsley, *The Edge of the Image* (Seattle: University of Washington Press, 1967) pp. 3-57, 96-169.

Weaver, Mike, *William Carlos Williams: the American Background* (Cambridge: Cambridge University Press, 1971).

Weimer, David R., *The City as Metaphor* (New York: Random House, 1966).

Whitaker, Thomas R., *William Carlos Williams* (New York: Twayne, 1968).

Whitehead, A.N., *Adventures of Ideas* (New York: Macmillan, 1933).

Whittemore, Reed, *William Carlos Williams: Poet from Jersey* (Boston, Mass.: Houghton Mifflin, 1975).

Zukofsky, Louis, *Prepositions* (London: Rapp & Carroll, 1967).

Index

WILLIAM CARLOS WILLIAMS AND THE AMERICAN POEM

MACMILLAN PRESS LTD.

Title: William Carlos Williams and the American Poem

Main Text: 11/12 pt Baskerville rom. u/lc. x 25 picas
Chapter Heading: 24 pt rom. u/lc.
Running heads: 11pt Baskerville ital. u/lc.

Typeset in Hong Kong by Graphicraft Typesetters